Are Textbooks Harming Your Children?

Norma and Mel Gabler Take Action and show you how!

James C. Hefley

mott media Box 236 Milford, MI 48042

Textbook Citations

All quotations from textbooks are taken directly from public records of the State of Texas, including legislative and textbook adoption hearings between the years 1962-77 where they were placed by sworn petitioners and witnesses, publishers' representatives, Textbook Committee members, Commissioners of Education, and members of the Texas State Board of Education.

Library of Congress Catalog Card No. 78-24251

ISBN 0-915134-38-1

Printed in the United States of America

Contents

Publisher's Foreword   **4**

Preface   **6**

Preface to First Edition   **8**

  1   Parents Have Rights Too   **11**

  2   School Daze   **27**

  3   Strike Two   **39**

  4   Big Government and "Biased" Economics   **52**

  5   Taking the Offensive   **62**

  6   A "Ten Year Pin"   **76**

  7   For the Love of Children   **91**

  8   The "Sexy" History Book   **108**

  9   X-rated Textbooks   **125**

10   Battling the Bookmen   **139**

11   The Truth about West Virginia   **157**

12   Charting the Future   **177**

Epilogue, "The Continuing Battle"   **194**

Appendix I   How Textbooks Are Adopted
in Various States   **211**

Appendix II   Values Clarification   **213**

Appendix III   Textbook Reviews   **215**

Appendix IV   Recommended Sources and Publishers   **216**

Appendix V   Recommended Readings   **218**

Appendix VI   How to Take Action   **219**

Appendix VII   Eulogy to Don Allen Gabler   **223**

Publisher's Foreword

The question posed in the book's title suggests that there is a connection between the content of school textbooks and the condition of the nation's children.

Textbook content has a twofold effect. First, children cannot learn what they are not taught, and second, what they *are* taught will affect not only the ability to perform basic tasks required of an educated person, but also moral development.

When textbooks convey the notion that one lifestyle is as acceptable as another and that all ideas have equal merit, why should students believe that it is important to follow grammatical rules or that one manner of expression is correct and another incorrect? Why do the multiplication tables constitute an important truth when textbooks demonstrate that truth is only relative to the situation in which one finds oneself?

Scores on the College Entrance Examination Board Scholastic Aptitude Test, the American College Entrance Examination and the National Assessment of Educational Progress as well as a host of other nationally-administered tests demonstrate that verbal ability, mathematical ability and writing skills have been steadily declining for more than a decade. Students are untutored in the basic facts of history and science and display even more appalling ignorance of the principles and ideals which are the foundation of their own nation and of western civilization.

The substitution of "look-say" methodology for instruction in phonics, modern math for computational drill, and street language for standard English in elementary school has created students who are not prepared to take more advanced and academically rewarding courses in high school. The result has been a proliferation of less demanding mini-courses at the high school level which in many cases serve to titillate and entertain rather than educate.

A Ford Foundation study into the causes of test score decline found that "Our gross data indicate a considerable enrollment decline in academic courses. Secondary pupils have been taking fewer courses in general English and mathematics.... These course enrollment declines parallel closely the test score decline patterns..." (in Annegret Harnischfeger and David E. Wiley, *Achievement Test Score Decline: Do We Need to Worry?* CEMREL, Inc., December 1975).

The deterioration of standards of behavior and language represented in the textbooks reviewed by Mel and Norma Gabler has not only resulted in weakening the academic disciplines but has also affected the ability of young people to discipline their own behavior.

When children are routinely subjected in their textbook readings to an image of man as violent, sadistic, and unreasoning, liberated from absolute standards of moral conduct, it is a powerful influence on their concept of the world, themselves, and acceptable standards of behavior.

Crimes of violence and anti-social behavior are increasing among young people. Though television is often blamed for setting examples of destructive behavior, the Gablers point out that what is seen on television or in the moving picture theaters is validated daily in public school classrooms.

Bad textbooks full of immoral content and violence, politically biased toward an increasing centralization of power as the answer to all problems, spiritual and material, will ultimately destroy the family, decent standards of behavior, and the basic principles of American government. It is evident that these texts have already caused irreparable damage to the ability of many to learn or even to want to learn.

The message of this book is that today's textbooks have sacrificed teaching to opinion shaping, basic skills to personality molding, and factual content to ideological propaganda of a kind that the majority of American parents would find totally unacceptable if they but knew of it. The purpose of this book is to create that awareness and assist parents, school board members, and concerned teachers to do something about it.

Preface

It has now been three years since the first edition, titled *Textbooks on Trial*, was published. Four hardcover printings have been sold. Norma Gabler has appeared on the nationally televised Phil Donahue Show and ABC-TV's "Good Morning America." The crusade for better textbooks, through the Gablers, has reached to New Zealand and Australia.

Politicians and progressive educators are getting the message. Not only through parent demands for better schoolbooks for their children, but also through tax referendums denying funds to public schools. The publicized "California Tea Party" vote of June 1978 in which California voters drastically cut back property taxes is, at least in part, a powerful symbol of the revolt. No longer will parents accept the excuses, such as too much television and lack of home discipline, given by the educational establishment to explain failing test scores and other problems. They are demanding a drastic change in educational philosophy—away from relativism, social adjustment, and the Dewey-inspired credo of secular humanism; and a turn to emphasis on skills, discipline, character building, and responsible citizenship.

While progressive educators are wringing their collective hands over the growth of private schools, concerned parents are asking: Why can't public education take lessons from private institutions? They cite Providence St. Mel High School, an all-black parochial school in Chicago's West Side ghetto. St. Mel's operates under a shape-up or ship-out policy. Students can be fined or assigned mandatory chores for being tardy or cutting class. They can be expelled for drug use and academic failure. Students may enter with low reading skills, but they must read at twelfth-grade level to receive a diploma. Before graduating, all students must take college boards, apply to at least three colleges, prepare financial-aid forms, and state their career goals. It is no wonder that eighty-five percent of the graduates go on to college in a neighborhood where ninety-five percent of students in public high schools are said to be on drugs and unemployed.

Sadly, because of a lack of funds, St. Mel's may have to close. Yet the cost per pupil in 1978 ran $1,300 a year, compared to $1,700 in Chicago public schools.

Textbooks, of course, are only part of the problem, but a major part. The fight for better texts is part of the struggle for a turnaround in public education.

This Revised Edition of *Textbooks on Trial* contains the full story of the Gablers as related in the original edition. It also includes a new epilogue with an update on present developments in the textbook crusade since initial publication of the Gabler's story.

JAMES C. HEFLEY
SIGNAL MOUNTAIN, TENNESSEE

Preface to First Edition

When Jim Adair, Editorial Director of Victor Books, called about a book on a crusade against objectionable textbooks, I wasn't interested.

Not that I wasn't concerned. I had read stories about "realism" in high school literature (profanity, sex, violence, radical revolts); "presentism" in history (where the past is capsuled into the present to discover meaning as they define it); "economic determinism" (where man's materialistic desires are said to shape the future); "behaviorism" (where children are conditioned to behave as master planners think they should). And I knew that college entrance test scores were dropping and employers were complaining about youth with high school diplomas who couldn't write a decent sentence.

As so many others, I thought if things were really this bad (which I doubted), something should be done. Perhaps write letters to one's Congressman, complain through the PTA, call up the superintendent of schools, write better textbooks.

But a crusade smacked of extremism. Boycotts. Book burnings. Marches. Angry confrontations with authorities. Such as had been reported in the national media about the controversy in West Virginia.

"This isn't what you think," Jim assured me. "The story is about a Texas couple, Mel and Norma Gabler, and how they've worked within the system in Texas. Why, they've done more to improve textbooks than anyone else in the country."

Jim is a longtime friend, level-headed, not given to sensationalism. Victor Books is a division of Scripture Press, a respectable, foundation-owned evangelical Sunday School publisher. But I felt they had missed the mark on this one.

"Well, the least you could do is come up for a conference with us and Mel Gabler. We'll pick up the fare."

It was the least I could do.

Mel was disarming at first meeting. A lanky, drawling, mild-mannered fellow, he didn't fit the image of the fire-breathing West Virginia protesters I'd read about.

8

He didn't wave a scare pamphlet under my nose. He merely flipped open a bag and handed me some textbooks. "Read a little," he said, indicating marked passages.

I read. I moaned. To read *about* the books was one thing. To read *the* books was another.

The more I read, the more disturbed I became. It wasn't just the gutter language that couldn't be printed in a family newspaper or spoken on TV. It was lessons on myths, with biblical stories worked right in among Roman and Greek tales. It was situations where lying, stealing, even sex outside of marriage was said to be OK, if that was your value system. It was gory stories of murder. Cultural studies of wife-swapping, mercy-killing. All in textbooks—mostly high school, but some running into the lower grades.

"Parental involvement kept these and a lot more out of Texas schools," Mel assured.

But what about the Gablers' tactics?

"We haven't been arrested, or broken a law. Mrs. Gabler has been honored by the Texas Legislature and by the Texas Mothers' Committee in the presence of the governor, with three of our state's top educators attending in her honor."

I was still not convinced. "What's so significant about Texas? You're a big state, but only one."

"Because books are adopted for the entire state, Texas is the world's biggest single buyer of textbooks. It influences the whole industry."

I kept listening. I signed the contract to write the Gabler story.

I didn't expect the research to be pleasant. It wasn't. I was alternately sick and angry. It seemed incredible that textbooks can have changed so much. Disgusting.

At the same time I was encouraged by what Mel and Norma had done. They've proven that ordinary people, if they work long enough and hard enough, can effect change for decency and morality. They've shown that the "public-be-damned" attitude of some academic and government elitists can be challenged. They've demonstrated that the worst textbooks can be kept out of the schools when parents and taxpayers exercise their rights under the Constitution.

I'll say it again: The Gablers are not extremists. Unless extremism means believing in faith, fidelity, family, work, freedom,

9

and America, while demanding that public school textbooks must not indoctrinate children in irreligion, lawbreaking, sexual perversion, doctored history, and the benevolence of Big Brother government.

This is their story, written from their viewpoint, and told simply so other parents and educators who share their ideals, and some who don't, may understand why and how they waged their crusade. It includes, of course, actual quotes from scores of textbooks, filed and/or read into the public record of the State of Texas.

It is written with sympathy, but without editorial judgment, so you, the reader, may decide.

JAMES C. HEFLEY
SIGNAL MOUNTAIN, TENNESSEE

P.S. The day the first draft of this manuscript was finished our sixth grader came home from school talking about a discussion of values.

"Tell us about it," we asked.

"We talked about lying and discussed if it wasn't sometimes better to lie than tell the truth. The teacher drew a line. At one end she wrote 'always'; at the other end *'never.'* Then she asked us, 'Where do you put yourself on the line?' "

"And where did you put yourself?" we wondered.

"Just as close to *'never'* as I could."

A good question for family discussion or Sunday School. But for public schools in the values clarification framework of situation ethics?

Now it's hitting home.

1

Parents Have Rights Too

The first floor conference room in the Texas Education Agency building across from the State Capitol is jammed with about 200 textbook salesmen, reporters, and book protesters.

The annual "trial of the textbooks" is in progress. Books proposed for use in Texas public schools against which citizen protesters have lodged complaints are before the State Textbook Committee, which serves without pay. The Committee is hearing public testimony by both protesters and publishers. The protesters who speak from previously filed bills of particulars may only speak against the books. The top salesmen of the American textbook industry are allowed equal time to defend their wares.

It is a time-consuming, costly process for citizens, publishers, and for the state. But Texas, in contrast to most other states where citizens have little recourse against objectionable books, prefers it this way. Dr. Donald S. Lutz, an associate professor of political science at the University of Houston, calls the Texas system of textbook hearings *before* adoption and purchase "an excellent example of the democratic system in action, a model for other states to emulate." It has also probably prevented stormy confrontations such as occurred in Kanawha County, West Virginia during 1974.

The salesmen are tense. Million-dollar orders are won and

11

lost in this room. Much of a year's work for a publisher can go down the drain, but the ordeal cannot be dodged if they expect to sell new books. Texas, like about half of the 50 states, has a state-approved list of textbooks from which districts must select. (For the salesmen, the object of the game is to make the list, which is limited to a maximum of five books per subject. It will usually be six years before the same subjects come around again in Texas. And books that "flunk" here will be viewed with suspicion by some school boards in other states.

This year, high school psychology and sociology books are before the business-like "court" which must decide.

Much testimony has already been given. Committee chairman Ed Irons now recognizes Mrs. Mel Gabler. A legal reporter is poised to record every word she speaks.

Eyes turn to the raven-haired, blue-eyed matronly woman moving to the witness table. A long-time adversary of the book publishers, she needs no introduction. By this year, 1973, she is probably the best-known battler for better textbooks in the world—certainly in Texas where in educational circles the name Gabler has become well-known.

She has already appeared in hearings held before the Commissioner of Education where testimony was recorded for study by the State Textbook Committee. Now she is back for an appearance before the Committee.

She is usually smiling, even when speaking against books. Today, educators, salesmen, and media representatives have never seen her so grim.

A heavy silence pervades the room as she pulls two books wrapped in plain brown paper from her attaché case. When she lifts them high, everyone can see that "X-Rated" is stamped across each one, front and back. The salesmen look questioningly at each other, wondering whose books they are. They need wonder no longer when she identifies them as *Sociology: An Introduction* and *Behind the Mask: Our Psychological World,* both titles of Prentice-Hall.

"These are so dirty I was afraid I might get picked up and charged with possessing pornography. I'll challenge anyone reading parts of [these books] . . . to tell me if [they're] . . . not rated 'X' at the very lowest. . . . Read this chapter . . . and see if you don't think it makes an all-out play for the homosexual. . . .

Personally, I don't see how members of this Committee can read this and . . . [not] get under the table and wash their mouths. It's that filthy."

She flips the pages of one of the books. "Here on pages 204 and 205 is a sex-related case study using four-letter words with animalistic behavior overtones. . . . In a test devised for embarrassment . . . the girl . . . was told to get in a booth and read the . . . vilest sex-related information on little three by five cards, down to sexual behavior for animals. . . . She also had to go back into the group for discussion."

The room is like a funeral parlor. Silence is broken only by occasional coughing. Everyone is aware of the biggest news story of the year: The murders of 27 young boys in Houston involved with homosexual perverts. Norma Gabler cited the summer tragedy in earlier testimony against these and other books which appeared to condone homosexual behavior.

The Prentice-Hall man now has a turn to speak.

Unsmiling and grim, he reads a terse statement: "We of the Educational Book Division [of our company] . . . have reached the conclusion that some of the material may be too mature for the high school students. . . ."

There are startled looks all around. Chairman Irons is no less astounded. "Are you telling us as a committee not to vote for your book?"

"Mr. Irons, may I put it this way: That would be a reasonable assumption."

Hawkins, Texas, 1961

At the beginning, Mel and Norma Gabler trusted textbooks almost as much as they did the Bible.

They lived with their three sons on a 68-acre ranch-farm just outside of Hawkins, a small oiltown in East Texas. It was a good and convenient life. The big consolidated school, built with oil money, was a couple of miles away and so was the church. Mel's job as a clerk for Humble Pipeline's district was just down the road. There was a public swimming pool, a baseball field, neighborhood ice cream socials, and a community picnic every Fourth of July. The people were friendly, fair, and trustworthy. Norma's parents lived only a half-hour's distance and within four hours they could be in Houston where Mel's folks lived.

Mel was eight years older than Norma, having met her when he boarded with her parents in 1938, when she was a 14-year-old school girl. They were married during his stint in the U.S. Army Air Corps during World War II, and four days before Mel left for the Azores Islands their first son, Jim, was born. After the war they followed Mel's job "all over" Texas—one year they moved seven times—before settling in Hawkins in 1958. Along the way they were active in Bible-believing churches. In Hawkins they became community pillars. In 1961 Mel was a deacon and Sunday School teacher and Norma superintendent of the youth department at church. The past year Mel had been vice-president and program chairman of the PTA. This year he was PTA president.

Their three sons drew them into PTA. Mel had less than a year of college and Norma only a high school diploma; they wanted their boys to go further. More important, they wanted them to become God-fearing, patriotic, industrious citizens.

For that, the boys needed a good educational foundation, and Mel and Norma wanted to do all they could to back up the local teachers.

They were already proud of their sons. Jim, 16, and a high school junior, was already taller than Mel's 5'10½". Paul, 14, was shooting up faster than a persimmon sprout. Don, the curly-haired nine-year-old practical joker, was the prize exhibit of the whole family. When he blew his bass horn from the back porch, the cows came running, stood around the yard fence and mooed. The older boys were more like their dad, easy-going and methodical in almost everything they did. Don, more like his mother, was a bit impulsive, laughed and smiled a lot, and could find humor in almost anything. All three boys enjoyed ranch life, especially cowpunching from the back of their pickup. They never tired of telling about their city-slicker dad lassoing Marty the bull around the middle.

The Gabler boys were expected to be respectful and they were. A black friend of the family was always marveling, "Your boys are the only ones who call me, 'Mister.'" And the parents' response was always, "They'd better."

In sum, the Gablers were the cream of self-reliant Middle America. They lived by the old landmarks, took child-rearing seriously, supported community institutions, sang "God Bless America" with a lump in their throats, and believed that the

American system of limited and divided governmental power was the best under the sun.

That system included textbooks until the fall of 1961.

Several times Jim tried to tell his dad that something was wrong with his textbook. Mel wouldn't believe him because he thought that all textbooks were perfect down to the last comma and period. Finally, rather exasperated, Jim asked, "If I bring my book home, will you take time to read it?" Mel agreed.

The next afternoon Jim brought home his copy of *Our Nation's Story* by Laidlaw Brothers, but before he handed it to his dad, he asked, "Dad, what did the founders of our nation intend to accomplish when they wrote the Constitution?"

Mel told him that they tried to establish a government which would be strong enough to unite the people, but which would leave them as much of their God-given freedom as possible, with most of the governing left up to state and local governments.

Jim said, "Not according to my book."

Handing Mel the book, he opened it to the chapter on the Constitution and showed 10 subheads about the Constitution of which two concerned governmental powers. One of these enumerated powers granted the new government and the other listed limitations on the states. There was nothing about any restrictions on the federal government and nothing about rights or freedoms retained by the people and the states. This set Mel on fire.

He passed the book to Norma and she too became very upset. They looked further in this and other history texts obtained from friends. Familiar stories and sayings of patriots were missing. In most they could not find Nathan Hale's "I only regret I have but one life to lose for my country." Nor Patrick Henry's "Give me liberty or give me death." Leaders like George Washington seemed to be downgraded. There was only a brief sentence in one book about the loyalty of his army at Valley Forge and nothing about his deep religious faith.

The emphasis appeared to be on modern history, the benevolence of Washington, D.C., and the building of world brotherhood through the United Nations. World Communism and its plan for world domination was hardly touched upon.

While the Gablers had never doubted the books their sons were studying, they had never really looked closely at them either, except to give occasional assistance with homework. The PTA didn't meddle in curriculum; national policy made that off limits. (In 1975 this policy was changed to allow local participation in curriculum.) The Gablers had always thought that school personnel knew best.

Just how were books selected? [1] Who decided which books to take?

They inquired at the school and were matter-of-factly told that in Texas a State Textbook Committee is appointed annually by the State Board of Education on recommendation of the Texas Education Agency. The Committee reviews publishers' offerings and recommends for Board adoption from two to five titles for each grade subject. Local district textbook committees then choose from the state-approved list.

Do parents participate?

Yes, the state and district committees can call on lay advisors. Who were the local advisors? The school office didn't know.

The system sounded good, but they wanted to know more about it. They wrote for information. While waiting for an answer, they received another jolt from Jim's schoolwork.

Jim had been assigned to memorize the Gettysburg Address. Since only a small-print picture of Lincoln's famous speech was in his text, he was typing it from the 1960 edition of the *World Book Encyclopedia*. "Mom, come look," he called to Norma. "I think something has been left out."

Norma followed her son's finger. ". . . that this nation shall have a new birth of freedom . . ." She read on to the end. *Under God* was not there.

"Mom, if it isn't in the textbook or the encyclopedia, where do I go to find the truth?" Jim asked plaintively.

The Gablers were now more determined than ever to help provide children with the truth. They began asking local school board members if there wasn't some way parents could screen textbooks before they were purchased. Nobody seemed to know if or where the books were available. Further, they received the distinct impression that some educators were resentful of their questions.

A newspaper story helped explain why. The Texas Society Daughters of the American Revolution (TSDAR) and a group

---

[1] See Appendix I: How Textbooks Are Adopted in Various States.

called Texans for America (TFA) had been appearing before the State Textbook Committee in Austin protesting new school texts. The article quoted them as saying the new books were anti-American, and gave short shrift to patriotism, morality, free enterprise, individual and states' rights—while promoting federal programs, economic determination, secular humanism, dirty literature under the guise of "social realism," the United Nations as an agent for world brotherhood, and many left-wing ideas.

The writer further noted that the TFA had dug up a requirement in Texas law stipulating that publishers and authors must sign a non-Communist oath before their books could be purchased by the state. This, along with protests of book content, had publishers and educators crying infringement on academic freedom by "book burners" and censors. The tumult was so great that the Speaker of the Texas House of Representatives had appointed a five-member legislative committee to investigate textbooks; public hearings were to begin in January 1962.

The Gablers read the article with great interest. They decided to take their complaint before the legislative committee.

The Campaign Begins

They talked to friends who asked to see some of the books. This interest encouraged them to begin sending information to people on their Christmas card list. Another outlet for publicity opened when they got enough courage to telephone a popular radio call-in program known as "Party Line" on powerful KWKH in Shreveport, just across the Texas-Louisiana border. During that fall either one or both of them called into this program each week. Letters began coming in, asking for help.

Meanwhile, they gathered materials. They wrote for textbook reviews available from America's Future, an educational review organization, and from the national DAR. They obtained copies of the TFA reviews. They compared history texts adopted in Texas with old histories preserved from another era. The more they read and compared, the more convinced they became that the quality of school curriculum had dangerously deteriorated.

Apart from the textbook project, this was one of their busiest years. They were cross-fencing their land, tending a 30-head herd of cattle, and Mel was building a three-car garage in addition to his regular job.

After the State Board of Education adopted the American history texts over TSDAR and TFA protests, the Gablers compiled a 20-page information booklet which parents could use when schools selected books for local school use early in 1962. One night they and their sons worked until dawn, collating the information for mailing to 1,000 persons. Their mailing list grew so rapidly that they had to spend another entire night collating another thousand booklets.

In January they were in Shreveport and called up Joe Fribley, the moderator of the KWKH call-in radio program on which they had spoken by telephone many times. Fribley frightened them almost out of their wits by insisting they be his studio guests that night for an hour and a half. They had never been in a radio studio in their lives. From the moment he introduced them on their subject, the phones started ringing.

Some callers complained about books their children were using, and asked what could they do. The Gablers offered to send the material they had compiled and referred them to their local school personnel.

Other callers felt the protesters were stepping out of bounds and that curriculum choices should be left in the hands of educational "experts."

"No, we parents have a stake in what our children are being taught," Norma countered. "And, don't forget, the books are bought with our tax money."

The time was up too soon, but they were invited back for a return broadcast.

Back home, disappointing reports began coming in from individuals who had received the review mailing. "I went to my school board and they laughed me right out of the room," was typical of some.

"I complained to the principal and he said I didn't know what I was talking about, that the quotes were out of context, and I had been misled," was another example.

It became clear to the Gablers that they needed to start in Austin where the books were adopted for state-wide use. The legislative textbook investigating committee now loomed extremely important. Other than help from two concerned businessmen, Mike Harvey, Sr., and his son, Richard, of nearby Tyler, Mel and Norma were spending their own money for the publicity campaign and travel expenses. Deciding that it would not be wise for Mel to take off work, Norma and Jim went to the state capital by train.

The First Hearing

Mother and son arrived on a cold, snowy Wednesday, January 24th. Norma had written ahead to be sure of a place on the agenda.

The room was filled with ranchers and professors, lawyers and businessmen, a few women, and a scraggle of long-haired, sloppily dressed University of Texas students standing at the back. "We'll hear Mrs. Mel Gabler first," Chairman W. T. Dungan announced. Norma was surprised at the quick recognition. Later she learned that the Committee had been impressed by the family's direct mail and radio campaign.

She had spoken in Sunday School and Training Union. Never had she faced such an assembly. Her knees jellied and her voice quavered as she began.

"I'm here to speak for myself, my husband, and our three sons who use some of the textbooks that will be talked about today. I would like to tell this committee why we are concerned about the history being studied in our schools."

There was a smattering of applause and a few boos from the back as she stopped to catch her breath. She continued as if nothing had happened.

"Let's take first a high school history called *Our Nation's Story,* published by Laidlaw Brothers, copyright 1954. It's quite different from the old histories.

"For instance, it never mentions that our forefathers came to this country for freedom, particularly religious freedom. Compare that to what Barnes' *A Brief History of the United States,* printed in 1885, says:

". . . They longed for a land where they might worship God in their own way, and save their families from worldly follies. America offered such a home. They came, resolved to brave every danger, trusting God to shape their destinies" (p. 54).

Ignoring the foot scraping, coughing, and boos from the UT students at the back, she read next from her son's textbook on the Constitution. "Under 'a,' 'Powers granted the new government,' page 165, we have a discussion of the so-called 'Elastic Clause.'"

"The insertion of this clause had enabled the federal government to adopt the powers originally granted in the Constitution to meet the needs of a nation in which great changes have taken place.

"There is much, much more about the power of the federal government."

There were shouts of "Get to the point" and "What's your objection?" But Norma managed to continue.

"All this is true, but the one-sided presentation amounts to a half-truth. The Bill of Rights clearly limits the power of the federal government to functions designated in the Constitution. Yet this book gives not one word in this discussion of the very, very important limits placed on the federal government."

"Mrs. Gabler," a legislator interrupted, "if you were queen of the United States—"

"I hope I never see the day when we have a king and queen," Norma shot back and resumed reading.

She took a second book, *American History for High School* (1961) by Ginn and Company.

"Page two. Our heritage, this nation's Christian heritage and the spiritual principles on which it was founded, are omitted and only a materialistic view given."

The disturbances and irrelevant questions continued. The chairman kept rapping his gavel. Norma kept on, but it was obvious few could hear. "Pages 656, 657. The Korean War is not properly covered. . . . The fact is not brought out that studies by the U.S. Army revealed that 75% of our war prisoners, either knowingly or unknowingly, cooperated with the enemy, and over one-fourth collaborated knowingly, because of their lack of knowledge of American principles, American history, and knowledge of how our system operates."

The noise increased. Norma raised her voice.

"Until recently I was naive enough to believe that history was history. However, I've had a rude awakening.

"Did you know that history can be, and is, written to reflect the political views of the writers? . . . Did you know that, almost without exception, Big Government is treated as desirable? In fact, the foundation of our nation on a heritage of Christian principles is generally slighted or ignored."

Norma's time ended and she stepped down, the boos still echoing in her ears. It had been the most frustrating half-hour of her life.

When there was a break in testimony, the Committee chairman thanked her for coming. She bit her tongue to keep from boiling over. Jim stood beside her, red-faced and angry.

"Mr. Dungan," he finally said. "Can I speak as a student who is using these books?"

Jim's request caught the legislator by surprise. "Well, uh, we've never had a student speak before. You have the right. But we can't put you on today. Come back next week."

"He'll be here," Norma promised.

Jim worked hard on his speech, staying up until 2 A.M. Monday morning to type up the final copy by a hunt-and-peck method so it would be completely his own.

This time Mel arranged for a day off work, and Richard Harvey flew him and Jim to Austin. They were there when the Wednesday hearings began.

Jim was introduced and the typical 16-year-old youth, a forgotten wad of gum in his mouth, strode to the speaker's table. The room, again crowded, was strangely silent as he began the speech he had so carefully prepared.

"I am Jim Gabler, representing myself. I am a student in Hawkins High School in Hawkins, Texas. I am in the 11th grade and have a 93 average for my first semester in American History. I plan to talk about *Our Nation's Story*. I am using this textbook now in American History. It is the only book used in this subject in our high school. I have covered the first 365 pages as well as the average student does. This is the first 17 chapters; in fact, I have a test on chapter 17 tomorrow.

"This book has puzzled me somewhat throughout, but especially the chapters concerning the Revolutionary War and the Constitution. I have always thought George Washington was one of our greatest patriots. After studying him in this book, I was left with the impression that Washington did little more than Baron von Steuben or Benedict Arnold.

"My earlier American History textbooks had a picture of Washington at Valley Forge as he was praying to God. I believe this to be a great piece of art since it shows George Washington's faith in our Father in Heaven. I have yet to find such a fine picture in this book."

After citing more downgrading of Washington, he turned to the Constitution, agreeing that "these items (the power of the federal government) should be included in history. But . . . the one section left out should be titled: Limiting the Power of the Federal Government. This is one of the main things which the Constitution provides."

Then he recalled a statement made by a witness the previous week that " 'the book is only a tool.' This is definitely not true. My teachers use the book as the final authority. I was not even allowed to elaborate on a World History test last year. The teacher told me that I was to put only what was in the book or it would be counted wrong. Does this sound like the book is only a tool? It doesn't to me."

Reporters described Jim as a "gum-chewing East Texas kid" and quoted liberally from his speech. The speech was reprinted in the South Texas Chamber of Commerce magazine and by other organizations. A Chamber official later told the Gablers it was one of the most requested items they had ever distributed.

When Mel's time came, the University of Texas students again were disruptive, especially when one of the members of the legislative committee asked, "Do you think anybody else could run the Post Office besides the federal government?"

"Yes, I think free enterprise could do it better."

The boos and catcalls drowned out the speaker and the chairman had to rap for order.

The division deepened as the hearings became the talk of the state. There was bitter name-calling and demands for certain "Communist sympathizers" and "pink liberals" to resign from teaching posts, and for the textbooks of "disloyal authors" to be rejected.

The Gablers felt the protesters were defeating their own cause by waging a war on personalities. They determined to stick to the content of the texts.

Alerting the Community

Till that time they had been able to obtain only a few history books. They tried to purchase books on other subjects and ran against a stone wall. The books were not for sale, school personnel said, nor could they be loaned out to parents. None told them that the state required publishers to sell textbooks to citizens at school prices. Undaunted, they asked the State Board member from their district for help.

Dr. B. E. Masters was the founder of four junior colleges and one of the state's most respected educators. He was himself disturbed by the trends in textbook publishing and promised to secure the books, provided they would not disclose the source because feelings were running high.

When the books arrived, Norma and Mel began reading, marking objectionable passages in red. One day she was in Longview and just happened to have several books in the car when she got the idea to show the books to someone with the East Texas Chamber of Commerce, whose area includes Houston and Dallas.

She hurried into the building and was directed to the office of Alf Jernigan, the assistant manager. When she entered, carrying an armful of books, he looked surprised. "Are you selling books?" he wondered.

She pushed an economics book across his desk and sat down. "Do you have children?" she asked. "Read this and see if that is what you want them taught."

He read a paragraph shaded in red. He read on, page after page, while Norma patiently waited. "This is a school text?" he asked incredulously. Norma nodded. "It's on the approved list in Texas."

"I'm amazed," he said solemnly. "It's terrible. I can hardly believe it. Thank you, Mrs. Gabler, for alerting me."

Norma put the book back in her brief case and reached for her purse. "Wait, don't go yet," Jernigan requested. "You have a message—a story to tell.

"I'll give you a list of people to see. Just drop in on them as you did me. Ask for five minutes of their time. Show them a book. You'll have them hooked. Keep going back. Your message needs to become known.

"And you've got to start speaking to groups."

"Me?" Norma replied incredulously. "I can't speak in public."

"Who else will do it?" he countered. "You know the story. You have the information. I can't do it for you."

Taking Jernigan's list, she followed his suggestion and went to key leaders from town to town, asking for just five minutes of each person's time. Invariably, reading a few paragraphs would evoke concern and the pledge, "I'm with you and your husband in anything you can do to keep books like these out of the schools."

Norma would then suggest that they write their legislators or some other official in Austin, and add, "That's where the problem is."

Some of the community leaders confronted local school officials they knew. To educators who would scoff that a "bunch of nuts" were behind the textbook protests, they would say, "I saw the books. Something has to be done about them."

Word spread along the educators' grapevine that the Gablers were getting copies of textbooks. Already upset by the legislative committee hearings, the pro-textbook people tried to find the source, without success. During this time a superintendent, known to be friendly with Mel and Norma, was mysteriously fired. The Gablers heard that he had been a strong suspect.

More Hearings

Meanwhile, the legislative investigating committee had left Austin and was holding hearings around the state. Crowds of spectators and long lines of witnesses appeared at every meeting. The investigation of books was now attracting nationwide attention. Book publishers were nervous.

A Midland, Texas witness read objectionable excerpts from junior and senior high school library books (required research resources for certain courses) into the record. The obsenities and explicit desciptions of sexual intercourse and perversions shocked listeners. Some clapped hands over their ears. Others cried for readers to stop.

One witness responded, "If it is shockingly objectionable for us to be reading passages from these books here in open meeting, how much more objectionable to force your child to read them in school?"

When the hearings in Dallas opened in June 1962, both Norma and Mel testified. Norma read from a Prentice-Hall home economics text, *Building Your Life* (1954), a paragraph about home relationships that she felt would stir youth to rebel against their parents.

"Are your parents inclined to be old-fashioned? Do they ever embarrass you by things they say or do in front of your friends? Are they often unreasonable?

"If so, perhaps you have tried to keep your feelings about it to yourself. But if you have talked to your friends about your difficulties with your parents, you have found that your friends have most of the same complaints that you have" (p. 123).

Her voice snapped in indignation as she commented. "That's all it takes for a teenager to have complaints about their parents, because we have two teenagers and a 10-year-old, and I'm sure they have a lot of complaints." She read more:

"If you and your classmates would all write on slips of paper the three things that bother you most about your parents and then have a committee summarize the results, there would probably be a large measure of agreement on troublesome traits in parents.

"Why do parents behave as they do?

"Is there any way you can help them to change? (pp. 193–194)

" 'Seeing the matter in perspective may be a good idea,' you say, 'but it is still just as aggravating to have to try to cope with parents who boss too much, who set old-fashioned and unreasonable standards, and who don't realize that a person has a right to some privacy in life!' " (p. 195)

"And it goes on and on," she concluded.

Mel hit high school economics books on the state-approved list. From Scribner and Sons' *Economics and You* (1956), he read questions which he said "subtly move the thinking of the student to the left":

" 'Should the government put a ceiling on the middleman's profits? (p. 201)

"Since banking is an important part of a nation's economic life, would it be advisable to make banking, like the Post Office, a government monopoly? (p. 260)

"Is it desirable for the government to set price and wage ceilings in peacetime? (p. 310)

"Should a national sales tax on all articles except food be established? (p. 480)

"The questions in this book," he stressed, "are slanted toward values the author wants you to have, because, after all, the questions covering the chapter are to see what the student has learned."

But it was not just the presentation of supposed "advantages" of Communism and the extolling of the benefits of Big Brother government that bothered him. It was also the failure of three of the five economics books to present fairly the American free enterprise system. "Unbalanced" economics texts, he charged, contribute to the economic "illiteracy" revealed by surveys among high school students.

He concluded with a personal citizen-parent "Bill of Grievances":

"The public school system of this country has . . . [become] a propaganda agency to support the projects, campaigns, crusades, ideas, and personal philosophies of a self-appointed group of educators that now asserts the right to dominate and control that system. There is no place in that system for individuals desiring to use their position or authority to promote any New Deal, Square Deal, Fair Deal, Re-Deal, or any other kind of Deal. It is a violation of our constitutional rights to make the public school system an instrument for the dissemination of the propaganda of any partisan or political group or other special interests in the community. The parents of the children of America have a right to a public school system where the instruction is based upon the truth. They have the right to oppose any and all school programs and activities where propaganda is substituted for the truth."

Unknowingly, Mel had laid down the *raison d'etre* for the crusade he and Norma would wage in the years to come.

2

School Daze

Dallas marked the last of the stormy hearings. In his report, Chairman Dungan reached four conclusions: (1) Pornographic and anti-obscenity laws should be "strengthened to cover some of the trash and filth called literature by some people, and require removal from school libraries." (2) "Inferior" history texts "should be replaced." (3) "Publishers should be required to submit more copies of a textbook up for adoption if necessary, but should be paid for them, and that the time allowed between submission of proposed textbooks and decision upon adoption should be lengthened in some cases so as to allow more study by interested persons as well as the textbook committee members." (4) "Most of the economics textbooks being used do a poor job of presenting our free enterprise system and what this country has accomplished under it."

Chairman Dungan's views brought respectability to the textbook protesters. The *Dallas Morning News* editorialized that "there are . . . books in the school system which deserve to be criticized and possibly withdrawn," adding, "If Rep. Dungan is an 'extremist,' we're happy to join him."

But a spokesman for the Texas State Teachers Association "feared" that the criticism of textbooks was an attack on the public school system, and that some of the objectors wanted to see free schoolbooks discontinued. Their campaign, he said, was "based on preserving an 'Americanism' of narrow dimensions." Predictable echoes came from many educators across the country who had been watching the Texas scene closely.

Most of the protesters felt their battle had been won. But the Gablers were not convinced. Friendly school board members and school personnel warned Mel and Norma that the books would continue to reflect the views of liberal educators and government bureaucrats. "Don't kid yourself," they said in effect. "The publishers sell to people trained under the same liberal philosophy in universities and teachers' colleges. In Texas they are entrenched in the TEA (Texas Education Agency). The TEA nominates the State Textbook Committee and the State Board rubber-stamps the nominations. The Committee selects the books and the Board approves them. The publishers make money and commission authors from the liberal educational establishment to write new books. And from there the cycle starts all over again."

"We're for you," the Gablers' friends in education said, "but we don't have much hope you can change the system. And don't use our names, or we'll be in trouble," they added. "Educational politics, you know."

The Gablers said they understood and would appreciate all the help these friends could give without risking their jobs. In response, one school official got the Gablers an account at the Texas Schoolbook Depository in Dallas (the building from which Lee Oswald would allegedly shoot President Kennedy the following fall). They could now order and be billed for any book being used in the state school system.

So in 1962 the chances seemed slim for the Gablers to ever attain much success for their cause. The national tide was flowing with the currents of progressive education. Outside of conservative areas such as East Texas, Big Government was riding a euphoric crest on John Kennedy's "New Frontier." People believed the political rhetoric issuing from Washington that the country would soon eradicate poverty, integrate the races, and travel in outer space. "Just a few more years," they assured. "A few billion more dollars." Government, science, education, and the new morality—in sum, humanism—were the four horsemen of promise that would bring in the secular millennium. Those who disagreed were branded, at best, as opponents to progress and, at worst, as reactionaries, racists, extremists, or warmongers.

Tucked away in East Texas, the Gablers didn't realize how great the odds were against them. They believed that when enough people knew, they would demand changes.

The more texts they read, the more strongly they believed that their traditional way of life was being threatened by the educational establishment. The texts contained seeds of moral, economic, and political change. What children studied about today, they would become tomorrow. The Gablers wondered how curriculum could have changed so much since they were in school.

They wrote and called upon traditional educators and scholars. They read books on the philosophy of education. Slowly, they began to understand what had happened.

History of American Education

The Gablers learned that the public school system had been brought to America by Dutch and English Protestants. During the colonial period and for over 50 years after Independence, schools were church and community controlled. They were to teach the Bible, basic knowledge and skills, and reinforce the basic institutions of church, family, and government.

The idea for a centralized school system was credited to Horace Mann, a liberal lay theologian. In 1837 Mann persuaded the Massachusetts State Legislature, to create the first State Board of Education in the U.S. As the first appointed secretary of the board, Mann visited Europe in 1843, where he was favorably impressed by the Prussian system of mass education. Returning home, he persuaded the Massachusetts legislature to establish a similar, tax-supported system. Massachusetts then became the model for other state centralized systems.

Mann had argued that the state should indoctrinate students in democracy and to further general welfare. The school was to be the fundamental instrument for accomplishing that purpose. Education was to promote *progress* in society by equipping students for roles in desirable social change.

The Gablers found John Dewey to be the second most influential figure in "progressive education," a popular philosophy though the term itself was waning in 1961. Dewey and other influential liberal ideologues built on Mann, but gave religion a lesser place than did the earlier educator. Religion, Dewey taught, was human in origin and would eventually wither away. Morals and values were also in the stream of evolution, and they too would change and reappear in new forms to fit the demands of society.

The Gablers saw that according to Dewey's beliefs, man was wholly a creature of animalistic evolution, born without any supernatural bent toward good or evil. As such, his behavior was learned through social experience.

They could now see how public education fit into the progressive philosophy. The schools were, as Dewey had taught, to be the main tool for shaping behavior [1] and thereby indoctrinating children into a pluralistic, democratic society.

It was easy for them to understand how this could be sold to idealistic educators and social planners, even to most professing Christians. Who could argue with improvement of children's behavior?

What frightened Mel and Norma was the philosophical promise of progressive education that there was no absolute transcendental God, Bible, or system of beliefs. If the history of past civilizations was to be believed, the stripping away of supernatural religion would leave a void to be filled by human gods. These human gods would use education to shape the masses in reaching their goals.

In studying history, the Gablers saw how America had been softened for progressive education and how "social" reformers had taken advantage of the prevailing conditions to magnify what they considered inequities.

Conditions after the Civil War were fertile for planting the seeds for humanistic social changes. The war had shaken the foundations of national unity. Immigration, principally Catholic and Jewish, challenged Protestant control of education. Profiteering by a few capitalist "robber barons" gave free enterprise a black eye. Industrialization and some exploitation of workers created a climate for the establishment of labor unions. Darwinian evolution and biblical higher criticism, exported from Germany, penetrated seminaries, persuading thousands of ministers-to-be that the Bible was only a human book.

---

[1] The aim of education is no longer to impart facts and knowledge, according to teachers' editions of textbooks. The aim of the educational establishment now is to change the social values of the child. (Away from values that have traditionally been considered fundamental, fixed, permanent, or absolute.) When Norma urges a return to teaching basics, she is often told that it is more important to teach a child how to get along socially than it is to teach academic skills.

During this same period, American Protestants divided over social involvement. Some said social ministry should be confined to charity for individuals. Others felt churches should also work to change oppressive social and government structures. The "social Gospelers" subsequently were swallowed up by secular humanists, while many conservative Protestants retreated into anti-social, end-of-the-world isolationism.

The result was obvious to the Gablers: Orthodox Christians had for the most part abandoned leadership roles in public life, including public education, to unbelievers. By the 1930s the secular humanists had obtained strong footholds in the teachers' colleges and were indoctrinating future educators with progressive education philosophy. Coming at this time, the Great Depression weakened faith in traditional systems of society and made the masses receptive to programs promising massive social and economic improvement. And what part was the school to play in this? Professor George S. Counts of Columbia University said in a 1932 monograph, "Dare the School Build a New Social Order?":

. . . Ignorance must be replaced by knowledge, competition by cooperation, trust in Providence by careful planning, and private capitalism by some form of socialized economy. . . .

The Gablers noted that by the end of World War II, progressive education had become the ideology of the National Education Association. They saw a report by an NEA affiliate, the National Council for the Social Studies, on "The Study and Teaching of American History" that helped explain the changes in recent history texts that had disturbed them:

Our principle for selecting what is basic in . . . history involves a reference to its predicted outcome. Our "emphasis" will be determined by what we find going on in the present. . . . Most of us have pledged our allegiance to an organized world community. . . .

. . . The teacher who adopts this principle of selection is as intellectually honest as the teacher who relies upon the textbook author—and far more creative . . .

This they understood to be in line with the promotion in textbooks of the United Nations as a global collective that would establish permanent peace. Under this new world government, national sovereignties would wither away just as organized religion would disappear, bringing fulfillment to the hopes of mankind.

As they continued their research, concepts that had puzzled them took on meaning. Irrationality could be rational if it advanced the progressive cause. Relativism in morality was reasonable if there were no absolutes. Syncretism in religion was acceptable if there was no ultimate authority behind any belief system.

To the Gablers, progressive education threatened to undermine church and home teaching of biblical Christianity and the principles on which America had been founded. It was materialistic, humanistic, atheistic, and socialistic; an ideology foreign to a nation whose motto was "In God We Trust."

It might be accepted by "educators" with impressive degrees. But it was dangerous and nonsensical to the Gablers. They agreed with David that "the fool hath said in his heart, 'There is no God' " (Ps. 14:1). If the world seemed irrational, they reasoned it was because of willful sin and disobedience to God by the human race as individuals. Foundation morals [2] were more fixed than the planets in their orbits. Christianity was unique and far superior to all other religions, including secular humanism. Truth was not to be drawn from a stew pot of world religions but from the everlasting spring of biblical wisdom. Change did not always spell progress, nor did newness guarantee improvement.

Why Fight It?
While the Gablers were still reeling over their awakening to the ideological direction public education had taken, the U.S. Supreme Court declared unconstitutional the official use of voluntary, nonsectarian prayer in the public schools. (A year later the Court would outlaw school authorized Bible reading and recitation of the Lord's Prayer in classrooms.) East Texas newspapers and pulpits were outraged. Public indignation ran high. Mel and Norma saw the Court decision as just another step closer to the goals of progressive education. At the same time they read in the papers that Max Rafferty, the newly elected Superintendent of Public Instruction in California, had called for a reversal in "our national educational philosophy" before it is too late.

The Gablers were stirred by what they saw as the basic issue—

---

[2] The teaching of morals, once eliminated from classrooms, is rapidly being returned, but based on a framework of situation ethics, generally called "values education" or "values clarification." For an explanation, see Appendix II.

robbing children of the heritage of family, church, and country. They could see only three possible ways of preserving this heritage for their children and grandchildren: (1) transfer their children to a Christian school teaching traditional values; (2) teach them at home; (3) fight the self-anointed system of secular humanism. The first two were out for them. Even if they could afford the tuition, there was no Christian school nearby. And they could be sent to jail for keeping their children home. The third was their only alternative.

"Why shouldn't we fight?" Norma told Mel. "It's our children, our tax money, and our government. And it's our rights that are being violated. If textbooks can't teach Christian principles, then they shouldn't teach against Christianity."

There was no recourse through the PTA. Talking to local school personnel was unproductive since nothing could be done about books already purchased, and since the district had to select from the State-approved list of books adopted for a four- to six-year period.

Their protests had to be made to the State Textbook Committee and the State Board of Education as new subjects came up for adoption each year. With the adoptions staggered from year to year to keep a balanced budget, it would take time. But if enough people could be recruited to prepare valid, convincing "bills of particulars" and then appear before the State Textbook Committee, the publishers might start thinking of parents. And because Texas was the largest textbook purchaser in the nation, the publishers might find it unprofitable to issue different editions and other states would benefit.

The Gablers were now looking toward the '63 state textbook hearings when new economics texts would be adopted to replace those criticized during the legislative investigation.

During the winter of '62 Norma covered East Texas like the morning dew, talking to community leaders and speaking to civic clubs and church groups. And a week was spent in the Texas panhandle. Her evidence was the 31 textbooks which she and Mel had reviewed.

"I want to emphasize that I'm not angry at anyone," she told a crowd in the Hereford, Texas Community Center. "My only purpose is to tell parents what their children are being taught . . . and what they are not being taught.

"Don't go jump on the teachers or the superintendent," she implored. "They are only working with the books available to them. Put the heat on Austin."

Turning to her table display of books, she said, "Texas has the finest textbook selection system, but often only poor books are offered. Take this approved American history. The story of the history of the 'Three Little Pigs' got more stress than the story of how 'The Star Spangled Banner' was written. And Francis Scott Key isn't even mentioned."

In February she went back to Austin to speak before the House Education Committee. The permanent standing committee of the Texas House of Representatives was considering a proposal by W. T. Dungan that a course on "Capitalism vs. Communism" be required by state schools.

The weather was snowy and many businessmen who had promised Norma they would come were unable to get there. One who did was Richard Harvey, a businessman in Tyler, who had continued to help financially. He said to the Committee: "The success of the Communists has been due in part to their ability to indoctrinate young minds in their philosophy of life, and we, as citizens, . . . cannot expect this country to long endure unless young people in our educational institutions are properly instructed about the free enterprise system."

Another was Maurice Doke, a publisher from Wichita Falls and a vice-president of the State Jaycees, who said, "The issue we face is not simply a matter of economics. We face a choice between godless ideology based on dialectic materialism, and the way of life that we Americans love and cherish. . . . We must teach young people about the brutality and ugliness of Communism; let them see Communism for what it is."

The legislators questioned the businessmen intensely. But they gave Norma the longest and hardest grilling.

She was quoting a newspaper article (*Dallas Morning News,* Feb. 23, 1962) that said only 5 of each 100 Americans joining the nation's work force each year had been instructed in economics when a legislator shouted, "Point of order! We all believe in free enterprise. We're here to discuss this specific legislation."

Eyes flashing, Norma declared before the chairman could speak, "If you all believe in free enterprise, then why do we have to come here demanding legislation to try to preserve it?"

"Please relate your testimony to the legislation under question," the chairman requested.

"Certainly," Norma smiled and held up a text *Understanding our Free Economy* (1956) published by D. Van Nostrand. "Here's a book which accurately portrays the free enterprise system. You can get this kind of book into the classrooms.

"But I'm not trying to select *a* book for the course. It's just that schools have many books on the evils of capitalism, but practically nothing about the evils of Communism."

She began reading again and was interrupted before she could finish a paragraph. For the next hour, she kept trying to present the case which she and Mel had carefully worked out. Repeatedly, she was interrupted, scolded, badgered, ridiculed, put down.

Back home she wrote to the Speaker of the House, who was from Tyler and whom she knew on a first name basis:

"I have never before been so sadly disappointed in a group of men as I was of the ones chosen on this committee. . . . Because of a so-called shortage of time, I was not allowed to present positive proof of the points I was attempting to make; yet the committee spent a whole hour questioning me on vague generalities. . . .

"This disappointment does not mean I've quit. I'm a fighter, so will continue to do my best to correct the present biased political view in which our students are being indoctrinated. We may not have a powerful lobby and public relations department on our side, but I am confident that the majority of parents and businessmen are solidly . . . with us."

He never replied. The Committee voted not to require the course which Dungan wanted. (It was 1973 before the State Legislature finally approved a course on the free enterprise system.)

The battle for a course on "Capitalism vs. Communism" had been a side issue. The Gablers turned back to the main fight. Their crusade was now a family affair. Mel answered correspondence and the boys stuffed thousands of envelopes. Norma kept on the go across East Texas and as far west as Amarillo, firing up supporters, extracting pledges from people to appear at the State Textbook Committee hearings on the new economics books in the fall.

The speeches she made and the marked textbooks she left in

editorial offices prompted a stream of articles about her views and the books. The *Amarillo Daily News,* in a long commendatory column, termed her "Texas' No. 1 Textbook Sleuth."

Some papers did long analysis articles and quoted extensively from criticized texts. The *El Paso Times* spotlighted an eighth-grade history, *The Story of American Freedom* by Macmillan, which had been adopted in 1953 and readopted in 1959. The *Times* writer quoted from a section on World War II to show how history had actually been changed to create a more favorable student opinion of the U.N. In the book the Allied forces had been re-named the "United Nations" forces, even though the U.N. had not been organized until *after* the war ended.

The *Times* said when the Commissioner of Education had been shown a first draft of the article, he claimed the book had been fully investigated and found factual. Then he had conceded some changes were made in later editions.

"If the material was factual, why was it changed?" the *Times* asked, noting "surprise" to find *The Story of American Freedom* had been recommended by both state and local textbook committees "which, according to the explanations, spend days and days and weeks and weeks reading and evaluating textbooks.

"Every day we hear impassioned pleas against obscene movies and literature. How many school children every afternoon carry into the home an armload of books which may or may not be good but which are never scrutinized by their parents?

"We suggest a program in textbook reading."

Norma had been constantly urging this program in her speeches and interviews—not name-calling or personal attacks upon textbook defenders. "Just read your children's textbooks, and decide for yourself," she challenged. "Then if you agree that better books are needed, help us do something about it."

May was an extremely busy month. Jim, their oldest son who had started them on the crusade, was graduating from Hawkins High School. The Honor Society president, he was anticipating college in the fall.

Tragedy at Home

After the graduation rush, the Gablers plunged back into the textbook melee. But new books were extremely hard to get. In one instance Norma had to drive 150 miles just to look at a book in a Textbook Committee member's home, and then she couldn't bring it back with her.

To compound the frustration, a spell of dry weather caused water problems at home. On a late June morning she had to go into town to wash clothes. Returning, she found Mel bending over their second son, Paul, who lay on the living room floor unconscious. A trail of blood ran from the door.

"Paul called me at work and mumbled, 'Dad, I've been hurt,'" Mel shouted. "I've called for an ambulance to meet us on the highway to Longview. We've got to get him to the hospital."

Mel and Norma, with the help of Coach Robert Lowrance (Jim's football coach), got their limp son into their little Mercury Comet and met the ambulance. In Longview a spinal tap indicated brain damage, so he was immediately rushed to a neurosurgeon in Tyler, 35 miles away.

At Tyler the neurosurgeon required Mel's permission to do a dye test X ray, explaining that there was practically no chance for Paul to pull through and if so, he would likely be only a vegetable. While he was mowing the pasture, a piece of steel had apparently ricocheted and struck him in his head.

Mel and Norma prayed, committing Paul "completely to the Lord," asking only that if Paul recovered he would be normal. Soon, they felt peace and assurance about Paul. Peace such as they had never known before.

In about two hours Paul was wheeled into the Intensive Care room where he was to remain 10 days. The dye test showed that an object an inch and a quarter long was embedded frontally on the left side of his head, having traveled through two-thirds of his brain, missing his optic nerve by a hairbreadth.

For the 10 days Norma sat and slept in the lobby just outside the Intensive Care ward. She and Mel were allowed to see him five minutes per day, morning and evening. On the sixth day he regained consciousness but gave no indication of recognizing them. The doctor counseled, "Don't expect too much."

On the seventh day, the nurse opened the door and called. Fearing the worst, Norma turned white. "Oh, I didn't mean to scare you, Mrs. Gabler. Paul needs a battery for his radio and he knew you were out here. I asked him how he knew, and he said, 'Because she told me she'd be there, and she never lies to me.'"

When the day to return home came, the neurosurgeon warned

that it would probably be two years before Paul would be making passing grades. Mel and Norma decided to let him return to school but they expected he would fail in every subject. Paul did return to school and worked so hard that he complained of headaches when he tried to do homework. Norma noticed tears. "Honey, what is the matter?" she asked.

"I've been reading all day and I still can't do this book report," he moaned. "I just can't remember."

But the doctor was encouraging. "The headaches are probably caused by tension. There is hope, but it will take a long time. You'll have to be patient."

Paul not only did not fail, but he made the honor roll and stayed on it until he graduated!

The textbook crusade had been shunted aside. It was now too late to file a bill of particulars on books to qualify for appearing at the hearings in Austin. This year, friends had to carry the ball.

3

Strike Two

Two persons who spoke in Austin before the State Textbook Committee's 1963 hearings against five objectionable new economics texts were Joan Slay, a medical secretary from Fort Worth, and R. K. Harlan, a real estate broker from Dallas. They had met the filing deadline with great difficulty. Some of the books had not been available for public inspection until late in the summer and one book, unfinished, came with pages blank.

Trying to escape being labeled as a "censor," Harlan pointed to a difference between objecting to books being placed in a public library or book stores and books to be used in schools. The five economics texts· were "the only books being offered," he said. "Teachers in local school districts [will] have no other choice but to select [from] . . . books one-sided in favor of economic determinism and federal spending programs." The books did contain some excellent materials—which state adoption rules didn't allow him to commend, but they were still "not good enough for Texas," he declared.

Mrs. Slay agreed. She singled out McGraw-Hill's *Economics for Our Times* (1963) as having "one page on the free enterprise system, six pages on socialism and Communism in which it defends liberal socialism, [and] two chapters on Big Government."

The salesmen for the publishers appeared edgy and said little, standing on their previously submitted written replies.

They were worried about the avalanche of letters and phone calls induced by the Gablers through the Texas Farm Bureau, the East Texas Chamber of Commerce, businesses, and newspapers. McGraw-Hill was particularly concerned about its *Economics for Our Times* which had been the subject of a letter to the Commissioner of Education by the powerful Morgan J. Davis, Chairman of the Board of Humble Oil and Refining company and the vice-chairman of the influential Texas Committee On Education Beyond The High School.

After examining the book, Davis had written the Commissioner, with a copy of his letter sent to Governor John Connally:

"This proposed economics text is as I evaluate it an out-and-out advocate of the welfare state and a system of socialism. . . . It does not give the young mind a choice between different concepts of the relationship of government and economics. There are many, many passages in this book which either openly advocate a governmentally controlled economy or infer that such an economy is the ideal for which we should strive.

"It is difficult for me to see how a student who accepts the text as written could be other than an embryo socialist in his thinking. Surely it is not in the tradition of Texas education to put a book of this type into the hands of our young people. . . ."

A copy of Davis' letter went to McGraw-Hill. In response, a vice-president of the publisher flew to Houston and asked a Humble officer to talk with the chairman. Davis reportedly said, "There's no sense wasting my time. I have seen the book."

But to the dismay of the protesters, three of the objectionable texts were adopted anyway.

New Math

Paul Gabler's continued improvement lifted the spirits of his parents, who were now puzzling over five approved "new math" programs. The new math troubled them. If average parents were befuddled, wouldn't children be also?

The math teachers at Hawkins were aware of parental unease. At their request, Mel, who was still PTA president, scheduled a meeting with parents.

When the question and answer time came, Norma asked the

head of the department, "Are you sure new math will be good for the kids? What if it's a failure?"

The teacher shook his head, "We've been receiving training to teach the programs. But we honestly don't know what will be the results."

"You mean you don't care?" Norma asked in growing irritation. "Suppose ten years from now it's a proven flop."

"Well, we hope not. We hope it will work."

Norma's face darkened. "Look, you aren't just talking about numbers, but about the mind of our youngest son who will be taking math this year."

The teacher could only shrug and say the department would do the best it could.

To satisfy their own curiosity and to be able to answer parents who would be asking them, the Gablers dug up information on the new math.

The innovation, they discovered, had been financed by the government's National Science Foundation (NSF) and private foundations, and printed by private publishers who contracted to pay royalties back to the government. Seeing the potential for profit in selling completely new math programs to American schools, the publishers had conducted a gigantic promotional campaign aimed at textbook buyers.

What the promotional literature did not include, the Gablers discovered, was the stated skepticism of some math scholars and even outright opposition of a few to the radical switch from traditional teaching.

They obtained from the *New York University Alumni News* (October, 1961) an article by Dr. Morris Kline, titled "Math Teaching Reforms Assailed As Peril to U.S. Scientific Progress." A world famous mathematician, Dr. Kline was director of the Division of Electromagnetic Research at the New York University Institute of Mathematical Science. The math scholar charged that the new math developers were from "the more remote and less scientifically motivated domains of mathematics," and that they neither knew what should be taught in the schools nor how students should think. He stated further:

". . . The Commission on Mathematics of the College Entrance Examination Board urged the changes in hundreds of talks and articles when the very proposals to make the changes were no further advanced than the discussion stage among the members of the Commission itself.

"During that time, high school teachers were told they would have to adopt the changes because questions would appear in college entrance examinations based on the new curriculum. If teachers wanted their students to do well on these examinations, they had no choice but to prepare them in the new material. No experimentation of any kind was ever attempted.

". . . Not only do these reform groups urge their respective curricula through articles and talks, but principals and superintendents are pressured into accepting them. It is implied that secondary school administrators who fail to adopt the reforms are guilty of indifference or inactivity. As a result, many principals and superintendents are urging it on their teachers just to show parents and school boards that the leadership is active."

The Gablers studied the new math books and other materials, and talked with knowledgeable persons. Then they prepared a list of reasons for questioning the new math, which they mailed along with the Kline article to their mailing list.

The list included the following:

"Those promoting this 'new' math are those who promised similar improved results for the sight-reading which has been disastrous for so many.

"On a moral basis there is fear that such abstract teaching to young minds will tend to destroy the students' belief in absolutes—to believe that nothing is concrete. This could be instrumental in helping erode their faith in other absolutes such as Christian faith.

"Are those who are concerned about this math just not capable of understanding it? Consultations with teachers, businessmen with considerable math, and mathematicians revealed that (1) it is 'planned confusion,' and/or (2) a complicated method of arriving at simple solutions, and/or (3) a few brilliant students will learn extremely fast, leaving the majority of students to plod along, never fully understanding it, especially since many of the present teachers are having so much difficulty that they question their own ability to teach it properly."

The mailing on the new math triggered a huge response from both school personnel and parents. The school people substantiated Dr. Kline's charge of "pressure" to go along with the new programs. But again, they asked the Gablers not to use their names.

The parents wanted to know how the new math could be removed from schools and the old books and teaching methods restored. The Gablers could give them no assurance this would be done. The five new math programs had been adopted at the state level. Districts could only choose from these.[1]

Biology: Blue, Green, and Yellow

Their sights were now on the '64 hearings when new high school biologies would be offered by several publishers. The three books receiving the biggest promotional ballyhoo had been financed and developed much like the new math. The NSF had provided $4 million of federal funds, and private foundations had supplied another million. The Biological Science Curriculum Study group (BSCS) had prepared the books and leaders of the American Institute of Biological Sciences had endorsed and promoted them. Three private publishers had contracted to print the books and pay royalties back to the federal government.

The three books would radically change the teaching of biology, weaving all of biology around the theory of evolution—from cover to cover. Each of the three used a different approach. The Blue book (so named because of the cover color) was molecular, the Green book ecological, and the Yellow book cellular. Friends from California, where the course was already in the schools, said the books delivered the boldest indoctrination in atheistic evolution and the strongest attack on the biblical account of origins that students had ever faced.

The Gablers hoped the BSCS books might be rejected because of the government financing. Austin had been ambivalent on this point, accepting the new math while declining a federally financed chemistry book. In rejecting the chemistry text the previous year,

---

[1] It was years later that most of their charges were verified in an article about the mass return of textbooks to more basic math content in *The Wall Street Journal*, May 31, 1973, which was headlined, "MANY SCHOOLS DISCOVER KIDS USING 'NEW MATH' CAN'T DIVIDE 100 BY 10," and included, ". . . Many of these kids can't add, subtract, multiply, or divide." The article concluded that the best of the 'new math' programs have only a 3% to 5% accomplishment rate.

the Commissioner of Education had warned, "This . . . could lead to the federal government determining what is to be taught in our public schools down to the last detail."

But there was nothing to indicate that the BSCS would be declined on the same grounds. Indeed, the Gablers learned, the biology course was already being used in some Texas schools on an "experimental" basis. This seemed to be a clear violation of state laws and Norma planned to so inform the State Textbook Committee.

They got the books early from out-of-state friends. Mel began reading and making notes. "No wonder they complained so much in California," he told Norma. "These are simply awful. They'll undermine the faith of thousands of students. We don't pay our taxes for that!"

They started a publicity campaign. Norma took summary reviews around to editors and businessmen. The editors were cordial, but the businessmen explained, "evolution isn't our thing." The Texas Farm Bureau was more encouraging and used their reviews in alerting the membership.

Unknown to the Gablers, several church groups were also upset over the biologies. Reuel Lemmons, editor of the respected *Firm Foundation* magazine in Austin called the BSCS books "extremely dangerous." In a June 30 editorial broadside, he warned members of the Churches of Christ:

". . . If the parents of Texas school children allow [these texts] to be adopted they will have entrenched sheer atheism in every biology classroom in the state." [2]

Lemmons saw the state adoption process as "one dim ray of hope" and called for his readers "to get these godless texts rejected if they cannot be changed."

By the time the hearings before the State Textbook Committee opened on October 14 in the Texas Education Agency headquarters building, the letters of objection filled two huge cartons. Dr. J. B. Golden, director of TEA's textbook division called it "the most voluminous protest in my 11 years with the Agency."

Press interest was the highest in anyone's memory. Every seat at the press table in the TEA Conference Room was taken and television cameramen and photographers stalked around the room

---

[2]Reuel Lemmons, Editorial: "An Extremely Dangerous Textbook Coming," *Firm Foundation*, June 30, 1964.

crowded with book salesmen and protestors. The presence of an NBC-TV crew indicated that more than Texas schools were at stake.

To bolster their case, creationists brought in scientists of stature. These men could only appear during time allotted to petitioners who had previously met the adoption procedure requirements. Dr. H. Douglas Dean, head of the Biology Department, Pepperdine University, represented Vernon L. Decker. Dr. Jack Wood Sears, head of Department of Biology, Harding College, appeared on the bill submitted by Reuel Lemmons and Hulen Jackson. Professor T. G. Barnes, the distinguished director of the Schellenger Research Laboratory and professor in the Physical Science Department of the University of Texas in El Paso, and an articulate creationist, appeared with the Gablers.

The Committee chairman laid down the ground rules: Each accredited petitioner, or his/her expert witness, would have 10 minutes per book or 30 minutes for the series, with publishers allowed matching time for reply. There were 15 citizen speakers on the agenda this year, nine of whom were there to object to the BSCS biology series. Norma was listed last.

The overall criticism was that the content put more emphasis on evolution than any science book ever studied in Texas high schools. The Blue book was the worst, protester Hulen L. Jackson noted, "devoting nearly 300 pages directly to the theory of evolution. It's not a textbook on biology, but a textbook on evolution." The Yellow and Green books had about 100 pages each on evolution, he said. In contrast, a biology presently in use had only 12 pages "devoted to evolution."

The protestors carefully defined the type of "evolution" to which they were objecting. Prof. Barnes said he could accept "special evolution" which called for "variation within limits," but not "general evolution." The BSCS books, said mathematician James White, were teaching as fact "unlimited [biological] change across all boundaries, across all limits, and across tremendous gaps in fossil evidence." He too, could accept "limited" change "because it is documented evidence," in agreement with the Genesis record, but not the "evolution or the development of man from . . . non-living matter."

The books defenders argued that the BSCS series was teaching evolution only as a theory in the spirit of scientific inquiry. According to Gordon Hjalmarson, a Houghton-Mifflin editor, the purpose of his Blue book was to teach "biology as a science, not as a group of isolated facts . . ." Scientific theory, said William B. Miller, science editor for Rand McNally, quoting from his Green book:

". . . [Evolution] is never 'proved' once and for all. But if it continues to account for new data as they appear, it becomes increasingly convincing. In short, 'proof' of a scientific theory means simply this: The theory continues to account for new evidence as it arises" (p. 547).

Admittedly, it is "much more difficult to prove the theory of evolution than certain others," conceded Don Meyer, representing Harcourt, Brace, and World, the publisher of the Yellow version. This was because the theory of evolution was "based, in such large part, on the past. . . . It will be further documented with time. We must realize that, among other things, only a spoonful of the earth's surface has been upturned even in search of fossils. What will be yielded in coming years we can only imagine."

The witnesses for the publishers kept claiming their books presented evolution only as a theory, with the protesters saying this was only a semantic disguise. Prof. Barnes pointed to a statement in the Yellow book that declared "scientists had yet to find any facts in nature or in the laboratory that cannot be explained on the basis of the theory of evolution" (p. 633). "Boy, that's a good one," the El Paso scientist snorted. "This . . . excludes any other possibility." Hulen L. Jackson cited a paragraph from the Blue book:

"It is for this reason that we have organized the contents of this book around the theory of evolution. But we have been able to show also that the gene theory and the cell theory . . . provide reinforcement for the theory of evolution" (p. 669).

And Dr. Dean told about a poll he had taken of high school students in California who had been using the BSCS books. ". . . Some of them were very religious, some . . . not religious at all, and I asked them, 'What was your opinion of the textbooks? Did you get the idea that evolution is true or is just a theory?' And . . . 98 percent of them had gotten the idea that evolution was a fact."

"We have no objection to the teaching of evolution as an unproved theory, which it is," said Dr. Sears. "But we object to a book that admits evolution is a theory and not just a fact and then continues to 'preach' . . . it as a fact and to examine all phenomena only on the basis of evolution as a fact." That, he said, "is a narrow, unscientific approach." Sears, who earned his doctorate in genetics from the University of Texas, declared that study of the fossil records had "convinced" him that "scientifically the evidence does not support evolution." But he added, "I do not think we will ever support or prove evolution or creation. I am confident we won't, but I believe the evidence for and against must be presented if a book is fair."

Vernon H. Harley, a Lutheran minister from Corpus Christi who spoke against the BSCS books, felt fairness would include identification of "biologists and other scientists who repudiate evolution," and he offered to prepare a list. "Does fear of exposing the weaknesses of the theory," he chided, "account for the failure on the part of evolutionistic writers to mention opposing interpretation and data?"

Harley further suggested: "It would appear to be in the interest of scientific integrity, impartiality, and fulfillment of responsibility for the authors to either eliminate evolution entirely from the textbook or for them to place it alongside opposing views and let each stand on its own merits without arbitrary interpretation."

The three scientists who spoke in support of the petitioners all presented evidence which they felt supported biological development within created species. The publishers' witnesses seemed impressed. During a break in the proceedings, three went to Dr. Dean and said, "We had no idea there was such scientific evidence for creation." Each indicated his company would be interested in publishing a textbook on scientific creation.[3] However, when the hearing resumed they insisted that creation theory should be excluded from high school biologies because such a theory was in the realm of religion.

It was the responsibility of "parents and clergy" to teach creation, said Houghton Mifflin's Gordon Hjalmarson. "It would not be proper for the public schools to usurp this right in the American tradition of church and state."

George Golden, a Baptist pastor from Arlington, said this dichotomy would "confuse the students." The schools should pro-

---

[3]See Appendix IV, Recommended Sources and Publishers.

vide "an opportunity to see the truth from both sides by presenting data supporting both creation and evolution."

But Hjalmarson and his colleagues could see no "conflict between the theory of evolution as presented in the Blue version and our religious beliefs." He added that he himself was a Congregational Church deacon, and that the supervisor of the writing team that produced the Blue book was an elder in the United Church of Christ.

The book opponents steadfastly maintained that the biologies presented an anti-religious point of view. Said the Lutheran pastor: "When biologists begin to speculate upon the origins of life, they also begin to dovetail with theology and actually become guilty of proposing an answer to a question which remains primarily in the field of religion. It is to this approach which, like religion, demands faith rather than concrete proof that we object. A theory that explains the origin of all life without God becomes atheistic religion advanced in the name and pretense of science."

And since texts were bought with public tax money and children required to attend school, argued attorney Vernon L. Decker of El Paso, an anti-Christian view expressed in schoolbooks was a violation of conscience and Section 6 of the Texas Constitution. To illustrate this contention, he quoted from the *Teacher's Manual* of the Blue version:

"Some [students] will come to the subject with preconceptions, many of which will serve as a barrier to the proper understanding of evolution" (p. 2).

"Now if the authors of this *Teacher's Manual* speak of preconception as a belief in the creation as explained in Genesis, then we feel that definitely this would be unconstitutional under the Constitution of the State of Texas. . . ."

The contrast in this debate and the 1925 Scopes trial over the teaching on origins should have been obvious. But some reporters who had predicted "another monkey trial" at Austin failed to see that the shoe of intolerance was now on the other foot. In 1925 Tennessee students were denied the teaching of evolution. Here in Austin, 39 years later, the protesters argued that acceptance of the BSCS books would deny Texas children the teaching of creation.

Dean and Harley went further and charged evolutionists with applying unscientific pressure to keep creationist views from being fairly presented. Dean said "several biologists" had not appeared at the hearings in support of creation "because of adverse publicity, because their college presidents and deans . . . forbade them to come." Some biologists, he added, had tried to get him not to come.

The Lutheran was more blunt. "We are sincerely alarmed by the fact that many evolutionists, using the claim of science for what is arbitrary classification and interpretations, are attempting to foist their beliefs upon an unsuspecting public and even upon fellow scientists in such a fashion that it often becomes scientific suicide to disagree with their position. We deplore this tendency toward intolerance whether in the religious or the scientific field. . . . We believe that the exclusion of God or refusal even to consider the possibility of explaining the origin of life from the viewpoint of creation is tantamount to intolerance and if you please, persecution."

Throughout the proceedings, Norma had been impressed by the courtesy and order observed. It was a pleasant dissimilarity from the rudeness she had experienced in the rough-and-tumble legislative hearings. When her turn finally came to speak, she asked the Committee to consider "two or three points . . . strictly from a parent's viewpoint:

". . . What a child is not taught is even more important than what he is being taught in the schools today.

". . . In appearing before investigating committees we have heard repeatedly that parents have been told that a . . . student must be given both sides of an issue. Now, we as parents, are pleading for the same thing . . . let our children be given both sides in the field of biology.

". . . The thing that means the most to me, particularly in light of our recent Supreme Court ruling, [is] our children will be taught atheism out of these books. . . . Why it is unfair to teach the creation theory to a child? Why can't they teach that?"

The Decision

That night the participants watched themselves on NBC television. The program included a warning by a publisher's representative that the biology controversy could start a dangerous trend nationwide.

The next day the Committee met to choose five new biology

books. Protesters and publishers' representatives waited for the verdict. If the Biological Sciences Curriculum Study (BSCS) were accepted, the salesmen could begin counting their commissions. If they were rejected, the protesters could count their blessings.

The decision was announced the following day. The BSCS Series would be recommended to the State Board for adoption. A Committee member who asked not to be identified by the press admitted arguing that the state would fail its students if the books were rejected.

Norma called Mel in deep disappointment. "How could they be so unfair?" she groaned. "But we'll keep fighting. They aren't in the schools yet."

She and Mel took the next step and appealed to the Commissioner. He refused to strike the books from the list. They asked that she be heard by the State Board of Education.

She was joined by Dr. Russell Lewis, a professor at Abilene Christian College who appeared in behalf of Editor Reuel Lemmons.

The BSCS books, he argued, were not adapted to the maturity of high school students who would use them. They violated the academic right of students to be informed of all sides. They failed to present a challenge for critical thinking. They contained untruths and speculation that would lead students to unproved conclusions. "There is no surer way," he added, "to undermine confidence in public schools than to adopt objectionable textbooks."

After Norma and other protesters had their say and the publishers answered, the board voted 14 to 6 to approve the books.

The decision was front-paged across Texas. "FIVE EVOLUTIONARY TEXTS ADOPTED" said the *Houston Chronicle*. "DARWIN DECLARED WINNER IN TEXAS 'MONKEY WAR'" declared the *Sweetwater Reporter*. It was infuriating to the Gablers that some reporters had still not seen the difference between 1925 and 1964.

The few changes required by the Committee and the State Board were minor and of little consolation. The Gablers were not uplifted. They felt that the cosmetics had not changed the body.

Only the local school district textbook committees remained. The Gablers could not appear before them all, but they could mail out reviews on the five books to help the districts choose. They recommended Holt, Rhinehart, and Winston's *Modern Biology* as preferable to the BSCS books.

The Gablers also sent reviews to Bill Wedemeyer, Research & Education Director for the Texas Farm Bureau. Wedemeyer used the Gabler's material in preparing a study report on the new biologies for the thousands of Bureau members across the states. He called the BSCS books "unacceptable" because they pursued a straight evolutionary approach, without presenting "an honest, straight-forward account of the creation." Furthermore, he said, the BSCS books had been promoted under the name of the American Institute of Biological Sciences, without the approval of all the Institute's 85,000 members. Wedemeyer recommended that Bureau members urge their local schools to select Holt's *Modern Biology,* which he said was "much milder" on evolution.

The Farm Bureau report added vast influence to the Gabler's reviews. The publishers naturally would not release sales statistics, but the feedback which the Gabler's received from districts indicated to them that *Modern Biology* was heavily outselling all three BSCS books combined.

4

Big Government and "Biased" Economics

The old farmhouse was fast turning into a textbook depository. Books and stacks of mimeographed reviews and photo copies of articles overflowed onto the back porch and into the rear of the garage. Dauber wasps were having a picnic. Then Mel was transferred to a job in Longview.

With Mel commuting, and the textbook work growing, the most sensible thing to do seemed to be to sell the farm and get a bigger house in Longview.

They built a ranch-style four-bedroom house on a sloping tree-shaded corner lot. The "bedroom" behind the garage was added to serve as the office. Books were stored in other rooms.

With all the hassles of moving, it was tempting to skip the 1965 hearings. But high school economics books were coming back. The controversial *Economics for Our Times* was even being offered again—a reminder that victory was far from being won. The Gablers felt that the publisher, Webster Division, McGraw-Hill, was counting on public forgetfulness of the objections raised two years before.

Norma began a travel-and-tell campaign to refresh memories. Again, she took books into offices, pointed out objectionable passages and asked that letters and telegrams be sent to the Commissioner of Education and the district representative on the State Board.

Because of the time and travel involved in reviewing the books, the Gablers were the only ones who prepared bills of particulars in 1965. They had also researched the history of economics and had a better understanding of economic theories and the direction the new books were taking.

The old books had been built around the classical theory that said self-interest was the strongest economic force, that the economy would prosper when trade and commerce were least controlled, and that prices, wages, and employment would fluctuate naturally according to supply and demand.

The new books appeared to follow more the beliefs of John Maynard Keynes that government should keep the economy balanced with "pump priming," making credit easy, and/or setting up public works programs when employment levels were low.

Keynesian programs, launched in the Depression, had opened the door to the heavy involvement in the economy which the Gablers believed had done more harm than good. Faceless bureaucrats sitting in plush Washington offices were stifling individual ambition and free enterprise and rewarding slothfulness. Increased government control and interference in the private sector, the Gablers felt, would lead to state socialism.

They saw a parallel between economics and biology. To them, it wasn't fair to teach the evolutionary theory of origins while ignoring creation. Nor was it fair to teach Keynesian economics without giving students a proper understanding of classical or free enterprise economics, especially since free enterprise was responsible for the United States becoming the richest and most productive nation in the world. Parents and taxpayers had the right not to have their children indoctrinated in a system of economics in which they did not believe.

They entered their strongest objections to *Economics for Our Times* (1963), stating in their cover letter to the Commissioner:

"We realize that a person's opinion of this book will depend to a large extent upon his own political philosophy. Those who believe in 'big brother' government—also known as the Welfare State, The Great Society, etc.—will find little fault with this book's content and will see only its excellent arrangement for teaching, its attractive format, etc.

"However there is a state requirement that Texas textbooks be objective. We urge the references given in this protest be carefully considered, in context. We believe that every fair-minded person who does this conscientiously will come to the conclusion that this book strongly indoctrinates students to favor government intervention in our economy. Omissions of the classical view of economics prohibits students from receiving an objective presentation of this subject."

In their 11-page bill of particulars, they grouped objections under three headings: (1) "Errors," (2) "Contradictions," and (3) "General." Some of their citations with comments in italics were:

ERRORS

"It is surprising how little increase there has been in the *relative* size of government expenditures. . . . Federal government expenditures, *other than for defense and security*, were under 1 percent in 1929 and are now only about 1.6 percent' (p. 353).

The Gablers' comments were, *"Instead of 1.6, the percentage should be approximately 6.4. U.S. Department of Commerce figures show $28.26 billion non-defense spending in 1960 out of a $441 billion GNP, which equals 6.4%. This larger figure can also be verified by comparing the charts in this book on pages 340, 352, 370, and 748."*

CONTRADICTIONS

". . . experience seems to indicate that present tax rates have not discouraged the incentive to work, save, and invest" (p. 369).

"Yet page 582 states, *'Many economists think that these tax rates, which are substantially higher than those in most European countries, have been a major factor in damping down the rate of growth.'* "

GENERAL

"The collection of taxes is a way of forcing people to save" (p. 106).

"Taxes to construct public property could be considered as 'savings' only to a collectivist. The idea of 'forcing' people to save is in violation of the basic freedom to utilize one's own property."

The 1965 Hearings

After their bills of particulars were in the mail, Mel helped Norma prepare for the '65 hearings. First taking the role of a publisher's representative, he attacked her positions from every angle he could conceive. Then he switched to committee chairman and gave her the third degree on procedural matters.

While this was going on, Don was in the back bedroom with his friend Steve Scobee. "I'd better go home," the Scobee boy said uncomfortably. "Your parents are having a, uh—"

"No, don't go," Don broke in. "Dad's just getting Mother ready for Austin. They never fight." Steve didn't seem convinced.

When Norma did get to Austin, she found herself the only petitioner who had qualified to speak. Pitted against her were the vice-presidents of three publishing houses who had flown from the East Coast for the hearings.

Before tackling the first of the five books to which she and Mel had filed objections, she explained her "reason for being here" as "our concern over . . . what our children learn. We have found in speaking during the last few years that children know little about the economic system under which our government operates. To us, it is alarming that they know so little about the free enterprise system. Many will say, 'Well, you surely want people to know that there is a role the government has in our economic system.' By all means, I think children should know the role which our government plays, and it certainly plays a big one. . . ."

She related a conversation with three San Antonio schoolboys who insisted that "men in Washington" knew better than local people in communities what was good for them.

"I told them we had lived on a farm for the past seven years. . . . We were not allowed to raise a grain of wheat, even for our own cattle. . . . These young boys . . . couldn't believe it. They said, 'Even for your own use?' We said, 'By all means, for our own use. We did not have a wheat allotment. We could not grow grain, wheat on our land." He [one of the boys] said, "Well, that isn't fair.' We said, 'But you told me a man in Washington sitting at a desk knows far more than you do or I do down in our own community.' . . . This is typical of young people today—how little they know of our economic system."

Then, taking one book at a time, she moved on to speak about specific objections. When she came to Allyn and Bacon's *Modern Economics* (1964), she noted that the publisher had said the Gabler's bill of particulars was written by "amateurs."

"We concur with the publisher that we are amateurs and not professionals. Were this book written for educated economists, our review would possibly be out of place. However, this book is supposedly written for students who know little or nothing about economics and nothing about the intent of the author. Therefore, we have tried to review this book from the viewpoint of those whose economic knowledge would be limited to what is learned in this book."

Of the three publisher's vice-presidents in the room only one made more than a perfunctory attempt to challenge Norma. Emerson Brown, vice-president of Webster Division, McGraw-Hill began his defense by suggesting that Norma's criticisms were not valid on *Economics for Our Times,* because she had used the wrong edition.

Norma reddened, but she had no recourse.

Brown did not push the point, but continued, "The question involved is: Does the book you publish represent the best economic thought that is agreed upon generally by economists in government, . . . business, . . . labor, . . . the schools? Is this the economics of the 20th century?" He looked at his book and smiled. "This represents the most modern economic thought. . . ."

Publishers Win Again

The next day the Committee voted to recommend the protested books.

Norma was embarrassed and disappointed. She was not only set back by the vote, but also by the failure of many businessmen to follow through on their promise to at least write letters. And when she checked *Economics for Our Times,* she found that the publisher had provided her with two different versions, identical in appearance and copyright date but different in some content.

While others might be lax, she and Mel would not quit. They appealed to the Commissioner and when he did not act, they prepared a petition to the State Board on *Economics for Our Times* and one other book. They said, in part:

"This is not fair, since there is a state requirement that textbooks be objective. Economic practices are presented as though federal economic policies are the criteria. Students are not advised that these federal policies are following unproven theories."

Copies of the petition sent to East Texas newspapers brought strong editorial support. Declared the *Tyler Morning Telegraph:* "*Economics for Our Times* is unsuitable as a textbook because of its lack of objectivity and real accuracy in discussing the economy of this country historically—both through omission and constant out-of-proportion presentation of government as a solution to individual and commercial economic problems. The authors have expounded what might be called 'central statism.' "

Norma was at the November 8 Board meeting to speak her petition. She had hardly begun, when Board member Jack Binion, a bachelor lawyer from Houston, interrupted, "Mrs. Gabler, would you please tell me and the members of this Board what qualifies you for us to listen to anything you have to say?"

Norma looked him squarely in the eye. "Yes, sir. I have three qualifications. First, I am a mother of three sons. Second, I am a taxpayer whose money pays for these books. Third, I am a registered voter, who by law you represent. Can you think of three better reasons?"

The other Board members grinned as Binion said, "Go ahead, Mrs. Gabler."

She continued speaking, trying not to be bothered by one Board member reading a newspaper and several others talking in low tones. But she had to stop when the paper reader called, "Mr. Chairman, why must we listen to this woman? We know how we're going to vote."

Chairman W. W. Jackson of San Antonio was not amused. "As long as I'm chairman of this Board, any citizen will receive a hearing. Continue, Mrs. Gabler."

Norma picked up her line of talk and tried to keep smiling. It was hard, but she finished.

After the book salesmen offered brief defenses, the Board debated the books. The Gablers' old friend and Board member from their district, Dr. B. E. Masters, was opposed to all five. "I hate to see our children taught the same kind of economics the Russians have," he said, adding that the five new texts all leaned toward a government-controlled economy. Two other Board members wanted to throw out only *Economics for Our Times*. In the end, the majority voted to adopt all of the contested books.

Again, Norma was dumfounded. Why couldn't the Board majority see what the books were teaching? Most were businessmen and professionals with a bent for public service. Norma felt they didn't like the encroachment of Big Government any better than she and Mel did. Why were they so willing to believe the line of the publishers and accept the recommendations of the Textbook Committee?

She went home and helped Mel prepare reviews for mailing to the districts. There were no books they could praise, since the five new economics books had replaced the old ones. No matter how a district chose, students would end up with a bad book, in the Gablers' estimation.

Other States Concerned

The one consolation was that Texas seemed to be far ahead of other states in allowing protesters to be heard. The reports they received from elsewhere indicated that people were complaining *after* objectionable books were already in the schools.

In California, for example, some legislators were upset over acceptance by the State Curriculum Commission of an eighth-grade history, *Land of the Free* (1964), published in California by Franklin Brothers. The objections had come up during budget hearings when it was discovered the Commission had committed the state to pay out over $1 million for the history.

Opponents claimed the book was slanted toward radical views in society. They cited as an example the treatment of two blacks, Booker T. Washington and William E. B. DuBois. Washington, who had urged blacks to study hard, learn trades, and start businesses, was given only two short paragraphs. DuBois, a black activist with a strong leftist philosophy, was lauded in two lengthy articles. The book ignored the fact that clubs named after DuBois were, according to the U.S. Justice Department, Communist-created and -controlled.

They further charged that *Land of the Free* showed the country in a bad light. The Boston Tea Party was described in a caption as a "mob scene" and the seizing of the tea on the ship as "hijacking," not as a protest by disfranchised American patriots.

Max Rafferty, the conservative Superintendent of Public Instruction, was upset that the book had been accepted. Rafferty said that some parts were "certainly not historical," and that a historian "has the positive duty of portraying all sides of every issue."

A member of the State Curriculum Commission assured Rafferty and the angry legislators that a major editing job would be done before the book went to press. Editors of the *Los Angeles Herald-Examiner* who had reviewed the book called for a "major operation," adding:

What we really need is a system whereby textbooks are not bought and paid for before they are screened. And that screening should be done with considerable thoroughness and the honesty that minds of young Americans deserve.

It was reassuring to the Gablers that others felt as they did about school curriculum. Even scholars were sounding warnings. While Californians were fussing over history, Mel and Norma read an Associated Press story that one of the founders of the new math was now having doubts about the "crazy turns we've taken" in the new program. Dr. Max Beberman of the University of Illinois, in speaking to the National Council of Teachers of Mathematics, was quoted as saying, "We're not doing a good enough job of teaching masses of children the very, very basic ideas and skills [in mathematics]."

He was voicing the Gablers' sentiments exactly. But they seemed to have accomplished so little. The protested economic books were in use. The federally financed biologies were on the approved list.

They sensed that public concern was greater than ever. Norma's speeches were always warmly received. She and Mel continued to be invited to the "Party Line" talk show in Shreveport and they had appeared on Allan Dale's radio talk show on 50,000-watt WOAI in San Antonio. Callers predominantly agreed with them.

The Shreveport program had made the Gablers popular in Louisiana. Norma was invited to speak to the Greater New Orleans Area Chamber of Commerce Women's Auxiliary in the Blue Room of the Roosevelt Hotel.

A high-ranking school official in New Orleans public schools had heard of the Gablers through educational channels. When he learned Norma was coming, he immediately demanded that the Chamber Auxiliary permit him to sit at the head table with the privilege of correcting her as she spoke. The irritated Program Committee took the request to the Chamber president who shot back a telegram saying the educator could sit at the head table, provided he kept his mouth shut.

Norma spoke about fairness and objectivity to all sides in curriculum. Afterward, the official greeted her with a smile, saying, "You're not at all what I expected."

A Run for Public Office

In the fall of 1967 Norma was wondering if there wasn't a better way to get more objective textbooks than spend so many hours reviewing books, and then making two or three discouraging trips to Austin every fall.

As a member of the State Board of Education, she would be an insider. Dr. B. E. Masters had announced his retirement because of ill health and had encouraged Norma to run for election as his successor. Both Norma and Mel had reservations, but with so many friends urging her to run, they decided she should try.

In February she had to register in each of the eight counties that made up her campaign area. Accompanied by her mother, she visited a different town almost every day. She asked support from local officials, shook hands at businesses and plants, and spoke to every group that would have her. No town was too small, no crossroads store too far out for a visit.

Often, people were amazed to meet a woman running for office. For example, in one town, which was too small for a post office, she surprised the local blacksmith at 7:30 A.M. When Norma explained that she was campaigning for the district seat on the State Board of Education, he looked even more puzzled. "I didn't even know that office was on the ballot. But anybody who can get up this early and come way out here will sure get my vote," he promised.

Everywhere she encountered ignorance about the office. Those who did know that the Board member was elected, didn't seem to think the office was important. The exceptions were school superintendents.

It was soon obvious that most school administrators were supporting her opponent as a representative of the Texas school establishment. One told her bluntly, "You are not our candidate." Another said insultingly, "We pick who runs for the State Board."

Another predicted, "The teachers will get out the vote for our man."

But her supporters were telephoning their friends. In addition, they bought a large newspaper advertisement. By election day there was more interest in the race than there had been in years. Political prognosticators predicted that her opponent would win by a large margin.

Instead, Norma lost by only a small margin of the votes cast. She carried Longview by a 2.5 to 1 majority.

Both she and Mel were exhausted. They took a vacation to Colorado with their son, Don, with Norma speaking along the way. By the time they returned, it was too late to file for the '68 hearings. Very few new texts were up for adoption anyway.

They were now aiming for '69 when biology and history textbooks would be considered.

5

Taking the Offensive

The Gablers had always felt themselves among the least qualified to wage a crusade against objectionable textbooks in their state. Others such as the Churches of Christ and certain businessmen had come in from year to year against books that aroused their ire. The Texas Society Daughters of the American Revolution could usually be counted on, but the TSDAR was handicapped by its media image of extremism.

So Mel and Norma felt the mantle of representing the masses of ordinary parents had fallen on them. They belonged to no political organization, had no vested interests other than concern for children, and sacrificed their own money, with help from the Harveys and a few others. Even those who didn't agree with their position on economics or biology had to concede that they were dedicated to public service.

Being "home folks" gave them a big advantage with East Texas media people, many of whom were already resentful of the northern and eastern publishing establishments. The Gablers had influential editorial friends on newspapers in Kilgore, Tyler, Longview, Borger, and other cities. All they had to do was send over copies of bills of particulars. The newspapers would do stories and often print strong editorials in advance of the Austin hearings.

One of their special editor friends was Ellie Hopkins who had been with the *Longview Daily News* and *Longview Morning Jour-*

nal since 1945. Hopkins had known Norma since she was a little girl and he was a deacon in a church she once attended. A respected, soft-spoken conservative, he had won several Freedom Foundation awards for his editorials and in 1969 was president of the Texas Press Association.

"I'm disturbed about these books," he told Mel and Norma. "This 'progressive' education really isn't 'progressive' at all. It's just a way to sell change."

Ellie Hopkins counseled them about cultivating good press and public relations: "Don't go into an editor's office as belligerent, loudmouth protesters. Go as ordinary people, seeking to do good for home, schools, and country. Go with reasonable attitudes, affirming your convictions, not flaunting them, and not trying to embarrass him. If you do, you'll get a better hearing and a lot more consideration.

"If you see you aren't getting your message across, or if the editor appears rushed, tell him you'll come another time. Then leave him in a position that will allow you to come back. It might not be an editor, but an official in Austin. You never know the pressures he's undergoing. Just keep a low profile and be persistent."

Hopkins also talked to Norma about speaking in the Austin hearings where big city newspapers, television, and the national wire services would be represented. "Watch your attitude and tone of your voice. You may be boiling inside, but keep your voice under control. Don't let a questioner get you excited or throw you off the track. If you have something of substance to say, the press will pay attention to you."

"The Textbook Committee members are picked new each year," he continued. "You don't have the chance to get to know them well. But the State Board members are in there a lot longer. When you know them well and appreciate them and they appreciate you, you'll have some influence. Remember they have all kinds of people coming before them, and some are pretty far out.

"Try to understand the book salesmen, too. They want to sell books. They feel they must do their job, and if they don't do it, somebody else will. So if you can, get on good speaking terms with them and listen to them.

"If you try to bully your way through, anywhere, you'll go right out the other side of the building.

"And always do your homework," he reminded. "Don't ever be caught short."

With both history and biology texts coming up for adoption, the Gablers had plenty of homework.

The last time around the Biological Science Curriculum Study (BSCS) "Yellow," "Green," and "Blue" biologies had been adopted for a six-year listing.

The Gablers had a reservoir of material from the '64 hearings. The basic objections which had gone unheeded then still seemed valid. (1) The books wove the study of biology around the assumption that evolution was fact; (2) evidence against evolution was not presented; (3) other theories of origin, specifically divine creation, were not considered. As in '64, the Gablers wanted the presentation of evolution as a theory, as long as it was discussed fairly, pro and con, and hoped creation would eventually also receive fair treatment. Objectivity, yes. Indoctrination, no.

They would, of course, need to check their old research against the latest editions of the biology books. Norma had not forgotten the "put down" on *Economics for Our Times* when the publisher had accused her of using the wrong edition.

There were 33 history books, 16 for eighth grade and 17 for high school. One of the eighth grade titles looked familiar. It was Benziger's *Land of the Free,* the book that had created a furor in California, where it had been published by Franklin Brothers.

They were able to purchase new editions of the biologies and three of the four history books they intended to protest.

Norma kept calling for the missing history, *The Promise of America* (1970) by Science Research Associates. Finally they told her, "It's here."

She drove over the next day and began making notes. Page 29 was blank. She thumbed ahead. Pages 33, 38, 43, 75, and 88 were blank. She started counting. There were 33 blank pages and the book ended abruptly at page 514. There was nothing to do but review the incomplete book and complain about it at the hearings.

Back home she shared the notes with Mel. He read them and composed a letter to the Commissioner of Education as a summation of their objections on this book. The letter said in part:

"The title [*The Promise of America*] sounds great, but its

content destroys the very concept of the founders of our Republic which it professes to uphold.

A student studying this text would feel ashamed of our heritage. From this book the student would never learn why our nation has progressed so that today 6% of the world's population produces half the world's consumer goods. Other nations have natural resources, intelligent people, but only in ours was there enough freedom from government control so that the tremendous energies of our people were released. Instead, this book advocates more government.

"Great pains have been taken to equalize historical figures. That is, great men are brought down to a mediocre level and relatively unknown men are elevated.

"To illustrate the misrepresentation and bias we are including excerpts. More could have been listed, but sufficient are included to illustrate the bias in this tentative format as furnished for review . . ."

They reached similar conclusions in reviewing the other three histories, Holt's *Discovering America* (1967), Benziger's *Land of the Free* (1969), and a Macmillan high school text, *History of a Free People* (1969).

They felt there was abundant evidence to "convict" the histories, not only in content but also in author attitude.

But past experience indicated that the State Textbook Committee paid more attention to publisher' boasts of relevance, new teaching methods, and the scholarship of authors, while the Gablers appeared as ordinary parents without the degree and authorship credentials that were the open sesame in educational circles.

The Gablers knew they had to have a way to get the committee's attention and make members hear what they were saying. A method which would also give a press angle for publicity.

One evening Mel returned late from depositing a packet of mail in the post office. Norma was sitting at her kitchen desk wearing an impish grin. Mel walked over and put an affectionate hand on her shoulder. "You've got something cooking. What is it?"

History Changed or "Changed" History?

"Remember the legislative committee hearings when we compared the new histories with the old books? Well, we can do that before the State Textbook Committee. We can even compare Macmillian's old books with their new one and ask, 'Has history changed or have the authors changed history?' "

Mel thought this a terrific idea.

They placed the old and new books side by side and began preparing their bill, which along with the publishers' responses, would go into the public record for the hearings.

In some instances, the difference was in the amount of space given. For example, they stated that William Penn, whom the old histories lauded as the first to propose a United States of America and who was called "the greatest among the founders of the American commonwealth" by historian John Fiske, was given only one page in *The Promise of America*. But the book devoted five pages to Penn's little-known secretary, James Logan, who wasn't even listed in the 1960 *World Book Encyclopedia*.

More often, the Gablers saw historical personages downgraded. In Macmillan's 1918 *History of the United States of America*, the Gablers found this statement about Washington during the terrible winter in Valley Forge:

"Amid the general discouragement one cannot but note the extraordinary fortitude of Washington. His soul was wrung with grief, but there is no evidence that his faith in ultimate success was shaken. His ability as a soldier was of a very high order . . ." (p. 260).

Whereas Macmillan's new *History of a Free People* (1967) said little more than,

"He [Washington] sometimes annoyed his men by his stiff manner and by a tendency to talk as though all were lost" (p. 65).

Sometimes it seemed that the important information, contained in old histories, was left out of the new books. For example, *The Promise of America* stated concerning the 19th-century socialist, Eugene Debs:

"[He] had been a Democrat all his life. But both Democrats and Republicans served the interests of the corporations. He concluded that no type of union could win against the corporations. The political and economic system of the country would have to be changed. The government must take over industry and run it for the benefit of the workers. Within a few years after he left jail, Debs helped to form the Socialist Party of America" (p. 361).

This paragraph on Debs was followed by one about union leader Samuel Gompers. Gompers' opposition to socialism, not shown in the book, was:

"I want to tell you Socialists that I have studied your philosophy . . . and watched the work of your movement the world over. I know how you think and what you have up your sleeve. And I want to say I am entirely at variance with your philosophy and your doctrines. Economically you are unsound; socially you are wrong; industrially you are an impossibility."

The Gablers met their August 1 deadline. The publishers got their responses in just before their September 10 deadline, leaving the Gablers less than a week to prepare for the hearings. Then on September 12 Mel and Norma read a disturbing Associated Press News story. The terse lead paragraph sent Mel to the telephone.

The Texas Education Agency's textbook committee will hear complaints Tuesday from Texans who oppose inclusion of the theory of evolution in biology textbooks.

"Why can't they get it straight," he complained to Ellie Hopkins. "We never have opposed the teaching of the theory of evolution. We only want fair play. They're still trying to hang the Scopes Trial around our necks. Where did they get their story?"

"Probably from a press release," Hopkins replied. "The TEA always turns one out just before the hearings."

"What about our side of the story?"

"If they don't have it, they don't print it."

"Could we send out a release?"

"There's no law against it. Write one up and I'll see that it gets on the wires."

Their first release was only four short paragraphs:

Tomorrow in Austin, Texas citizens who have met the necessary state requirement, will appear before the State Textbook Committee as petitioners against certain biology textbooks.

The petitioners are requesting that the theory of evolution be taught to Texas students because they have confidence to believe that students can be trusted with pro and con evidence. This is in accord with the principle of science which requires that any discussion of a theory must include all evidence, both 'for' and 'against.'

Students are entitled to form their own opinion from all the evidence, not just evidence selected to support the view held by the authors of these books.

Within hours the Gablers' story was spread across Texas. Reporters seemed amazed to learn that they were only asking for objectivity. Every state news broadcast for three days mentioned their purpose in objecting to the biologies. Every newspaper they saw had balanced news articles.

The history texts came up before the biology books. Norma first outlined the charges detailed in her and Mel's bills of particulars: They demoted national heroes; they trivialized important historical events and wasted space on frivolous material; they followed a negative slant that would make students ashamed of their national heritage.

She began comparing the new histories with the old ones, using Macmillan as her prime example. Each time, she asked the Committee, "Has history changed or has the publisher changed history?"

She turned to SRA's *The Promise of America* and noted the publisher had called her and Mel's objection to the book's handling of John Hancock unjustifiably critical. She quoted the publisher as saying, "The Gablers err concerning John Hancock, on page 95 for example. . . ."

Eyes flashing, but with her voice firmly under control, Norma declared, "It would have been very difficult for us to have read page 95. Or pages 96, 98, or 99—shall I continue listing all the other pages that were blank or had blank spaces for pictures? How were we to know what the publisher intended on page 95 or any of the other pages?

Committee Chairman Julius Truelson, the Fort Worth Superintendent of Schools, agreed that Norma had a "valid complaint" about the book with the blank and missing pages. He put the salesmen on notice that any books considered for future adoptions would have to be made available complete by the time specified by State Board policy.

The SRA salesman and his Macmillan, Holt, and Benziger counterparts were all brief in their replies. One called the new histories "more realistic than used to be typical of school books." He argued that if books did not mention mistakes and shortcomings of historical personages, U.S. history "would not be convincing" to students and their study would be "untrue and inadequate."

But the Committee was not quite convinced and proceeded to reject the Macmillan, SRA, and Benziger books.

Norma's testimony against the four history books on which she and Mel had filed bills whipped up a flurry of favorable press attention. *The Dallas Morning News* (Sept. 25, 1969), for example, delivered a particularly hard-hitting editorial by David Hawkins titled, "We Need to Resume Yea-Saying." The editorial said in part:

Texas Textbook Commissioners had a harder-than-usual time this term trying to find a good American history text. The new ones offered by the publishers didn't give them much choice. They had to settle for the text that was least offensively anti-patriotic.

You wonder why the commissioners feel impelled to change texts for the worse. The new ones, we suppose, give students accounts of more recent history, but what good is a view of the cold war that proclaims Russia's intentions as peaceful? That is what the new history text tells Texas students.

If there's anything to choose between our system and its rivals, our history texts ought to make it plain. But there's a dearth of good texts, and history itself figures more and more infrequently as a high school subject and less and less as the kind of national yea-saying that it should be.

The new Texas text is called *Discovering American History*, 1967 [Holt]. Critics say it doesn't make much of a search and that it frowns at what it finds. How much satisfaction, you wonder, did the author get from belittling national heroes and neglecting patriotic events but telling schoolboys that Russia's intentions are peaceful?

One of the rejected texts was worse. After calling the Boston Tea Party a "riot" it went on to observe that the arrest of Communists after World War II was mere persecution of unpopular opinion—like the opinion of the Rosenbergs, we suppose, that Russia ought to have our atomic secrets!

. . . We don't have to reinterpret or falsify to make the sum of our history plain to our students and the world. But we do need to re-emphasize . . . the . . . beautiful. We need once more to call the roll on the heroes who breathed life and meaning into our commitment—into our historical premise that freedom is a sounder omen of national endurance than the Russian proposition that the same history that exalts them dooms us.

We need to resume yea-saying.

Biology Texts, Round Two

The biologies were a different story.

As expected, the arguments over the new editions of the Biological Science Curriculum Study (BSCS) biologies and three others which were called "evolutionary" were a rehash of '64. Reuel Lemmons, the Church of Christ editor, was back to protest their "one-sidedness." "I have no objection to a chapter on evolution in a textbook in biology," he said. "It would be incomplete without it. But I'm pleading with this Committee to give us science books that are science books and not bibles in the evolution of the human being."

Norma declared, "All we're asking is that the theory of evolution be taught as a theory with the students allowed to study both pros and cons." The BSCS publishers, she complained, had "censored" evidence against the theory of evolution in attempts to "brainwash school children."

A letter to the Committee from the assistant pastor of the huge First Baptist Church of Dallas echoed these claims. Speaking for the senior pastor W. A. Criswell, then president of the Southern Baptist Convention, Melvin Carter said the books presented the theory of evolution "as fact," and that the Blue book in particular violated "the spirit and the word of the law requiring textbooks to give both sides of an issue."

For the most part, the salesmen for the BSCS publishers stood by their editors' responses to the protesters' bill of particulars.

Chairman Truelson sought a compromise, suggesting some word and phrase changes that he hoped might satisfy the objectors. In one instance, he asked Allyn and Bacon's man, "What's wrong with your book saying evolution is a theory instead of evolution is a fact? That's the way it's always been. It might not solve her problem but it would solve mine."

The salesman stated his editor had agreed to change "evolution is a fact" to "the author believes evolution is a fact."

But Norma insisted this would "make no difference. The students will believe what the book says."

The Committee vote was interesting. For a book to be recommended, at least 10 of the members had to vote for a book. On the first ballot four of the five books received sufficient votes but none of the three BSCS books was included. On ballot two, the votes were divided between three BSCS books and one non-BSCS book. Thereafter, every vote was for one of the BSCS books but it was the eighth ballot before the Yellow book received enough votes to be placed on the recommended list. The Green and the Blue books were eliminated.

Most newspaper coverage of the evolution controversy was on a far different plane than five years before. The Gablers were getting their message across that it was the evolutionists who were dogmatic, and some even bigoted, while the creationists were only asking for equal time. One of the fairest articles, in their opinion, was written by Dick Shaffer of the *Dallas Times-Herald,* a newspaper that had earlier said editorially, "fundamentalists have no business seeking to edit . . . textbooks to make them conform with mistaken theories of Creation . . ." [1] Shaffer said there was "more to" the Texas evolution battle than "a replay of the Scopes Trial," adding,

"The Austin reaction also may signify that the religious groups that have opposed evolutionary theory since the days of fundamentalism proper are gaining strength. . . ."

The articles and editorials kept the biology books in the spotlight while the Gablers made their follow-up appeals to the Commissioner and the State Board.

During this time, and unknown to the Gablers, a University of Texas botany professor who reportedly believed that "evolution is in fact at least as well-proven as the idea that the earth is round and that the moon has a back side," protested that Norma had violated state law in the Committee hearings. Dr. Irwin Spear quoted her as having said she " 'preferred the biologies other than the BSCS books because there was less emphasis on evolution.' " This, he argued, was speaking in favor of a textbook which the law said a petitioner could not do. He asked that the two books she had "favored" be removed from the list of recommended texts.

---

[1] Dick Shaffer, Editorial: "Evoluationary," *Dallas Times-Herald,* Sept. 21, 1969.

Commissioner J. W. Edgar disagreed, noting that Norma's statement had come in answer to the Committee chairman asking, "Are you satisfied with those biology texts which were not protested?" In rejecting the professor's request, the Commissioner said Norma in her reply "acknowledged that the official regulations did not permit her to speak for books under consideration, and that she confined her answer to a general statement defining her position on the teaching of evolution."

Dr. Spear continued to press his complaint. In a second letter he quoted Norma from the hearing record as asking that only books be approved that " 'relegate . . . the evolutionary theory to a chapter or maybe two. . . .' " He also cited the Committee chairman's request that Allyn and Bacon change " 'the author believes it (evolution) to be a fact' " to " 'evolution is a theory.' " He said these statements might "have unduly influenced the selection of books that soft-pedal evolution, to the detriment of the education of the school children of Texas," and again asked the removal of the two books.

The UT professor further asked the State Board to

". . . reexamine its rules on textbook adoption that permit persons with no particular training or expertise in a field to gain a public forum, as well as an opportunity to influence the adoption of books by public agency, without an equal opportunity for other interested parties to be heard . . . It would have been easy to discredit the testimony of Mrs. Gabler and Mr. Reuel Lemmons, but nobody had an opportunity to do that because the publishers are the only ones who are given opportunity to do so, and they generally prefer not to antagonize anybody."

Two Sets of Rules

Still having no knowledge of this interchange, Norma came to the November Board meeting with three "expert" witnesses to testify against the BSCS biologies.

Norma was first allowed to present complaints. Certain publishers hadn't been getting their books to the designated libraries on time, she said. Some books placed there were older editions of those being offered for adoption. And SRA had sent *The Promise of America* with "many, many blank pages."

"What do you publishers have to say about this?" Chairman Ben Howell asked.

"We submitted our latest additions in supplement form," one replied.

Jack Binion, the bachelor Board member who had once challenged Norma, spoke up. "This doesn't cut the mustard. You're supposed to supply for public viewing complete editions of your books."

State Commissioner J. W. Edgar defended the publisher, saying the regulations had been fulfilled because "the people [the Textbook Committee] charged with making selections had all the material before them."

Norma refused to be deterred. "We're supposed to be able to see the completed books, too. It's embarrassing to have a publisher say that I'm quoting from the wrong edition, or I didn't read the whole book, when he left pages blank. I'm just asking that the publishers be required to play by the rules."

"You have a point, Mrs. Gabler," Chairman Howell conceded. "This is a procedural matter. We'll take it up at our May meeting. Let's get on with what the petitioners have to say about the books they're appealing."

Quickly Chairman Howell laid down the ground rules: 10 minutes for the history text and 15 minutes for each biology text. The book salesmen would have equal time for responding to the Gablers' complaints.

To conserve time, Norma introduced her three witnesses immediately: Dr. T. G. Barnes, who had appeared at the 1964 hearings; Dr. John J. Grebe, the "father" of the petrochemical industry, and director of Basic and Nuclear Research for Dow Chemical Company for 41 years before his retirement; and Dr. Richard H. LeTourneau, president of R. G. LeTourneau, Inc., and former president of LeTourneau College.

The witnesses had come many miles at their own expense. They had meticulously prepared their objections to the biology books. But with each having less than 12 minutes, they could only hit the high points of their presentations.

In arguing against one of the biology texts, Dr. Barnes declared, "I find in this textbook a total bias toward evolution and a total censorship against alternative theories . . . it is almost a faith. Ironically, it begins, 'In the beginning . . .' "

Dr. LeTourneau held up his watch and said, "If evolution has any prudence at all and we can have life created from absolutely nothing, through the process of evolution, why can't we go out here and dig in our back yard and find some Accutron watches? . . . This should have been much easier to evolve than the life that we are trying to say evolved from nothing."

Dr. Grebe said, "In addition, I am offering a reward of $1,000 to the first one who will give one clear proof of the evolution hypothesis, or even the basic mathematical treatment of the subject that would elevate it to the rank of a scientific theory. No scientific theory should have to wait 110 years for proof now that information on facts of nature doubles every five years."

The three men spoke courteously, to the point, and kept within their time limits.

The book salesmen said they would stand on their written responses.

Then to Norma's complete surprise, Chairman Howell introduced the University of Texas professor, Dr. Spear, and told him the Board had "plenty of time" to hear him.

The professor said he was there to refute testimony of "so-called experts" who had spoken untruthfully to get their philosophy into biology books. He wondered why anti-evolutionists had never "written their own text and opened it up to public scrutiny. They can't find a professional biologist who would write that kind of text." Rambling on, he charged that the petitioners against the BSCS books had taken quotes of biological scientists out of context in building a flimsy case against evolution. Finally he got to the point of why he had come and asked the Board to reject the two biology books which he claimed Norma had commended.

Time was never called and he sat down at his own pleasure. Then the Board voted to approve all the books which the Textbook Committee had recommended.

Though the Board did not honor the professor's request to remove the two books he had questioned, Norma was not appeased. She felt the Board had brazenly violated its own rules in hearing a man at length who had not filed an official bill of particulars. She was angry, hurt, and embarrassed, feeling that the Board had treated her own distinguished witnesses shabbily in allowing them so little time when they had traveled so far, and then permitting the professor to ridicule them.

Dr. Edgar came toward her. "Thank you, Mrs. Gabler, for bringing your three friends. We are honored."

She fought for composure. An awkward silence hung between them. Finally she spoke. "Dr. Edgar, the Board hasn't heard the last of this. They have violated my rights. They have let a witness insult three great men, a witness who did not qualify to appear. When does the Board meet again?"

"In January," he replied.

"I'll see them then and they'd better be prepared."

6

A "Ten Year Pin"

"Mel, we can't let them get away with this. They broke the rules. Our rights as parents have been violated. Our witnesses were ridiculed without a chance for rebuttal. The State Board is going to hear me again. I'm going to demand to be heard."

Mel was fuming inside. But he kept his indignation under control. "We'll write a letter and . . ."

"You bet we'll write. To the Board chairman. The Governor. And we'll talk to Ellie Hopkins. This is as far as I intend to be pushed. We'll fight for our rights as parents."

When they cooled down, Mel and Norma realized they had time to think about what to say in the letter. The next Board meeting wasn't until January, two months away.

Their annual mailing of book reviews demanded priority. This year they decided to rate the five books adopted by the State for each subject in numerical order from best to worst as they saw them, giving a mini-review of each book to help districts decide. For the biologies, they rated Holt's *Modern Biology,* 1969 edition, first, calling it

> . . . the only one of the five adopted biology texts which will allow teachers to teach objectively. It is written in the tradi- tional manner in that evolution is covered in two separate chapters in order that this subject may be emphasized to the degree desired by the teacher. It has not been revised to con-

form to the government criteria of weaving all of biology around evolution.

Christmas was now upon them. And in the rush and happiness of having all their boys home, the appeal was put aside.

After New Year's, Mel composed the firmest, frankest letter they had ever written to public officials:

. . . We spend many, many hours and much expense . . . to help the children of our State; carefully abiding by the rules of procedure which the Board has established. We must meet the deadline for filing bills of particulars, giving page, paragraph, and line for 'questionable' portions together with reasons for considering them objectionable. We must request permission to appear before the State Textbook Committee, and have only five days to appeal their decision. If the Commissioner of Education also recommends a book we have protested, we must meet a dealine for requesting an appearance before this Board. To miss one of these steps, or even to be late, disqualifies us from further participation. Meanwhile, the publisher has the advantage of appearing at the Textbook Committee hearing *after* our appearance, receiving the same amount of time allotted to petitioners.

However, a double standard seems to exist. . . . A man, who had *not* filed a bill of particulars, asked and received permission to rebut Mrs. Gabler. . . . Not only was he allowed to speak *after* petitioners and publishers, but he was told to take all the time he wished.

Members of the Board, why was Dr. Spears given his choice to appear at the time he wanted, even though he appeared illegally? We, who conscientiously try to abide by the Board's rules, are never given a choice. We must *always* be first, with the publisher having the distinct advantage of appearing last.

. . . Available scientific evidence can be interpreted to support *either* evolution or creation, depending upon the philosophy of the scientist making the deduction. To select *only* facts which support a dogma and to disregard facts which support the opposing view is grossly unfair to Texas students who are entitled to objective interpretation of evidence. This is *exactly* what Mrs. Gabler and the men representing her were requesting.

In contrast, Dr. Spears was asking for a continuation of biased indoctrination in direct violation of the Board's own published requirements for objective teaching. (See 7.18, p. 121, Section II, *Policies of the State Board of Education.*)

Dr. Spears had the same opportunity to file protests as all other citizens of Texas. Instead, he was allowed to protest the two books that he alleged Mrs. Gabler considered good books, not on the basis of compliance with Board procedure, but strictly on the basis of being against them because Mrs. Gabler was supposedly for them. This was a false premise because one of these books was as bad, or worse, than the books we protested. There just wasn't time to file a bill of particulars on it. We never could secure a copy of it.

. . . In opposition to Dr. Spear's argument, that someone should be allowed to rebut the petitioners who were asking for objective teaching, it should be pointed out that the publishers already have an overwhelming advantage:

(1) They do not have the great difficulty of obtaining books for examination. We have to drive many miles and/or wait many days to examine copies.

(2) They have the services of personnel skilled in this area.

(3) They can utilize answers . . . given . . . in other states.

(4) Most of those professionally involved are blind to much of the questionable textbook content, because their philosophy is basically the same as that of the textbook authors.

(5) They can afford to hire representatives to promote their books because many millions of dollars are involved; whereas, we must stretch a tight family budget.

We expect an answer from the Board regarding the unethical treatment of petitioners at the November 10th meeting. . . .

Norma and Don made the six-hour drive to Austin and delivered the letter personally to Chairman Howell on the morning of the Board's scheduled January meeting.

His face darkened as he read it. Still, he didn't see how the matter could come before the Board, since it wasn't on the agenda.

"I know the rules say you should file ahead of time to be heard,"

Norma said sarcastically. "I'm just playing your game. You let the professor appear and he hadn't filed properly."

The chairman said he would still have to bring it before the Board. "If you get two-thirds of the vote—"

"You'll hear me, or I'll take you to court. I'll—" Norma suddenly checked herself. "Mr. Howell, I'm a Christian and shouldn't have threatened you. But I do have a right to be heard, and I intend to be at the February 2nd Board meeting. I'll be back."

The Board on the Defensive

On January 24th Mel wrote Chairman Howell a follow-up letter, confirming Norma's intentions to attend the February 2nd Board meeting. They called Dr. Grebe and he agreed to fly in from Arizona. The *Borger News-Herald* would send a reporter.

They met in Austin and went together to the TEA building on the 2nd. The conference room was dark.

Commissioner Edgar came out to greet them in the foyer, looking surprised. "Why, didn't you know? The Board meeting is next Saturday in El Paso."

Norma stood stunned. She shook with anger and frustration. Moving closer, she pushed a finger close to his nose. "This is the end. The Board has lost the ball. They are going to hear me, and the sooner they hear me the better, because beginning today I am going to start telling it like it is. Everybody in this state is going to know what is happening in Austin."

Returning to their motel, Norma called Mel, who felt as though the world had dropped from under him. He felt especially bad because Dr. Grebe had missed his birthday in Arizona to fly to Austin at his own expense. Then Dr. Grebe came on the telephone and very gently said, "Remember Romans 8:28—'All things work together for good to those who love God. . . .' Just wait: the Lord will receive the glory for this."

This encouraged Mel and helped make a more pleasant trip for Norma, Don, and Dr. Grebe as they headed for San Antonio, where Norma was to be on the popular Allan Dale talk show over WOAI for two hours that night. Mel called Dale and told him what happened and that Dr. Grebe, the inventor of synthetic rubber, would be with Norma for the program.

The *Borger News-Herald* reporter returned home and wrote a full-page story for his newspaper.

Back in Longview, Mel whipped out a press release about the shifting of the Board's called meeting to El Paso.

Quoting himself and Norma, he declared:

We have clear proof that the . . . [Board] broke the state laws in its November action. These are laws passed by the legislature, not just Committee rules or Board rules. It's another glaring example of the strange double standard which the state education establishment lives by in its activities.

Their editor friend, Ellie Hopkins, put the release on the wires. "Now you must go to El Paso," he told Norma. "I'll have the wire services cover you there."

Meanwhile, she went to Dallas for an hour and a half radio program over powerful KRLD and a 30-minute TV program over Channel 4, where the host said, "Tell it like it is." Norma spelled out her grievances.

A letter came quickly from the Board chairman. He said he had just read the Gablers' January 24th letter and had called Dr. Edgar to learn that Norma had come to Austin on February 2nd with witnesses.

He claimed a "misunderstanding" of the January 5th discussion with Norma. He had thought the Board was to decide at the February meeting if they would take any action on the appeal. The El Paso meeting had been set months before, he said.

He owed her "more than apologies" for not keeping his mail current and offered to pay for the fruitless trip to Austin. But she declined the expenses because of her policy never to accept anything from public officials.

A Board member told Norma's friend, Elsie Livers, "The Board has made mistakes and will make others, but will never make one like this again."

Norma arrived early the following Saturday at the Ramada Inn in El Paso where the Board was to meet. As the members entered the meeting room, she smiled and greeted them as if nothing had happened. Chairman Howell and others shook her hand. She sat through the proceedings, saying nothing.

During a break, a UPI reporter interviewed Norma. She hoped that the newspapers would print something just to keep pressure on the Board. In the evening when she went to dinner, a news vendor was yelling, "Special! Mother protests evolution books!" She grabbed up a copy of the *El Paso Herald-Post*. There, splashed across the front page, five columns wide, was the story that a mother was denied to right to be heard.

At the next month's meeting the Board listened respectfully, with only one interruption, as she lectured them about the "double standard" of "strictly enforcing rules on those of us who are asking for objective textbooks, while suspending the rules for those who oppose our efforts, and for allowing publishers to offer books which had not been made available for citizen review before the filing deadline." When she concluded, Chairman Howell thanked her and requested "any suggestions you and your husband may have for improving the selection process."

The Gablers anticipated little action. They did not expect the Board to go as far as it did in the May meeting when three policy changes, all victories, were approved:

(1) In the future, science books would have to "carry a statement on an introductory page that any material on evolution is presented as a theory rather than as a fact."

(2) "Textbooks presented for adoption, or selections contained therein, should not include language blatantly offensive which would cause embarrassing situations in the classroom or cause interference in the learning atmosphere. . . ."

(3) Student texts and teaching manuals would have to be placed in the regional educational centers for public review in advance of the petitioners' filing deadline.

Publishers were duly warned that books submitted improperly would not be eligible for adoption.

It was the best send-off the Gablers could possibly have as they began their summer work on bills of particulars for the 1970 fall hearings.

A Ministry to School Children

Still this was a time of decision for Mel. Very active in various church positions, including Sunday School superintendent, he was weighing textbook work against church work, when a friend told him, "You're doing more good for the Lord with your textbook work than all of your church work combined. Parents are looking to you for leadership."

However, Mel still wondered how much they were really accomplishing. They were not educators or scholars. They lived on a shoestring, putting money into the textbook crusade that could not even count as a tax deduction. And who were they to buck a huge billion-dollar publishing establishment with its batteries of Ph.D.s?

While thinking and praying about this, he asked advice from close friend Glenn (Fay) Livers. Fay promised to pray with Mel for the Lord's guidance and about a week later said, "I'll tell you how I feel. We can find someone else to do the church work, but I know of no one better qualified to work for better textbooks than you and Norma."

"Look at it this way," Fay continued. "I go to the jail regularly and talk to the prisoners. That's a very special ministry which the Lord has given me. Perhaps the Lord has given you and Norma a ministry to school children."

Mel resigned from his church offices and began devoting practically every waking hour to textbook work other than his clerical job for Humble, handling and purchasing pipe, fittings, and supplies.

Among the world histories, they concentrated on Allyn and Bacon's *A Global History of Man.* They felt it was veined with liberal bias that sometimes bordered on leftist propaganda.

Their bill noted that this "world history" treated the American revolution in only one paragraph "as just one of a series of revolutions and *not* as the revolution which was in contrast to most other revolutions and in particular the current usage of this word." The U.S. in modern foreign policy frequently appeared as a "bad guy," an "interventionist"—for example, where the book said that in the minds of "many progressive Latin Americans" the 1965 Dominican Republic involvement was launched "to block necessary and long overdue social reforms."

Communism in a "Good Light"
They charged the book did not present a balanced picture of Cuban, Russian, and Chinese Marxism.

The Cuban revolution was mentioned alongside the Mexican revolution, they complained, without comparing the different ideologies. Castro was portrayed "as a people's liberator in a just cause."

While "faults" of the Soviet Union were "pointed out" and "atrocities admitted," the Gablers believed the book's "overall impression" of Russian Communism was ". . . of a dark, heavy cloud, with a bright silver lining that is beginning to show. Difficulties are directed to the method of Communism, never the system."

But they reserved their strongest criticism for the 76-page discussion of Chinese Communism, prefacing a long list of quotations with a citation from page 444:

". . . Marxism turns the people toward a future of unlimited promise, an escalator to the stars."

"It is unbelievable," declared the Gablers, "that the above would appear in a textbook written in America."

The publisher countered in great detail, insisting that the book was "a world history text, not an American history text"; that quotations showing alleged favoring of Communism were "extracted" out of context; that the text "neither endorses nor approves of these [Cuban and Mexican] revolutions, but "does provide" a factual account; that the accuracy of the accounts of American military interventions in Latin America during the 1950s and 1960s could not be "disputed"; that the Soviet and Chinese systems were presented objectively.

After filing their bill the Gablers had had two history professors review *A Global History of Man*. At the State Textbook Committee hearings Norma read their statements into the official record.

Dr. Robert H. Selby, head of the History Department at Le-Tourneau College, disputed the publisher's argument that the description of Chinese Marxism as "an escalator to the stars" was taken out of context.

"In the section on China I found the following ideas . . . [in] the context of the material. One, Marxism has been good for China. Two, Christian missionaries were evil. Three, all Westerners were imperialistic, evil men bent on the rape of China as a people. Four, Chiang Kai-shek and the Nationalists were evil for China. Six, Chiang has only been able to keep the Nationalist cause alive on Formosa because of the aid of the United States. He has no popular support. Seven, all true Chinese people support Mao.

"It seems clear to this reviewer that any sort of reading of the section on China . . . in context or out, reveals a very clear support of Marxism, attempting to prove it is in truth an escalator to the stars."

Dr. Anthony Kubeck, Chairman of the Department of History and Political Science at the University of Dallas and an authority on American foreign policy, commented in part:

". . . the loss of China to Communism has been a subject of controversy among academic circles. It is only fair, therefore, that any author of a public school text should balance his material for the benefit of our young minds. In my view, the author does not do this. His description of recent Chinese history . . . is one-sided, leaning towards a sympathetic view of Mao Tse-tung's brand of Communism and critical of the Republic of China under President Chiang Kai-shek. It simply is not accurate to describe Communist China today, as the author does. . . . Internal conditions in Communist China today are completely different from the way the author describes. . . ."

Allyn and Bacon considered the adoption of the book so important that they sent a vice-president, Richard Carroll, from their Boston office to speak in the hearings. Carroll reiterated that the questioned excerpts were "either quotations taken out of context, or they are quotations to which the Gablers and others have rendered their own subjective evaluation . . ." The book, he said, "had already been taught successfully in thousands of classrooms. . . ."

To Norma's dismay, the Committee voted to accept *A Global History of Man*. But they rejected nine other histories which she and Mel had protested.

What is "Good Literature"?

The high school literature books were different from anything the Gablers had filed on before.

They stated in the preface to their bill on Macmillan's *Gateway English* (1970) series of "cluster books" which had been partially financed by the U.S. Office of Education:

"The aim and purpose of a literature course at any educational level should be to awaken an appetite in the reader for more knowledge, more understanding, more experiencing of the unknown: worlds not open to him in any other way. It could be called 'enlightenment.' While three of the four textbooks presented have some good qualities, the overall theme is the same that is presented everyday in newspapers and television, revealing man at his worst, most defeated and without hope, or rebellious and lawless. Perhaps this is what the authors call reality and seeing things as they are, but this is not good enough for the impressionable young mind!"

They presented summary evaluations of some of Macmillan's small books:

"This book [*Something Strange*] contains some of the chilling, horror-type stories that seem to appeal to the morbid imagination of this age's youth; but so much time spent thinking upon strangeness can make it almost seem normal. The characters in 'The Jam' are dope addicts. 'The Hitch-Hiker,' which follows, has an identical climax, both written to horrify. 'The Birds' was made into a Hitchcock movie, so is well-known, but in reading it there is so much more blood and gruesome detail that the reader feels the need to escape and cleanse himself from such horror. 'Zero' leaves the impression that it is normal for children to hate parents and for parents to be indifferent to the needs of their children. Everything in the book is conducive to causing emotional instability in the impressionable mind.

"This [*Rebels and Regulars*] is another very depressing book. As far as the language used, it is in keeping with the characters and plots of the stories, but not the sort of language the thoughtful parent would approve of in his children. There is throughout the book the undercurrent of 'a cause,' which gives a prejudiced viewpoint, always picturing the white man as the villain against different minority groups or individuals. Typical of the stories is 'The Cyclists' Raid,' which is militant, lawless, defiant, and completely without consideration for the individual. . . . A whole semester of concentrating upon rebellion as pictured in these stories will have a negative effect upon an impressionable young person. It becomes more honorable to rebel than to obey laws or consider the rights of others. . . .

"This book [*Ways of Justice*] indicates that justice is whatever an individual decides it should be. 'Junkie Joe Had Some Money' shows bullies getting away with murder because the only witness is intimidated. In 'Manuel,' a kindly act is rewarded with utmost cruelty, written in vivid detail. 'Mateo

Falcone' tells of a young boy who is bribed to reveal the hiding place of another, then his father kills him. Nothing here to indicate love or understanding is possible between parents and child. 'Marijuana and a Pistol' gives all the sordid details of a maladjusted youth who smokes 'weeds,' including the uncontrolled giggling and vomiting. 'They Grind Exceedingly Small' is a story about the person who has money, taking advantage of the poor, hard-working, underprivileged—indicating that all money and power are in the hands of the cruel, wicked, dishonest, and undeserving. . . ."

The stories so sickened them that they cut the bill of particulars short, and said:

"We feel it is a waste of paper and the Committee's time to continue our review on each story.

"Couldn't half of the stories in this series tell about people living together in harmony, love, understanding, and helpfulness?

"Is reality only negative? Does not reality also include the many acts of kindness between races that is evident across our nation? It must be remembered that qualities such as morality *must* be taught. They do not come naturally. Education without morality will result in a depraved society.

"Our conclusion is that if these books do not contribute to rebellion, lack of respect for authority, sadism, violence, and disillusionment, they will most certainly defeat the whole purpose for studying literature in our schools; for there is absolutely nothing presented here that would open the wonderful world of the printed page to our youth and cause them to want to pursue reading for the pure joy of doing so!"

Two days before the committee hearing, much of this bill on the Macmillan *Gateway English* series appeared in an editorial "If Parents Only Knew" by Ellie Hopkins in the September 13, 1970 *Longview Morning Journal.*

. . . If parents only knew, they would mount a storm of protest that would lead the State Textbook Committee and the Texas Education Agency to reject many of these unworthy books.

And concluded,

Textbooks are for reading, for teaching, for inspiration. But what is the U.S. Office of Education trying to do with such sordid rubbish, which it encouraged with financial support for this book project?

At the hearing Macmillan's regional sales manager then spoke briefly, repeating his editor's statement that the books were for "disadvantaged" students.

The second literature series was just as disturbing to the Gablers. Their son Don called the *Voices of Man* (1970), published by Addison-Wesley, "sick, sick, sick." Mel and Norma made the same basic criticisms that they had made of the *Gateway* series. The stories were "filled with cruelty, crudity, hate, and rebellion, without presenting any positive or enriching aspects of life, which are also 'reality.' "

The publisher, Addison-Wesley, did not even file a letter of reply. Nor did a representative appear at the hearings to defend the books. "I don't blame the publisher," Norma declared. "It will take some stretching of the imagination for anyone to take up for this type of literature."

Then she read excerpts from the story of a girl named Angelique, who lived in a ghetto apartment with her parents who were gone much of the time. She hated the little brother for whom she had to cook. Norma felt the story typical of the entire Addison-Wesley series:

". . . She turned and buried her face in the pillow, biting the fabric furiously, beating her fists and kicking her heels. An impulse, hot, urgent, and familiar, rose in her. She wanted to kill, break, destroy, smash something into a million pieces. She jumped up from her bed and slammed the door, . . . digging her nails into her wrists, trying to bring pain sharp enough to overpower her emotions. Hatred possessed her. She heard the light click off downstairs, and the voices grew fainter. Len [her brother] was going out, but he would be back. She suddenly imagined his blood spilled hot and red, and she moaned and gripped her hands together convulsively. It was not a new thought to her. It seemed he was everything she hated, everything that taunted and troubled her and held her back from what she wanted. If he were dead everything would be all right.

"She opened the door and listened. They had gone, and it was dark below. She walked softly down the stairs and into the kitchen. . . . Len's jacket lay in a heap on the floor;

that meant that he would be back in a moment. She would kill him.

"She picked up a long knife which one of the boys had used to cut bread, and looked at its sharp-scraped edge. She would kill him. She sat straight in her chair, one hand resting on the table, the other holding a knife between her knees, concealing it in the folds of her nightgown. She kept her eyes steadily on the door and Len came in. He looked at her, startled, and then glanced away. He started to walk around the table. "In a minute," she thought, "he'll pass me, and then his back will be turned. Then I'll kill him." Her fingers tightened on the handle of the knife.

"Suddenly he turned and faced her. 'Look, Angelique,' he said, . . . 'I'm sorry about Rick, but you didn't have to get scared or anything. He just talks a lot.' Angelique released her breath slowly and her fingers loosened from the handle of the knife. Len glanced around. 'Ah . . . look, . . . I know I bug you, but I am sorry. Look, would you like for me to do anything around here? Wash the dishes or anything?' "

Norma's time was running out. She skipped four paragraphs and read the ending.

"She walked a little unsteadily to the sink and turned on the water mechanically. She felt odd and free and limbless. Her emotion had gone, leaving a vacuum. Her hatred had shrunk and dwindled and run into itself, until it was only a tiny waiting pool deep in her mind. Her fatal impulse dropped below the level of her consciousness and lay like a black lilypad, waiting to be stirred" (pp. 75-77).

Norma stared at the Committee chairman. "What I would like to know is this: Regardless of the level . . . is this what we have to use under the guise of literature?

". . . This is not fair to any student, disadvantaged or otherwise. Why only the negative side of life? Shouldn't he be entitled to stories that would speak of love, warmth, beauty, and motivation toward the higher matters of life?"

The Textbook Committee rejected five of the protested literature series, but accepted Macmillan's *Gateway English* books for grade 12.

Mel and Norma filed their customary appeal to the Commissioner. He declined to rule against any of the Committee's choices.

Mel began preparing their appeal to the State Board while Norma hit the speaking circuit to arouse public support. Ellie Hopkins, now president of the Texas Press Association, again helped with a strong editorial against the Macmillan books. It appeared in the November 2, 1970 *Longview Daily News.*

It is well known that Christianity was removed from textbooks on the pretext that the state has no right or authority to teach religion. Now, morality is being removed on the premise that texts should be neutral (reference to an instruction in the teacher's manual: "Please refrain from moralizing of any kind." Students may indeed "tune out" if they are subjected to preachy talk about "proper English" and the moral obligation to "do one's best" in class and to "lend a hand" to the underdog in a battle). But note that the vacuum of morality in the texts has been and is being filled with content that reeks of sex, crime, drinking, drugs, civil disobedience, lawbreaking, violence, police brutality, rebellion. Failure to teach moral implication in human action and relationships is to convey an acceptance of these other things as being the "norm," rather than problems to be corrected.

There is a way to avoid use of these books by Texas children, and that is to remove the entire series.

The day following Hopkins' editorial, the Commissioner of Education announced he was eliminating the *Gateway* books after having recommended them two weeks before. The explanation was that the publisher had not "cleaned up the language" as requested and as required by the new Board policy adopted the previous May.

Honor Due

The next Monday, November 9, Norma appeared with others before the State Board and made a last-ditch effort to get *A Global History of Man* dropped. James Whiteside, the Board member from Lubbock, moved that the book be taken from the list. Whiteside, who had had the book reviewed by a Lubbock teacher, said the teacher found it even worse than the protesters had claimed. But when the vote was taken, his resolution was overridden 10 to 5 and the book was kept.

During the break that followed the voting, Norma mingled

with the Board members. By this time she had gotten to know some pretty well. Jack Binion, the Houston lawyer who had once challenged her qualifications to appear before the Board, spoke to her cordially. "You win some and lose some," he said.

"Yes, and we're going to win even more," Norma said confidently. "We're going to keep the pressure on you guys."

"That's your privilege, Mrs. Gabler."

A couple of other Board members came toward them. Paul Greenwood from Harlingen recalled, "It was 1961, I believe, when Mrs. Gabler got involved with texts. Maybe we ought to give her a ten-year pin," he suggested.

"Are you sure that I deserve it?" Norma asked with a straight face.

"Yes, you deserve it," Greenwood replied.

7

For the
Love
of Children

The Board had approved Allyn and Bacon's *A Global History of Man,* but the Gablers kept fighting. On the rating sheet they sent to the districts, they marked *Global History* as the most objectionable of the five high school world histories on the new list of recommended texts.

Richard Carroll, the vice-president of Allyn and Bacon, who had appeared in the hearings, was concerned. On February 12, 1971, he wrote the Gablers a long letter about the good points of *Global History,* as he saw them, and the philosophy behind the book. He sent copies of the letter to Commissioner Edgar and State Board members.

Global History, he said, had been successful in other states because the students appreciate the objectivity of the materials. They are not propagandized with superficial, emotional statements; they are given the objective facts from which they can form lasting, meaningful judgments.

Like it or not, we do have a credibility gap problem with our youth. The syrupy emotionalism, devoid of real facts, and an unwillingness to admit shortcomings, that characterized social science education in the '50s and '60s, has contributed to the problem America faces today with a significant portion of its youth.

Perhaps we place more confidence in America's teachers

and students than you do. We do not have your fears that somehow this text will weaken our country. We know that the opposite is true—teachers and students using this text will gain a better appreciation and understanding of their country and the world. They will learn that ours is the greatest country in the world; they will also learn that we can all contribute to making it an even greater country by working within our constitutional framework to remedy the ills of our society.

They will not receive a "pablum" treatment that will leave them vulnerable, at a later stage of their lives, to the entreaties of those who seek to overthrow our system of government. In short, we reject your interpretation of this text. You, and every citizen, have the right to challenge our texts—we welcome your interest and hope that your motivations are sincere. Our only plea is that you be objective in your appraisals.

You have set yourselves up as the supreme judges of the motivations and activities of over a hundred people involved in the authorship and editorial processing of the text materials. You discount the thought that these people can be God-loving and God-fearing individuals who also want to preserve and protect their country.

In my opinion your presumptions and your current activities with respect to our publication, *A Global History of Man,* abuse the rights of all of us, whether or not we be residents of Texas. It is, after all, our country, not just yours.

The Gablers replied by asking for titles of "syrupy" history textbooks "containing patriotism and emotion . . . produced in the '50s." Carroll answered, wondering if they had "understood" his letter. He referred them to "any bibliography of social science textbooks published in the '50s and early '60s."

The Gablers asked if he had ever "personally read" *A Global History of Man,* and requested again a list "of what you consider 'syrupy emotionalism' in American history textbooks . . . published in the '50s and '60s." Carroll replied that since it was apparent "that what constitutes an acceptable textbook depends entirely upon your personal interpretations and opinions," he saw "no purpose" in continuing the correspondence.

Publisher on the Defensive

By this time Norma, in speaking engagements and radio talk programs, had made *Global History* a cause celèbre around the state. It gained greater notoriety when Carroll flew from Boston to San Antonio to accept Allan Dale's offer of two hours equal time for a reply to Norma's earlier appearance on Radio WOAI.

Introducing the book, Carroll noted it had been developed at Northwestern University in the late 1950s under a Carnegie Corporation Fund grant to "try and improve world understanding" for American high school students. They had been fed the American viewpoint, he said, but had not been given the reasons for revolution in China and Cuba. American high schoolers, he argued, should understand these reasons if "challenges to our own American democracy and threats to our own freedoms" are to be avoided.

It was obvious that Dale had some doubts about the book himself.

Dale: Let me pose a question. The White House Conference on Youth recently asked 5,137 youths: "Do you agree that everyone has a chance to get ahead in this country?" Only 39% of them thought they did. Somewhere along the line—if this is the thinking of youth today—we have missed teaching what this country is all about. . . .

Carroll: I . . . agree that there is a tremendous need for better teaching of social studies . . . [and] how we teach values to students in the U.S. Right now the social studies area in American school curriculum is going through considerable change. There is a revolution taking place based upon the teaching of history, social studies, economics, anthropology, the philosophy of religion—all of which are parts of social studies—from a conceptual approach rather than the traditional rote learning that has been drummed into students for many years. And the other part of it is this inquiry approach that's being used. I'll put in a little plug for my own company. We have developed such a program for elementary grade education entitled *Concepts and Inquiries*. It seeks to bring about change there, too—to expose the child at those grade levels with real value situations, so the child can develop a system of values [that] will have a lasting effect on the child's behavior.

Dale: Are you trying to tear down the U.S. with that book?

Carroll: I hope not. But I do hope that people studying it will come to a different conclusion than the Gablers.

Dale: It would have suited me better if you had changed some things.

Carroll: The book is for American high school students. I think, Allan, you'll have to admit you're a little bit past that time.

Dale: Have you read the book?

Carroll: Yes, at the time it was published originally, in 1962. . . . Since then a little over a million students have studied from it in one of three editions.

Dale: Let's get to one of the main bones of contention. There's no U.S. or Europe included in the world's major culture areas. Why?

Carroll: We had good reasons. . . . The student already had a heavy concentration of history in Western civilization. What the student hasn't been getting is material on the Asian world . . .

Dale: The critics say the book shows the Communist world in too good a light.

Carroll: I disagree completely . . . Take the unit on China. The book is trying to explain why Communism was successful there, contrasting the old Confucius approach with Communism . . .

Dale: Words happen to be my bag. Did you count the number of "revolutions" in two pages?

Carroll: No, I didn't.

Dale: I don't see how—somebody would have to really work at it to put that many [32] "revolutions" in two pages [in reference to Cuba].

Carroll: There are very good reasons. There are all kinds of revolutions. The authors are talking about radical social change, not passing judgment on whether revolution is good or bad. One of the greatest—I don't mean in terms of the best—social revolutions that occurred recently was in Cuba.

Dale: Another thing brought out was that the book said Marxism turns people toward a future of unlimited promise, an escalator to the stars. That's on page 444. I think it's been changed. Was this correct?

Carroll: Well, . . . as a result of the Texas hearings, we felt there was so much confusion over this that we had better pin it down a little bit and modify it by including the phrase, "The Communist leaders say . . ."

Dale opened the phone and listeners began expressing opinions pro and con.

"I heard the Gablers and now I've heard this man's rebuttal," a woman caller said. "He hasn't convinced me at all. Any world history that leaves out American culture . . . is pure bunk and shouldn't be used in our schools. He is trying to get American children to accept the mind of the Communists. . . . After hearing him, I think the Gablers are absolutely correct."

A teacher differed. "I heard the Gablers, too. They're self-appointed critics, not highly educated. I'm so glad you [Carroll] are here."

The conversation moved to the book's paralleling of the Cuban and Mexican revolutions.

Dale: The book says [p. 335], "The Cuban Revolution . . . has proven much more radical than the Mexican [revolution]; but both revolutions share certain common characteristics." You're liable to get people down here [Mexican-Americans] all over you on that one. . . .

Carroll: You also should put in the line about Latin America having had a few genuine social revolutions. Once again, I come back to my definition that revolution causes drastic social change.

Dale: But I doubt that people . . . who think highly of the Mexican Revolution of 1910 would like to be lumped with the Cuban revolution.

Carroll: In overall evaluation, I'd have to agree, Allan, but our criterion is: Did that revolution in Mexico bring about social change?

The calls came faster. A college student praised the Russian revolution for "bringing people from the 13th century," adding, "the average Russian peasant today is many times over better off than his grandfather." Another said, "I hope this discussion will impress upon parents the necessity of checking out textbooks now in the schools. They're going to get worse before they get better."

People were still calling when Dale announced that the time

was almost up. At Dale's invitation the Bostonian made a closing statement:

"I hope people listening tonight will be very, very concerned as parents. I'm a parent myself, and I'm concerned about the books. If you have the opportunity, you should take advantage of it. Know what's in your schools. Know what books are being used."

The next evening Norma called Dale on the air. "Did you notice, Allan, that he [Carroll] didn't ask any who favored him if they had read the book, but to those who objected, he did ask that question?

"I noticed also that some of the callers who took up for the book said we should . . . tell all our [country's] faults. As I told a Lions Club last week, 'If you have a small child and you repeatedly tell him from the day he was born all the things that are wrong with him, when he gets older, he will become frustrated and feel hopeless.' This is exactly what's happening to our young people today. This comes from hearing so much more bad than good in your country.

"Oh, I wanted to ask Mr. Carroll how many copies of his book [*Global History*] he's sold in Texas."

Dale, still on the air, replied, "Well, he told me confidentially— but I'm a blabbermouth, 'Texas sales have been very poor.' And he gave you and your husband credit for it."

The Gablers were happy, but not jubilant. Because *Global History* was on the Texas list, it would have added sales appeal in other states. And with a $23 million adoption coming up in the fall of 1971, a flood of other "progressive" books would be coming to their state. There could be no let-up in arousing parent concern and in preparing for the next set of hearings.

Appeals to the Public

While Mel earned the living, Norma continued on the speaking circuit. In Nacogdoches County she spoke to the district meeting of the Texas Federation of Women's Clubs. "When a teacher is told she cannot teach morals, but is given instructions for spending days on a new kind of lawbreaking, civil disobedience, we must say *if* parents only knew what their children are being taught they would mount a storm of protest.

"These texts—the *Macmillan Gateway English Series*—were

written at federal government expense. The content includes stories on dope addicts and strange and gruesome situations . . . which leave the reader with a defeated and hopeless attitude. They were written to reveal man at his worst. Thanks to public pressure, the Commissioner took them off the list."

Turning to history and economics: "Textbooks today major in the defects and faults of our government, in our free enterprise system, and in our society. Too often they decline, or refuse to point out, the successes and achievements of our system. The mild patriotism, if any, with their indoctrination in the weakness and problems of our American system has made our youth think, 'The American system has failed. It must be replaced.'

"And we parents wonder why some young people are dedicated to the destruction of our American way of life.

"Each generation has the responsibility to pass their heritage to the succeeding generation. As parents, we have fallen down. Today's youth have received a distorted version of our heritage. It is late, very late—but not too late.

"We, the parents, should demand that a true and unbiased picture of the American system be presented to our young people. If this 'equal time' plan could be used in textbooks and in the schools, we guarantee that young Americans will develop a keen appreciation for the heritage which is theirs.

"If not, we will soon see a real revolution and the death of a great nation.

"The training we give our children is important—very important —for youth holds the key to the future of this nation."

The Nacogdoches County speech aroused so much interest that it was printed in full in one newspaper.

Between speeches, Norma checked new books in "friendly" school districts to see if publishers had made changes demanded by the State Textbook Committee relating to evolution, profanity, and other points of contention. In many instances she found they had not.

Someone asked a member of the State legislature, Rep. Bill Blythe of Houston, to investigate. Blythe did and introduced a resolution in the legislature that strongly urged the Commissioner of Education to require that the publishers make the changes, corrections, additions, or deletions requested by the State Textbook Committee. "If the wishes of the Textbook Committee are not carried out," Blythe declared, "then there is a serious question as to the lack of control of the quality of textbooks to be used by Texas students."

Despite strong editorial support from East Texas newspapers, Blythe's bill was defeated. But Norma intended to present the complaint to the Board later in the year and insist that they make the publishers adhere to the new rules which had been issued the previous year.

A busy summer was ahead. Their son Paul was getting married in July. And, just as Richard Carroll had promised on Allan Dale's program, a stack of "revolutionary" new social studies was coming down the publishers' pike for adoption.

As had happened with the BSCS biologies, the social studies had provoked a battle in California the year before. The heat of the fray had been in Glendale where a dissenting member of the local Board of Education, Dr. Joseph Bean, delivered a fiery resignation speech on the evils of public education in general and the poison of behavioral science as expressed through the new social studies in particular, tracing the core ideology of the new social studies back to John Dewey.[1] The Gablers got copies of Bean's speech, which was also printed in booklet form, and studied it carefully. Many of Bean's ideas later appeared in their bills of particulars.

After studying Bean's speech, the Gablers were eager to check the new social studies against what he had said. But by mid-July only the Harcourt Brace Jovanovich series for the first grades, *The Social Sciences: Concepts and Values,* was in their regional center at Kilgore.

The materials covered six grades and included both student and teacher books, and Norma could only examine them in the center and take notes. They needed a set of books to examine at home. Mel wrote the publisher two letters, asking to buy the books. When there was no response, he made two long distance phone calls, reminding them that the State Board had recently ruled that publishers had to sell their books to citizens in advance of the adoption hearings. The publisher did not reply.

By this time, the other social studies had arrived. After reading through them, Norma felt they were all objectionable, but Har-

[1]Joseph P. Bean, "Public Education—'River of Pollution,' " Fullerton, Calif.: The Citizens Committee of California.

court's was the worst. She told the Downtown Kiwanis Club in Tyler:

"Fifty years ago these books would have caused the wholesale firing of everyone responsible for even offering them because it is *not* the function of our schools to regulate the child's social development, to change his values, to reorient his faith—yes, to even determine his philosophy.

"Beginning with a six-year-old child, the books instill the idea that he *must* change, his community *must* change, the 'family of man' *must* change—and all in a predetermined way. Everything is questioned. There is an emphasis on change but *none* on absolutes. In fact, much of both the pupil's and teacher's editions consist of open-ended questions with seldom a firm answer. These social studies texts utilize inquiry as the means of learning—not the imparting of knowledge by the teacher. This approach is used specifically to teach the child that there are no absolutes, no certain values, that what he learned from his parents and his church is to be discredited or at least disregarded.

"Tampering with the minds of children is the most dangerous aspect of the 'new' social studies. Of course, it is innocently termed a change in behavior. No teacher should be forced to use this type of book because it will no longer be her duty to impart knowledge. Rather she is to act as a moderator, and she is to 'heal.' Yes, 'heal.' This is emphasized repeatedly in the series published by Harcourt. Now, if a child needs healing, it is obvious he is considered to have an unsound mental condition."

The Gabler Family—Together

The Gablers worked feverishly during the first three weeks of July. Norma curtailed speaking and concentrated on the Harcourt books at the regional center in Kilgore. Then Mel joined her at home after work and they typed far into the night. Paul, whose wedding was approaching, and Don, the youngest, who worked nights at the Holiday Inn three miles away, ran errands and helped with household routine. Jim would be arriving shortly from Washington, D.C., where he was doing his service stint as an officer at Walter Reed Army Hospital.

Long before, the Gabler household had ceased to be normal. The textbook crusade was a year-round passion. Norma was continually on the go. Mel worked late at the office to compensate for time taken with people calling for book information. Norma tried to cook regular meals when she was home, but there was always the telephone ringing and the constant press to get out a mailing or meet a deadline for Austin. The boys and Mel had understood and cooperated.

Each member of the family had his own color of cups, plates, and saucers. Norma's was green, Mel's red, Jim's yellow, Paul's pink, and Don's blue. This was so each could always wash his own dishes after eating or snacking. The parents realized they would soon be alone. After Paul was married, only Don would be left at home, attending college during the day and working from 3 till 11 P.M. Another year or two and Don would be coming home only for holiday visits.

Because Norma was away from home more than Mel, she had tried to find time to spend with Don. He often drove her to Austin and speaking engagements. Though they were always rushing, she treasured the times they had together at home.

The best time was when Don came home late from work. Norma would make him a cup of hot chocolate and he would stretch out on the rug beside the cone-shaped fireplace which he and Mel had installed in the den. There, for an hour or two, the long-legged, handsome, 6' 4" blonde 19-year-old would talk with his mother about college, girls, textbooks, and events of the day.

Don was to be an attendant at Paul's wedding and Jim was to be the best man. But on the wedding day there was a mixup in schedules, and Jim was late getting dressed. The boys ended up switching roles, with Don serving as best man.

After the Saturday wedding, the Gablers returned home on Sunday by way of Galveston, where Don talked his grandmother into wading in the surf. On Monday Mel and Norma drove to Dallas for a speaking engagement.

Returning home about midnight, they saw lights ablaze in houses along the block and cars parked bumper to bumper. "Oh, Honey, something has happened to Roger [Don's best friend who lived at the end of the block]," Norma said in concern. But Mel pointed to the police car parked at their house. What had happened, and to whom?

It was Don. He had been riding with young Steve Scobee, a nephew of Richard LeTourneau. In trying to stop for a traffic light just four blocks from the Gablers' home, Scobee's car had skidded on the wet pavement into the path of an oncoming station wagon. Both youths had been instantly killed.

The Gabler and Scobee families attended the same church and were close. The Scobees went to Don's funeral at 10 o'clock Tuesday morning and the Gablers returned for Steve's rites at 2 o'clock that afternoon. After the second funeral, Jim and Paul Gabler and Steve's brothers went to tell the driver of the station wagon that they knew he was not to blame and held no hard feelings.

"I tried to stop," he sobbed. "I jammed my foot so hard on the brake that the pedal broke."

Jim and Paul had a high regard for Don. They said, "Don is everything we ever hope to be." Jointly, they wrote a eulogy which became a source of comfort and strength for numerous individuals. It was printed along with Don's brief autobiography and is still being sent out by the thousands.[2]

Mel and Norma found solace in their faith. "We don't know why God allowed this to happen, but we know that He makes no mistakes," Norma told sympathizing friends. "We're just thankful to have only precious memories of Don." The wedding pictures were a comfort. "Now we know why Don was the best man," Mel said.

For a short time their whole world stopped, but Norma, who was due to testify in Austin in a matter of days, said, "Oh, Mel, how can I go to Austin when my heart hurts so much?"

Mel reminded her, "Don would want us to continue for his sake. Besides, who else can go?" As before, God gave them an inner peace and the strength to return to their work with the textbooks proposed for Texas schools.

Norma had long been known for her cheerful spirit. From tragedy she learned how to lift the spirit of others—she learned to smile till this became her trademark.

Back to Work

Rededicating their efforts for the sake of Don, they went back to work, introducing their bill of particulars on Harcourt's social studies program by asking:

"To whom does the child belong?

---

[2] A portion of the eulogy written by Don's brothers appears in Appendix VII.

"If students now belong to the State, these books are appropriate. If students still belong to parents, these books have absolutely no place in Texas schools.

"The author clearly states that these books are designed to change the behavior, values, and concepts of the child, based on the premise that the teacher is *not* to instruct, but to moderate and to 'heal.' "

Then in 27 single-spaced pages they cited hundreds of objectionable statements and directives. They objected to the teacher as "healer." "A teacher should . . . teach, instruct." They opposed emphasis on problems: ". . . If a child is continually told only the 'bad' about his personality, he will eventually begin to believe, accept, and act out these qualities to the exclusion of the 'good qualities.' " They charged invasion of privacy, citing from the Level 6 book one of many examples of "spying" in the instructions to the teacher:

"Have the class go on 'Independent Investigation . . . observing cultural patterns.'

"This investigation should be done by observation, not by questionnaire or interview. People can be very sensitive to the neighbor's child asking 'how much do you have' questions, even for scientific purposes" (TE [Teacher's Edition], p. 43).

From the Level 3 Green book they cited what they considered "attacks on family life" and "invasion of privacy":

from the Bill of Particulars: The eight-year-old child is to *first* decide his own values—before the parent's values are to be considered, after which the differences are to be explained with no indication in either the student or teacher's edition that the parent's mature judgment is to be valued more than that of the eight-year-old child.

from the Text: "After you decide what you value, ask your parents what they value. Do you and your parents value the same things? Why or why not?" (SE [Student's Edition], Green Level 3, p. 106; TE, p. 115, in some printings)

"Some children may use these to strike out at parents; they can be helped by such questions as 'Do you think your parents really value money for itself?' or 'Do you think it's parties they really value, or is it having friends around them?' The same approach might be taken to any child who defiantly claims only antisocial values for himself . . . (TE, Level 3, p. 115).

Bill: They note:

1. "strike out at parents"
2. Parents are portrayed through loaded questions as being materialistic and selfish.
3. Parents are compared note the wording "The same approach") to "any child who defiantly claims only anti-social values. . . ."

Text: "Does your grandmother or grandfather ever want you to do something in an 'old' way?" (TE, Green Level 3, p. 115)

Bill: This question plus the example given as a "short problem story" can only implant in the child's mind that "new" is better than "old" which is not necessarily true.

They opposed change for the sake of change,[3] stating:

A student would gradually be indoctrinated with the false idea that there are no absolutes, because there is a continuous emphasis on changing values, facts, ideas, etc., with no corresponding emphasis on the fact that there *are* permanent and unchanging absolutes.

They objected to group decisions,[4] claiming:

Much of the student's learning from the use of these books would be through class or 'group' consensus. Thus, the child

---

[3] The Gablers clarified: "Individual quotations cannot portray the cumulative effect on students of a continual reference to change. One must examine the entire series to grasp the deviousness and danger of textbooks which are gradually but effectively directing student minds away from basic Christian values.

"The combination of (1) stressing *change*, (2) *questioning* just about everything, and (3) *no* acknowledgement of anything fixed or *absolute* must, as steady dripping of water, gradually indoctrinate students away from traditional, basic, biblical, exact values."

[4] The inquiry method's use of open-ended questions with no right or wrong answers would be an effective means of changing student values, the Gablers reasoned. Each class would reach its conclusion, determined solely by whatever the class members decide, in discussions directed by the teacher, who would be free to add input in whatever direction desired. Thus, 100 different classes could come to 100 different conclusions for the same question. Each would be as acceptable as the other. However, the Gablers believed that the conclusions reached by a majority of the members of each class would generally be in a predetermined direction if discussions were limited to the provided or suggested source material.

will gradually begin to depend upon peer pressure to arrive at group decisions. Eventually it will become difficult and then practically impossible for the child to make individual decisions. Not standing firm for one's own view weakens the ability to think individually, blunts convictions, and allows gradual indoctrination toward the group view or group consensus.

They also objected to inadequate teaching of citizenship, belittling of parents, bias, paucity of facts, and continual asking of questions.

Paul F. Brandwein, the author and director of Harcourt's school department, responded that there was "not the slightest intent to belittle parents." "Indeed," he said, "the purpose is to strengthen the family." He denied or disagreed with other objections. He said, for example, "Scholars in the field . . . widely accept problem-solving as a major approach to the teaching of children." He defended and defined the role of the teacher as healer.

The schools do indeed make provision for the health and handicaps of children; further, educators acknowledge that the knowledge, skills, and attitudes which make it possible for children to meet the needs of a modern society with its complex social and technological environment are indeed under the purview of the schools.

He quoted from one of the teaching manuals:

"Because teaching aims both to enable and to ennoble, the teacher, by example, is compassionate, and would have the children be so. For competence and compassion are the marks of the educated person. In serving the ends of compassion and competence, a teacher heals" (TE, Level 1, p. 9).

Healing, he declared,

. . . in the sense of teaching is thus always related *in context* to educational aims. The petitioners have quoted out of context, and thus related the term 'heals,' out of context, to medical aims.

"What's Your Angle, Mrs. Gabler?"

The debate resumed at the September hearings in Austin. Norma put some previous objections in question form.

(1) Do Texas parents want their children reared to adulthood, unable to think as individuals, placing all reliance upon group decision-making?
(2) Will Texas parents want to relinquish all controls over the social development of their own children?
(3) Do Texas parents want hostile children?

Brandwein, a revered name among educational psychologists, was there to further defend his books. When he began speaking, there was noticeable silence. It seemed to Norma that the teachers and administrators serving on the Textbook Committee listened in awe.

He again denied the Gablers' charges that the social studies were anti-parent. "The American system is strong," he said, "because both parents and teachers want their children to be as compassionate as they are competent." He noted that the books had already been used in pilot studies throughout the nation, including Texas. "We do not find invasion of privacy," he continued. "We do find the children have gotten what we would consider the Judeo-Christian ethic that their neighbors are as important as themselves."

In a requested explanation of the inquiry approach, Dr. Brandwein stated, ". . . Before a person asks a question, he must have the facts. And the reason we believe that children of six, seven, and eight do have information, is that they have been brought up in a different culture, with an instrument known as TV. . . ."

The Committee wanted to complete the hearings in one day. Because each social studies series had six student and six teacher's books, Norma estimated that she was allowed less than 30 seconds a book. She was further upset by what she felt was "rude" and "roughshod" treatment given Mrs. Chet Baker and a new petitioner who were objecting to obscenity in stories by James Baldwin and Norman Mailer in literature books and to "look-say" sight-reading in first-grade books.

When her time came to speak again, she candidly expressed her feelings. "I'm appalled at the rudeness of some members of this Committee. These witnesses have a right to be heard and it's obvious that you don't care to hear them. I am ashamed of you. You haven't picked on me, so I feel I have a right to say this."

"Well, you've said it," a Committee member interjected.

"You bet I have and while I'm at it I'll say something else. I've come here for years, and when you work as hard as I've worked, such disrespect is uncalled for.

"It's particularly hard this year. A month ago I lost a young son in an auto accident. I should be home, but I'll never quit coming down here to Austin. Furthermore, I'm going to file charges with the Board of Education about the discourtesy you've shown witnesses."

The room was tense. The Committee members sat unsmiling, unspeaking. Finally, someone asked that Norma's statement be stricken from the record. "No, I want it recorded," she protested. It was removed anyway.

The Committee met to vote on its recommendations the next day. Interest was centered on the social studies for six grades where 16 publishers were competing for five places on the list.

The Committee accepted on the first ballot social studies by Field Educational Publications, Macmillan, Silver-Burdett, and Harcourt. The inclusion of Harcourt was a bitter pill for Norma, who sat among the salesmen.

One more social studies from among eight other competing publishers would be accepted. The Committee chairman called for another ballot. None received the 10 votes necessary for acceptance.

On the sixth ballot Laidlaw got nine votes to six for its closest competitor. Laidlaw was one of the two that Norma had complained about to the Commissioner for failing to get books to the regional centers on time.

A Committee member asked the Laidlaw salesman if his company would remove a drawing on page 40 of the sixth-grade book that suggested evolution. He agreed.

The Committee cast a seventh ballot. The room was tense as publishers and protesters waited the report. Finally, it came: 13-2 for Laidlaw.

The suspense was over. Salesmen who had lost crowded around the Laidlaw man to offer congratulations. An Associated Press reported ventured to ask what the decision was worth to his company.

As later printed by the wire service, the Laidlaw salesman replied, "Oh, about a million." He estimated his company would sell $3.5 million worth of the books and would make a net profit of about one-third.

After all the voting was over, the crowd moved toward the exit. A salesman pulled at Norma's sleeve. "Mrs. Gabler, I've never understood why you come here year after year. Why? Everybody has an angle. You aren't doing this for nothing."

Norma did not feel like answering. But she did.

"My only angle is that I do it for love of the school children of Texas."

8

The "Sexy" History Book

Don's death and the defeat over the social studies had made 1971 a hard year for the Gablers. But they were determined to keep fighting.

Despite all the rule changes, it still seemed to the Gablers that the educational establishment was not cracking down on violations by publishers. There was nothing to do but to keep appealing to the Board, keep appearing in person, and keep the media aware.

Their newest appeal included four complaints of rule violations: (1) some publishers had not been getting their books to all the regional centers on time. (2) at least two of the new social studies series and a science text had been used in Texas, either as replacements or as supplements to adopted texts, before the 1971 adoption hearings. (3) the rights of citizens to be heard fairly had been violated by some State Textbook Committee members. Testimony time had been limited to 30 seconds per book. (4) student and parents' rights had been infringed upon by the Committee's recommendation of the new social studies—"an experimental program designed to change the behavior of children."

The complaints were well-publicized by the Borger, Longview, Kilgore, and Tyler newspapers and other media before the November 13th Board meeting. In addition, Mrs. Chet Baker, the Texas DAR textbook committee chairman, prepared a 12-page newsletter that was circulated across the state.

The Board met on a balmy fall Saturday when the excitement of football was in the air. The Texas Longhorns, nationally ranked and rolling toward the championship of the Southwest Conference, would be playing that afternoon in the nearby University of Texas stadium.

The Board had a full agenda. Chairman Ben R. Howell ruled that petitioners would be limited to 15 minutes each. Norma protested that this would allow her only 15 seconds per book and she couldn't even give the authors and publishers in that time. But the chairman refused to extend the time. She could only state her objections to the social studies in broad principles. Mrs. Baker then spoke against three literature books which she said contained "obscene and immoral" stories by authors such as James Baldwin and Norman Mailer.

The Board members didn't seem upset by the social studies, but some were riled by the English literature texts and other books on recommended reading lists. Board member Paul Matthews of Greenville said his daughter had read one of the books on the recommended reading list and "it is so filthy that we should have replaced it with *Playboy* magazine." Another member proposed that the literature books be rejected, but the majority said no. After hearing other petitioners, the Board voted nine to eight to accept all the Textbook Committee's choices.

The Board dispensed with Norma's allegations of rules' violations in short summary fashion. Again, Norma protested that they were riding roughshod over herself and other witnesses. In the cross fire discussion that followed, she overheard a Board member say that the witnesses were not being treated fairly and another reply, "We don't have time to discuss it."

A few minutes later in off-the-record informal discussion, she overheard two Board members talking about the football game. "Now we know why they're in a hurry," she told Mrs. Baker. "They'll remember this," she vowed.

The meeting was dismissed shortly after noon, in time for Board members to make the opening kickoff. Norma hurried back to Longview and reported what had happened to Editor Hopkins. He suggested editorially to

> . . . the Board majority that its arrogant attitude in summarily disposing of protests . . . may not stand as the last word on the matter. . . . It is interesting to note that a big

football game was waiting to start in Austin at 2 P.M., and there was reference to the game heard in some of the unofficial remarks of one or more Board members.

Norma appealed again, charging violations "of our civil rights as citizens, parents, and taxpayers," saying the Board showed "obvious bias" and "denied time to properly present evidence of serious potential damage to the minds of students in the textbooks. . . ." She asked that the Board rescind its hurried November vote adopting the books and vote again after hearing more testimony. Chairman Howell replied that he had polled the members and found the majority opposed to another hearing. He therefore considered the matter closed.

The Gablers were both upset and puzzled. Upset because children would be subjected to the new social studies for the next six years. And puzzled at what seemed to them to be the Board's blindness to the content of the books that, in their estimation, kept getting progressively worse.

Ellie Hopkins had advised Norma to study the Board members; get to know them as individuals. She had listened to their discussions in meetings on books and other school matters as well. She had tried to be friendly, without seeming to be coquettish, during coffee breaks. They all seemed to be decent, leader types—businessmen, bankers, doctors, lawyers, accountants. They served without pay and didn't talk in "educationese," the language frequently used by publishers, editors, and TEA personnel during the hearings. Some could act quite independently at times. Carl Morgan from Jasper, who had attended Cornell University, had a way of saying, "I don't want to hear your educational jargon. Put it in language a country boy can understand." If Morgan was in doubt about anything, he would invariably vote against it. His place was known as the "no" seat on the board. Jack Binion, the crusty bachelor lawyer from Houston, had warmed up. Once he had made a publisher apologize to Norma for calling her a "damn liar" over a statistic during a hearing on an economics book. "I don't always agree with Mrs. Gabler," he said, "but I do have great respect for her. She has always conducted herself like a lady, and you'll act like a gentleman if you want to sell books in Texas." And a new petitioner told Norma, "When I first inquired about textbooks, Mr. Binion referred me to you. He said you knew more about books than anybody else in Texas."

How the Boards Work

"What I can't understand," Norma frequently told Mel, "is how these Board members can go along with most of the books the Textbook Committee recommends year after year. I doubt if very many, if any at all, really read the books, but they get our bills and testimony at the Committee hearings, and some, I think, listen to our appeals. Then when the showdown comes, they still vote for the books. Well, not always, but most of the time.

"I go out and talk to civic clubs, to editors and businessmen, to ordinary parents," Norma continued. "I get them to read the books for themselves. And 90% of them are appalled and wonder how Austin can keep buying such books. Why aren't the majority of Board members concerned? Why don't they make the publishers give us better books?"

Norma was asking these same questions during a visit she and Mel had with Jim and Joanne McAuley. Mr. McAuley was a business executive and Mrs. McAuley was a new member of the textbook brigade.

"Norma, have you or Mel ever served on the board of a corporation or a public institution?" Jim McAuley asked.

Norma laughed. "No, except Mel is a deacon in church."

"Well, don't deacons usually go along with their preacher, unless he does something wrong?"

"Sure, they figure he has a call from God and special training."

"Boards in secular life work the same way. Take the trustees of a corporation. They don't have time to be experts in the business. So they hire professionals and depend on them. Our State Board of Education is no different."

A light was dawning. "The professionals are the people in the Texas Education Agency," Mel said. "And they select the Textbook Committee each year."

"Right. The Board looks to them for recommendations."

"And the TEA people are influenced by their peers. They respect the authors and editors whom the publishers send down to testify for their books. You should have seen how goo-goo they were over Dr. Brandwein," Norma added.

"Then you women come in without the credentials of degrees and authorship and expect the Board to listen to you. Put yourself in their shoes. Why should they take your opinion when they have hired experts to give them professional advice?"

The analysis hurt, but Norma could see his logic.

"I've seen the Board members get their hackles up, but sometimes I wonder if they really understand the establishment's double talk.

"If they think they're being snowed," McAuley continued, "they won't stand for it. But they won't make a public debacle and fire their executives right there. That would reflect on their own wisdom in hiring them in the first place. They'll wait till later and make some changes."

Norma kept nodding. "I'm beginning to get it."

"Also, have you considered that textbooks are only one of the Board's responsibilities?"

"I know they have other things to do. I've listened to the discussions on budgets, vocational schools, and personnel problems. I've always felt textbooks were the most important. I guess I've expected them to become full-time experts in this field. But no matter what else they have to do, I'm going to keep at them until they do start reading books."

McAuley smiled. "I hope you succeed."

Mel had been listening closely. The conversation caused him to look again at something Dr. Joseph Bean had said in his resignation speech to the Glendale, California School Board several years earlier:

When a new trustee is elected to a local Board of Education, he intends, of course, to represent the residents who elected him. But usually the new board member, within a matter of six weeks, finds himself representing the educational establishment instead of the residents. When parents come before the board to make requests, they are often treated rudely and as enemies of the board. Rarely will a board member continue to identify with the parents and to serve them and their children. With their districts 90% controlled by the federal and state governments, parents live under complete tyranny when their own local boards identify with the administrative staff instead of the people whom they were elected to represent.

These new insights into the State Board's frame of work were not particularly encouraging to the Gablers. Still they were determined to keep chipping away to make the Board more responsive to the people it was supposed to represent.

"Behavioristic" Social Studies

New grievances continued to crop up. The Board was still allowing some schools to experiment with curriculum that had not gone through the adoption process. The prime example in the spring of 1972 was the new federally funded National Science Foundation's program for fifth grade, *Man: A Course of Study* (MACOS).

Parents in Arizona tipped them that MACOS was the worst social studies imaginable. It was already in their schools and was probably also being taught in Texas under the camouflage of a pilot study. The Gablers checked and indeed it was being taught in several Texas schools.

Further investigation revealed that MACOS was the brainchild of Jerome Bruner, a Harvard experimental behavioral psychologist. As was the case with the BSCS biology books, the National Science Foundation looked for a private publisher to develop the course under an NSF grant. After 58 publishers turned it down as too controversial or expensive, a contract was signed with a new publishing company, Curriculum Development Associates of Washington, D.C.

MACOS was intended to teach "the universal bond between all men" through a series of "discovery" lessons on a variety of cultures. The aim was to "have children step outside of their own cultures to question values they may have already learned."

The required training the teachers received forbade them to initiate any questions on their own. All questions came from manuals which had to be followed exactly. Nor could the students look for answers in extracurricular resource materials of their own or their parents' choosing. All answers were to be obtained from the course books, simulated games, and films. To the Gablers, it was the perfect example of a closed system of government indoctrination for neutralizing the values taught by church and home. The Gablers got the complete course and studied it with growing apprehension.

One simulation game was to be played for a week. The victor had to procure enough seals to provide for his own survival. He could only do this by "starving" his coplayers. The lesson that the price of surviving is killing was reinforced by a story of an old woman left to die on the ice because she was no longer useful to her society. The book word for this was "senilicide," a term impressionable fifth graders were expected to learn. This was covered in two student's books and two teacher's manuals, and the students were to play-act leaving the elderly to die.

Norma included this story and others in her speeches. She told one civic club, "After looking at textbooks for 11 years I thought I was unshockable. But this wins the prize for being the worst. Fifth-grade children, at an age when they are most impressionable and curious, are led to 'discover' the life-style of the Netsilik Eskimo tribe of Canada. And what do the Netsiliks practice? Cannibalism, infanticide, murder of grandparents, wife swapping, mating with animals—the most degrading things you can imagine. And what is the teacher to say about all this? She is not to make a value judgment. The children must decide with the clear implication that if the Netsiliks want to live this way, then these crimes against God and nature are all right. The whole idea is that one culture is as good as another and that the values of no cultures are absolute."

She pointed to the story of a man named Tunequ, "who consults with the spirits who tell him to save his own life by eating his wife. He begins by eating her clothing, and then by feeling her sides for flesh. When she ran, he stabbed her to death and ate her, collecting her bones in a heap. That's on page 98 of the teacher's book for that culture. This 'delightful' story is followed by another about Itqilik, who eats his brother's frostbitten feet, and then decides, since little brother is useless anyhow, to finish him off, gourmet-style. The 10- or 11-year-old child will then study a myth about a jealous mother-in-law who kills and skins her daughter and covers herself with the daughter's skin so the young son-in-law would take her as his wife."

The Gablers protested again to the State Commissioner of Education that the use of MACOS or any other un-adopted course in state schools was clear violation of state law. Their protest went officially unheeded but shortly thereafter, she was advised that the MACOS films were being removed from the Dallas Film Library, and there had been a definite reduction in the number of Texas schools using this fifth-grade program.

1972—Starting Another Cycle

It was time to start work on the books for the next annual adoption. The year 1972 appeared to be one of the biggest years ever with scores of American histories, economics, world geographies, and civil government texts competing for places on the coveted state list. And there was a very special wedding on their agenda; Captain James Gabler and Gloria Huisingh had planned their ceremony for late May, 1973 in Gloria's hometown, Denver, Colorado.

When Mel and Norma finished reading the new list they concluded that the objectionable trends in books had accelerated.

A sampling of summaries which they filed with their bills of particulars:

ECONOMICS (High School)
The American Economy, Houghton Mifflin, 1972

The discussion of free enterprise is weak. Socialism is praised and only its so-called advantages and appeal are presented. The Karl Marx theory of "from each according to his ability to each according to his need" is used four times. It then goes on to make a strong case for Communism and advocates peaceful coexistence. It states Russians are convinced their system is better than free enterprise and will remain "sold" on it (p. 409). In contrast, it is suggested on page 396 that Americans may turn to revolution as a means of correcting social problems under our American free enterprise system.

Economics: Principles and Practices, Merrill, 1971

Advantages and benefits of the free enterprise system are minimized and the command economics given preferential treatment. Capitalism is associated with old-fashioned, primitive, and traditional, while change and innovation are equated with advanced societies, and command economics . . . [as breaking] from restrictive customs. Pictures of the United States show our worst aspects and pictures of Russia their good aspects. There is a heavy emphasis on American problems with the implied cause being that capitalism is unable to solve them . . . uses mind and value changing behavioral science techniques.

AMERICAN HISTORIES
(Fifth grade, eighth grade, and high school)
Liberty and Union—A History of the United States, Volume 2, Houghton Mifflin Company, 1973

We were shocked at this publisher's contention that it is

possible to curse prayerfully. In the story related on pages 423 to 426, we objected to the use of profanity since this is in direct violation of the published procedure for textbook adoption. There were seventeen "damns" in eighteen lines, plus four other references to God's name in vain.

The publisher attempts to justify the cursing by stating:

"These oaths seem to be more prayerful than blasphemous. To whom does one appeal if not to God when all seems lost and the hopelessness or horror of a situation is apparent?"

In the context of the story, these expressions will have to be considered profanity. . . .

We reemphasize that prayerful cursing has no place in a textbook.

Many Peoples, One Nation, Random House, 1973

This fifth-grade text is sick, very sick. It engenders racial hatred through a heavy emphasis on discrimination. An example of how our "wonderful American heritage" is taught to fifth-grade children in the present tense:

"No nation on earth is guilty of practices more shocking and bloody than is the United States at this very hour.

Go where you may and search where you will. Roam through all the kingdoms of the Old World. Travel through South America. Search out every wrong. When you have found the last, compare your facts with the everyday practices of this nation. Then you will agree with me that, for revolting barbarity and shameless hypocrisy, America has no rival" (p. 88).

Quest for Liberty and Perspectives in United States History, Field Publications, 1972

These high school texts are especially offensive, being more sociology texts than history. They gradually, convincingly, and very effectively direct students away from fixed values to pragmatic relativism. Students, at the conclusion of the study, would have great difficulty in holding any favorable considerations of fundamental Christianity, respect for parents, personal morality. . . .

WORLD GEOGRAPHY (High school)

Man and His World, Silver-Burdett, 1972

An overemphasis on environmental problems through appeals

to the emotions. Strong pro-evolutionary bias in disregard of scientific evidence which supports sudden creation if arranged objectively.

Geography and World Affairs, Rand McNally, 1971

A world affairs text concentrating on people more than on geography. A liberal-left indoctrination course which eulogizes leftist activities.

CIVIL GOVERNMENT (Eighth Grade)

Civil Government (3 paperback books—boxed), Ginn, 1972

These texts seem to be designed more for agitation than education. Students are required to consider issues and then fumble with decisions in order to make judgments on them with only minimum information. Thus their conclusions must be based primarily on their imaginations. The students are led to think that they are making up their own minds, whereas, under a competent teacher they are being skillfully manipulated in their learning process through directed discussion. Under an average teacher the students will despair and under an immature teacher the course will be disastrous. Responsibilities are neglected while rights are emphasized completely out of proportion. Many of the topics are potentially explosive and could lead to anguish and despair even though exact answers are not expected from the open-ended questions. The course seems dedicated to changing students' values, actions, and behavior, instead of imparting traditional basic facts and knowledge.

It was hard for the Gablers to decide which of these and others were the worst books. Mel showed some of the proposed civil government texts to a police chief. He read a few pages and moaned, "This will legitimatize lawbreaking. It will be like sticking a match to gasoline."

Within the time limits, they could prepare bills on only a few of the books. They concentrated on a Houghton Mifflin civil government series of eight paperback books titled *Justice in Urban America* (1970, 1972) and a Macmillan [1] fifth-grade history called, ironically, they thought, *Search for Freedom* (1973).

Judging from past experience, Norma packed for only a three-

---

[1] Also published by Benziger.

day stay in Austin. This year for the first time there would be three state hearings, about a month apart. The first would be before the Commissioner. The record of this hearing would go to the Textbook Committee which would then hold a hearing. Then, as in previous years, petitioners would be entitled to last-ditch appeals to the State Board.

Another surprise came when the Commissioner announced that petitioners could take all the time they wished in the first hearing, both in their presentations and in their rebuttals to publishers, which had been granted two years before. Norma was ready to shout, "Hallelujah!" The appeals and the publicizing of results were beginning to pay off.

Getting a Hearing

The Commissioner's hearings lasted seven and a half days, in addition to the break for Saturday and Sunday. After the third day, Norma told a group of book salesmen in the coffee shop below the conference room, "You'll have to get used to seeing me in the same dresses. I'm not leaving until the chairman says, 'Hearings adjourned.' "

There were eight paperback volumes in the *Justice in Urban America* series. The Gablers had picked the two they felt were most offensive: *Youth and the Law* and *Poverty and Welfare*. "But I'm objecting to the whole series," Norma said in the hearings.

In general she believed that throughout these books (to teach citizenship) there was "overemphasis on lawbreaking, violence, prejudice, and poverty."

A case in point was a picture of two militants burning the American flag on page three of *Youth and the Law,* with the caption stating that the act was illegal. She noted that the publisher had said in his response to the Gablers' bill of particulars that there was a reason for picking the pictures. "A picture can usually be understood by illiterates . . . [and is] capable of creating a mood . . . that could compel feeling."

The picture, Norma said, "shows two militants burning the flag, our United States flag. We objected strongly and bitterly to this, because I see no excuse, whether it's to show they are violating the law [or not], because they [the publisher] have just made the statement even an illiterate can read a picture. . . . Most students will be far more influenced by the picture than they would ever be by the caption.

"Go through and look at the pictures. . . ." Her bill had called attention to many pictures of youth fighting, stealing, defacing property, violating the law, and taunting law personnel. "I think there should be more showing people upholding the law; . . . at least half of the pictures should show something constructive for youth to do instead of something violent . . . could not some of the pictures have been with our youth, both black and white . . . [with] sacks picking up the trash . . . instead of showing the filth in this yard . . . ?"

In *Poverty and Welfare* she found much to question since it was supposed to teach citizenship. On pages 62 and 63 there was a welfare application form, but there was no job application form, so she asked, "Would you believe that it is now more important for a . . . student to learn to apply for welfare than it is for him to apply for a job?" Then, quoting from the publishers' reply,

It is unbelievable that anybody would want to withold this kind of information [welfare application form] from our young citizens.

"This is for 14-year-old children. . . . An application for employment would relate to the rights and responsibilities of a citizen in the official Proclamation [the Texas call for adoption of books which meet the state's requirements for teaching citizenship] much more effectively than does the welfare form. . . ."

"This text [for teaching citizenship] does not encourage individual initiative to look for work; it has no information . . . [for] obtaining employment . . . personal skills . . . [which] would have a direct bearing on poverty by providing students with something constructive to overcome poverty rather than to believe, as this text would indicate, that solving poverty and providing work is a governmental responsibility."

In her bill, Norma had called attention to the use of the word "poverty" 168 times in this 83-page book.

Houghton Mifflin's salesman replied, in part, that the books had been developed by a foundation related to the Chicago Board of Education and the Chicago Bar Association with the avowed purpose of fighting rising juvenile delinquency. "Not, as the petitioner has indicated in her complaint, to aggravate it. That . . . is the most unusual interpretation.

"The virtue of these books," he continued, "lies not in that we are informing students for the first time of these problems. The virtue . . . lies at last in facing some of the problems squarely in classroom materials and showing students how to operate our society's time-tested machinery . . . for solving these problems—that is, the legal process."

He replied to Norma's criticism of negative pictures. For example, he quoted the caption under the students burning the American flag:

"The flag is a symbol of the United States. Its destruction is illegal. The burning is a symbolic attack on the U.S. political system!"

"Then, it goes on to ask the following questions:

"What do you think causes these young men to burn the flag? Does the action go beyond citizenship? Does their approach differ from that used by young people in the picture on page 2? Which strategy do you think might gain the most satisfactory response from the government?

"Now, page two . . . shows a picture of young people working in a political office doing a very positive thing. And that is balanced treatment, from Houghton Mifflin's point of view."

Norma responded, ". . . Take a good look at page two. If you will notice the pictures on the walls, there is no one, not even a child in the third grade, that won't tell you that's against the Vietnam War. That has to be a militant group and they're usually against everything that is concrete and sound in this nation." She later added, "The picture on page two was listed by the publisher as a constructive picture. We ask, 'Constructive for whom?' The picture shows several young people with a number of posters, all of which have been classed as being activist or revolutionary, including 'End the war in Vietnam' and so-called 'peace signs.' "

In defense of the questioning employed in the books, he said, "This type of questioning is not a recall question, it does not call for an automatic answer from a student for a school solution that he might have been previously exposed to. Instead, it calls for the student's own conclusion, supported by his own sound reasoning."

In her lengthy rebuttal, Norma reminded the publisher of a Texas policy that "supersedes" the specifications for the 1972 civil government books:

" 'The textbook contents shall not interfere with the school's legal responsibility to teach citizenship and to promote patriotism.

" 'Textbooks adopted . . . shall not include selections and works which contribute to civil disorder, social strife, or flagrant disregard for the law.'

"Whether I like the technique [of questioning] or not has nothing to do with it. It is the questions that are asked. It places and casts doubt on the mind of the child.

"The books do play up the problems . . . [but] if we are going to have reality, then we ask, why is reality always negative? Does not reality also include the many acts of kindness between the races across the nation?

"It must also be remembered that a quality such as morality must be taught. It does not come naturally. Education without morality will result in a depraved society.

"We know we have the problems. But to get a series of books that only play up and enlarge problems, play up poverty to such an extent that the child becomes more overwhelmed with problems. . . . [Well,] if there were more answers given to them, I could possibly justify some of the books."

Perhaps because the hearings were so long and the books so many, the debate over the *Justice in Urban America* series received little publicity. After a second and much shorter hearing, the Textbook Committee recommended the *Justice in Urban America* books for adoption. Then in a surprise move the Commissioner took the books off the list, saying they had too much emphasis on poverty.

The big news flap in '72 came over one chapter in Macmillan's *Search for Freedom* (1973).

Marilyn Monroe vs. George Washington

Norma objected to the book "equating" farm union organizer Cesar Chavez, Martin Luther King, Jr., and Mahatma Gandhi "with Jesus," while it "can't even say that Benjamin Franklin once used prayer to calm a troublesome Constitutional Convention." She then complained that the fifth-grade history gave "Marilyn Monroe, a 'sex symbol,' six and one-half pages, while it only mentions George Washington five times and doesn't tell anything about his life or what he did. That isn't fair."

Macmillan's salesman retorted, "There's nothing sexy about my book."

The Commissioner interrupted to say, "I don't believe Mrs. Gabler called it exactly that."

The salesman courteously conceded his error and continued. Among other defenses, he claimed that Franklin's request for prayer at the Constitutional Convention could not be included because of religious grounds. It would not be constitutional, he said.

During lunch Norma worked on her game plan for rebuttal. When the hearings reconvened, she was ready.

"The publisher says there is nothing sexy in this book. If you will turn with me to page 386 you will see the same picture you saw on the cover of *Life* magazine. I call that a sexy picture of Marilyn. Now read back on page 385:

"As Norma Jean [her name before she became Marilyn Monroe] grew older, the boys noticed how pretty she was. When she walked down the street, men turned to watch her; she knew just exactly how to walk. . . .

"Now let's look at the discussion questions at the end of the chapter. Number three is interesting:

"What problems did Marilyn have in her marriage to Arthur Miller? What did she seem to enjoy most about being his wife?

"Those questions are for fifth graders.

"That's enough. But I did want to mention again that Marilyn got six and one-half pages in this fifth-grade history while George Washington is only mentioned five times. I don't think so, but I'll ask: Is Texas ready for Marilyn to become the mother of our country?"

The crowded room exploded. There was a commotion at the press table as reporters raced for outside phones. As soon as Norma stopped speaking, she was pressed for interviews.

The UPI man in Austin later told Norma that his wire service had received requests from 10 foreign countries for the story. "You've made education hard news around the world," he said.

Many American newspapers gave the story front-page billing. A sampling of headlines:

"WASHINGTON FADES, MARILYN SHINES"
" 'SEXY' HISTORY BOOK ANGERS TEXAS MOTHER"
"MARILYN GETS TOP BILLING: GEORGE RATES
A FOOTNOTE"

The *Dallas Morning News* made the book the subject of an editorial on September 22, 1972:

Mother of Her Country

Movies, they say, are better than ever. Do movie stars improve grammar school history texts?

Mrs. Mel Gabler of Longview, who keeps up with texts offered Texas schools, has her doubts and made them plain at a hearing held by the Texas Education Agency in Austin the other day.

How about a fifth-grade history text, she asked, that gives Marilyn Monroe seven [sic] pages and a picture and limits George Washington to a dozen [sic] skittish lines?

How about this same text, *Search for Freedom,* likening Martin Luther King and Cesar Chavez to Jesus Christ—but omitting reference to Benjamin Franklin's call for prayer at the Constitutional Convention because, to use the words of the publisher's representative, that would be teaching religion?

We don't know any more than Mrs. Gabler what Chavez in the role of the Saviour is supposed to teach, but like her, we would have thought that Franklin's prayer was the historical fact and Chavez's new character a figment of modern historiography.

As for Marilyn Monroe's historical significance, maybe there is something we don't know about this tragic beauty who died by her own hand after several marriages failed.

But for setting historical examples for children, we would prefer Molly Pitcher if anybody is going to figure as Mother of Her Country. She was short on beauty, from all accounts, but quite a warrior in the Revolutionary ranks—right along side her husband. They say George Washington had a good word for her.

Then to almost everyone's astonishment, the Textbook Committee approved *Search for Freedom* on the first ballot. Norma appealed the Committee recommendations to the Commissioner, reminding him again of the Marilyn Monroe chapter. He removed the book from the list.

When the Board met later and heard Norma's protests against the Committee's recommendations of other books she had protested, people were still talking about the "sexy" history book. The Board members, as they had the year before, approved the Committee's choices. Several laughed about the Marilyn Monroe incident. One recalled to Norma, "I sat down to breakfast and opened my newspaper. There you were, Mrs. Gabler, on the front page. Then I read the story and put my head down on the table and laughed till I almost cried."

"Let this be a lesson to you," Norma smiled. "If I can't beat you with facts, I'll keep books off the list because of stupidity."

The publisher's representative was disappointed at losing the sale. But he was not angry. Later he told Norma, "Everywhere our salesmen go in the United States they're asked about the 'sexy' history book."

As a momento of the incident, he sent her a copy autographed: *For Mrs. Gabler, the very fair protester who went coast to coast with this text on newspapers, on radio, and on TV (without trying). I hope this is the last copy you will ever see with pages 384–390 (Marilyn Monroe) in it. With kindest regards.*

9

X-rated Textbooks

Macmillan's "sexy" history book produced a lot of wry laughter as Norma spoke around the country in the spring of 1973. But she and Mel saw no humor in the crop of psychology and sociology books being offered for the fall adoption hearings. Some of the books seemed to condone and even encourage homosexuality, a concern that heightened to dismay and anger when the brutal murders of 27 young boys by Houston homosexual deviants were uncovered.

Before the fall hearings opened, the Gablers prepared a news release on the books against which Norma would be testifying. Using that release and other information, Texas newspapers ran stories under eye-popping headlines. For example, the *Austin American-Statesman* announced: "TABOOS FALL IN SOME PROPOSED TEXTS." The Austin paper said some of the new books treated homosexuality and lesbianism as legitimate life-styles and taught that there were exceptions to almost all moral laws. And the *Longview Daily News*, in an editorial titled "NEW TEXTBOOKS OFFER BIZARRE MATERIAL," declared, "It leads one to wonder who is the sickest—the subjects about which these textbooks are written, the authors, the publishers, or those public officials who may seriously consider adopting this type of trash for young students in Texas."

The first hearings before the Commissioner of Education opened on a damp Monday, September 18th, in Austin. One of the first books on the agenda was *Inquiries in Sociology* (1972) by Allyn and Bacon, Inc.

To arouse interest, Norma announced, "This book suggests on page 151 that in the eyes of some, the garbage man is socially more important than the doctor because he removes filth that causes and spreads disease while the doctor only cures people after they get sick." Then getting more to the point of her main objections, she charged that the book encouraged negativism, racism, moral permissiveness, rebellion against parental authority, and was biased against Christianity. She gave examples of:

(1) Negativism: "This text has many, many pages on negative content. Why cannot an equal amount of constructive content be added? [Persons] successful in business, leaders in scholastics, sports, drama, music, science . . . who have overcome handicaps, and who do not harbor hatred and prejudice. This . . . would encourage and motivate students to do something worthwhile.

"The pictures (pp. 2, 4–13) portray indecisiveness, vagueness, depression, monotony, the lack of hope and futility. . . ."

(2) Racism: ". . . [White racism] is disproportionately emphasized compared to the racism practiced by many blacks, which is not mentioned. . . . We wondered why there were not pictures of those who are not activists [compared to pictures of Malcolm X, James Baldwin, Stokely Carmichael, and H. Rap Brown]. . . . It is not quite fair to . . . give them status in the text."

(3) Moral permissiveness: "Morality has not properly been portrayed," she said quoting: '. . . It's tactless, if not actually wrong, not to lie under certain circumstances' (p. 37). The text clearly teaches that little white lies are not only acceptable but are necessary in certain instances. This is . . . a situation ethic."

(4) Rebellion against parental authority: "There is a disproportionate emphasis in 'parent-youth conflict' on pages 57, 81, and 107. Students who have [little conflict with their parents] would [be convinced to] expect more [conflict]." She cited:

"The family cares for and instructs the dependent young. Unintended functions of the family may be to extend the period of dependency too long, and to imprint the child, often unconsciously, with the parents' prides, passions, and prejudices" (p. 144).

"This is . . . a point against the home and the parent."

(5) Anti-Christian bias: "It's the way it [the book] presents Christianity":

"[Christianity] didn't help the black man to gain dignity and equality in America, for Christian love was the white man's love for himself and for his own race (p. 129).

"The [Lutheran] minister was an austere and formidable man, the spokesman for a stern God who was ready to condemn forever anyone who deviated in the slightest from absolute good (p. 90).

"Both she and Joe had been raised by Baptist parents, and this meant they were raised strictly. They heard the Gospel preached from the time they were born, preached in church and preached at home. It was a hard religion. . . . There was no in-between, so after a while you took care to be pure" (p. 104).

"This isn't fair to blacks, Lutherans, and Baptists," she said. "Lutheranism certainly teaches the doctrine of salvation by faith in a loving God who died Himself to impart to His children the absolute good." Baptists "preach . . . [that] the Gospel is 'good news.' "

In conclusion, Norma pointed to 10 pages in the Allyn and Bacon text which she claimed dealt with "changing the beneficial values of students. . . . Our schools [must] not be turned into mass experimental centers to develop humanistic citizens of the future, students indoctrinated with behavioral predetermined conclusions."

Time was called. Allyn and Bacon's salesman responded, "Thank you, Mrs. Gabler. I think you have been doing your homework. This is a great country where we can sit here and respectfully disagree. This . . . program was developed by both high school teachers and distinguished sociologists. The sociologists . . . lent the subject expertise while the practicing teachers lent the practical methodology for the subject. The materials were first pilot-tested and then field-tested nationally with over 250 teachers . . . in about 32 states . . . so we feel that we did our homework in these materials.

"In this program we are concerned with the way things are, not the way things ought to be. However, these two are related. It is hard to get to where you ought to be if you don't know where you've been."

He then tackled some of her specific objections.

"We do not intend to demean doctors. . . . In the two pages after the one you discussed, we do have a comparison of the prestige of various occupations. Please note that the first one listed is that of the physician. . . ."

The Commissioner interrupted. ". . . Do you know how the company got trapped in this . . . statement, 'While the doctor only cures people after they get sick'? Well, well; you need not answer."

"I think we do show that physicians rank at the top in occupational preference," the salesman commented.

The Commissioner added, "After making that statement, you'd better."

The Allyn and Bacon man turned back to Norma's criticisms. He pointed to some pictures on pages 4–13 that were "not bad"—a family on a swing, people voting, Boy Scouts, etc. "We think we do have a balance."

"Black activists," he said, "were 'part of history' and therefore had to be included."

About the "little white lie," he suggested, "If someone really looked bad in a hospital, would you really say, 'Gosh, how bad you look'?"

On the parent-youth conflict (p. 59), he noted that the "previous sentence before your quote contains the phrase, 'The parent has the privilege as well as the responsibility of authority.' "

And he had "to take issue" with her view that "the material was against Christianity."

Norma came back smiling in rebuttal.

"That first question about the garbage man and the doctor . . . [should] be removed."

"The text clearly teaches that little white lies are not only acceptable, but necessary in certain instances. . . ."

"The basic thrust of this text is geared toward agitation and not elucidation of sociology. Textbooks should discuss authority of parents over children as being desirable and necessary for the child's own good rather than suggesting it is something that a child must bear.

"Why not look at parents from a positive point of view? Why not secure all the knowledge, virtue, wisdom, and common sense that a child can acquire from his parents? . . . Or . . . maybe this thought has just escaped the publishers.

"This textbook suggests students question, experiment, challenge, and debate issues of life, much of which have been settled forever in history. I think this would possibly create confusion for the student.

"Much in this book . . . needs to either be rewritten or changed to make the book acceptable."

Undermining Values

The Commissioner announced the next book: Holt's *Introduction to the Behavioral Sciences: The Inquiry Approach* (1969).

Norma noted that the publisher had replied in his bill to only 12 of 56 objections. "This indicates," she said, "that 40 of our specific charges were irrefutable."

She termed the book "a behavioral science . . . a means of changing behavior. . . . If I want my child's behavior changed, I will do it at home. But I don't feel the classroom is the place to do it."

To make her point she summarized a section on child training (pp. 254–255).

"We find that children who are taught obedience, respect for rules, and parental authority are prejudiced children: whereas, a child who is disobedient, has no respect for authority, or his parents, doing whatever he wishes, is not prejudiced, but develops basic ideas of equality and trust."

Then she followed a pattern of reading quotes from the text and giving critical comment.

Text: ". . . To be successful in our culture one must learn to dream of failure.

"From the point of view of the other children, of course, they were learning to yap at the heels of a failure. And why not? Have they not dreamed the dream of flight themselves? If the culture does not teach us to fly from failure or to rush in, hungry for success where others have failed, who will try again where others have gone broke? . . . (p. 59)

". . . The central obsession in education is fear of failure. In order not to fail most students are willing to believe anything and to care not whether what they are told is true or false. Thus one becomes absurd through being afraid; but paradoxically, only by remaining absurd can one feel free from fear. Hence the immovableness of the absurd . . . (pp. 59–60).

". . . School is indeed a training for later life not because it teaches the three Rs (more or less), but because it instills the essential cultural nightmare—fear of failures, envy of success, and absurdity . . ." (p. 61).

Comment: "This appears to be completely twisted reasoning."

Text: "As they do this exercise, the student should be developing the concept of cultural relativity—the idea that the 'rightness,' 'goodness,' or 'badness' of a particular kind of behavior can be judged only in terms of the culture in which it is found. For instance, is it 'bad' for people to eat the flesh of other human beings, as people do in a few societies which practice cannibalism? Why does this seem so horrifying to most people in our society and so natural to people in those societies which accept the practice? Why do many people in our society find it reasonable and logical to cook people in electric chairs after they have committed certain kinds of crimes? (Cook them, but not eat them.)" (*Teacher's Guide*, pp. 32–33)

Comment: " 'Cook them in electric chairs' is an intellectual gem. We presume it is, or is it a chipping away against capital punishment?

Text: ". . . Man in modern industrial societies is rapidly becoming detached from nature, from his old gods, . . . from his body and his sex, from his feelings of love and tenderness . . . (pp. 167–168).

"For a very few, religion can still provide a special sense of embracing belonging and selfhood; but for most, religion is but a Sunday meeting house and nursery school, and a recreation center, which cannot adequately define the entire person" (p. 170).

Comment: "This conveys the false idea . . . that the student might as well forget about religion, because it is . . . practically something of the past. This simply is not true. Many today still have that faith. It is worth noting that as the humanistic religious tones . . . have increased in . . . education, it has been paralleled by an increase in disrespect, destruction, crime, burning of the flag, etc."

At this point the hearings adjourned until the next morning when Holt's salesman presented a defense. Some of his principle points were:

(1) The book was the fourth in a series that resulted from a scholarly social study project carried on at Carnegie-Mellon University in Pittsburgh. One objective was "to develop within the students the ability . . . to be independent thinkers and to try to be more responsible citizens."

(2) The materials reflected the views of many contributors with some 58 different "readings" taken from magazine articles, books, etc.

(3) The materials dealt with the behavior of youth "as they are in school, [and revealed] some of the problems that exist in trying to show the students the part they play. . . ."

(4) "Examples such as cannibalism might be shocking, but we're simply trying to get students to look at . . . how culture is formed."

(5) The statement on religion (p. 170) stated a position "many students who feel alienated take."

"The raising of questions does not guarantee objectivity," Norma contended in rebuttal. "Instead, the questions are designed to have the student come to a predetermined conclusion. A student indoctrinated in this manner is firmly convinced that he is right 'because he came to his own conclusion,' without realizing that the subject matter provided him had been carefully selected to assure this eventually.

"These books are not instructing psychology. . . . These books are treating students with psychology. What chance does an immature student have against a trained and capable psychologist, whose values are obviously entirely different from our traditional values as clearly and repeatedly portrayed in this book. . . . [It] is not fair to put the burden on the classroom teacher to attempt to teach behavioral change. Parents will blame the teacher and this will place her in a most embarrassing situation."

Homosexuality Taught

Prentice-Hall's *Behind the Mask: Our Psychological World* (1972) was next.

"Prentice-Hall," Norma reported, "replied to our 18 pages of bill of particulars with only one paragraph. So, there again we felt that they had no way to discredit our objections. They would be foolish not to reply. This text also makes homosexuality appear acceptable. It attacks Christianity and the family. It belittles morality and derides law and order and has much evolutionary dogma."

Her rapid-fire quotes from the book, followed by commentaries, kept the reporters scribbling at the press table.

"It is thought-provoking to carry creativity training to its ultimate extreme, as at least one author has done. He suggests that if we wanted to truly induce completely creative thinking, we should teach children to question the Ten Commandments, patriotism, the two-party system, monogamy, and the laws against incest" (p. 61).

(*The Texas Tribune* [Oct. 17, 1973] commented: "In that one neat packaged statement, the authors have managed to plant the seed of doubt in the minds of impressionable young students concerning our entire moral, social, religious, political, and national framework of values.")

Text: "This process is called 'sex-role development' and means that we are trained gradually in the ways of behavior as a male or female. Put another way, we learn how to be a man or a woman sexually and adopt that role—as if we were in a play—until that role becomes second nature" (p. 37).

Comment: "This theory rejects God who stated that He made us male and female. You are either a male or a female and there is just no way to get around it."

Text: "And a majority of inmates at a state reformatory said they had been regular churchgoers, and one-half of them felt churches were effective forces to good" (p. 117).

Comment: "We challenge the accuracy and the honesty of the above, having just talked to a police chief who stated that in his many years of law enforcement, the percentage of offenders who have been regular church attenders has been rare."

Text: ". . . Children have been brainwashed: books have been published of such heavy moral tone that the youngest of today's readers would wince. In a book typical of the 1830s, . . . the plot went something like this: Guests urged a child to eat something his father had forbidden, since the parents weren't home. 'Very true,' (. . . my parents aren't here), the child said, 'but God and my conscience are.' Sometimes when you are in the library, page through this amazing book, which covers all the wacky things children went through in order to survive in the grown-up world. The book is entitled *The Child and the Republic"* (p. 100).

Comment: "There is no excuse for this ridicule of parental discipline."

Text: "Just this sort of behavior produced some rather humorous medical advice of the early 1800s; the doctrines taught at some religious revival meetings were said to be safe if you stayed at home and *read* them, but actually going to the meetings was extremely dangerous, because the large group of revivalists might be overwhelmed by contagious hysteria. One particular sect, . . . was held responsible for spreading 'epidemics of insanity' " (p. 71).

Comment: "Is it really necessary to depict religion in such a disparaging manner?"

Their bill of particulars called attention to:

Text: ". . . Teenagers are merely trying to sift through the garbage adults have been handing out for years" (p. 120).

Comment: "Why not anything beneficial about adults?"

Text: ". . . Admittedly, the issue of sex outside marriage is open to many arguments, both for and against; it doesn't make any difference what side of the fence you are on—the problem lies in our snickering attitude toward sexual behavior (p. 124).

". . . In some states a person convicted of certain homosexual acts, such as sodomy, may receive a prison sentence of 60 years to life. . . . It makes one wonder who is the more bizarre, the people who support this legislation or the homosexuals. One almost gets the impression that sex of any type, even between husband and wife, is illegal. As a matter of fact, it is, in most states . . ." (p. 130).

Comment: "It does make a difference. God has standards of right and wrong."

Text: "Dr. Hoffman blames society for the ills of the homosexual underground: society, he maintains, by its prohibitions and laws *makes* homosexual behavior abnormal. In other words, he is saying, it is not so much the act of homosexuality that causes grief, but instead the laws that prohibit it and the society that finds it repugnant.

". . . Many countries today have legalized homosexuality—which doesn't make it 'normal' or 'moral,' but does help to ensure that it won't be considered a terrible crime against nature as it is in most of the United States" (p. 130).

Comment: "This text certainly makes an intensive effort to indoctrinate students with the idea that homosexuality should be accepted as a way of life in direct contradiction to the fact that God has identified this act as wrong regardless of the beliefs or actions of society about this abnormal relationship."

The Prentice-Hall salesman replied briefly and broadly. In part, he said, "The heart of this criticism is that the text 'tends to discredit the student's faith in traditional values.' . . . The protesters are, of course, entitled to their viewpoint. If however, school systems wish to have secondary students study psychology as professional scholars in the field approach it, the prescriptive views contained in this protest should be disregarded. Psychology is the study of what is, not what should be; it is a science, although a very inexact one, not theology. It should not be made the servant of someone's own personal beliefs."

Norma's rebuttal was brief and sharp.

"You made this statement: 'Psychology is the study of what is, not what should be. . . .' I did not know psychology also included the advocating of breaking the law, and that if you felt the law wasn't right, then it was OK to do it, regardless. Also, in homosexuality, I feel that we have a valid reason for objecting to that. . . . One just has to consider Houston, Texas. . . . One of those 27 [victims of homosexual murders] could have been my son. . . . The parents of Texas are not going to put up with that kind of teaching, now or ever. . . . I believe that our society has not sunk that low. . . . The book is not only stupid, but . . . absolutely, completely out of the . . . realm of psychology."

Have We Reached that Level?

Prentice-Hall's second book, *Sociology, an Introduction* (1972) came next.

Norma noted that the publisher had given only eight lines in written answer to "pages" of criticism. "I gave up typing [objections]," she explained, "because it was almost more than I could stomach."

Then she grimly continued the pattern.

Text: "Can one really understand the lesbian or the Afro-American without being one?" (p. 172)

Comment: "The implication is: No, one cannot."

Text: "A large proportion of male homosexuals are socially hyperactive. . . .

"It is in the 'gay world' of bars, restaurants, gyms, beaches, etc., that such extroversion manifests itself.

"The gay bar is the most frequented of these and serves as a meeting place for friends, an opportunity for sexual contact, and a clearing house for homosexual news and information. . . .

"There may be a considerable difference between the attitudes and styles of life that characterize the clientele of different bars. *Mixed bars* may cater to all homosexuals of both sexes, *cuff-linky bars* are limited to college and the upper white-collar types, *swish bars* are for the more overtly groomed and effeminate, *TV bars* are for the transvestites, and *leather bars* are for the tough, sadistic, male homosexuals" (pp. 378-379).

Comment: "Take a look through this and read how they decide on page 381 who will be the male and female. I have never seen such an extensive course . . . it's more of a 'how-to' than it is about the subject."

Text: "We're [Hell's Angels] bastards to the world and they're bastards to us; when you walk into a room, you want to look as repulsive and repugnant as possible.

"An Angel's initiation into a club may include having the other Angels urinating on his levis and gang------- his girl . . ." (p. 398).

Comment: "By the time you get through reading such pages like this, you have to believe that you are reading pornography. . . . If this is the best that we can come up with, I don't think we need the course in sociology."

The Prentice-Hall salesman returned. "Mrs. Gabler, I agree with you. Unfortunately, in a sociology text which is the study of society and the people in it, it is difficult to eliminate all statements that might be offensive to someone. Invaluable sociological insight can only be provided by the study of areas which may be considered taboo to some. There can never be a sociology text that is unanimously accepted. The purpose of this text is to present the comments of one expert about his own field, containing his considered views, which to others, may, and often do, seem to be limited, biased, and incomplete." And with that he stopped.

Norma was equally brief with her rebuttal. ". . . The publisher . . . [says] that [this] 'sociology' is a study of society and the people in it. I find that very difficult to believe. I will not accept the fact that . . . people have all reached this level in our society."

Norma had one more book to protest: *Psychology for You* (1973) by W. H. Sadlier, Inc. (published by Oxford Book Company).

Her objections centered on the book's "attack on Christianity," as particularly expressed in two chapters titled, "Mythology and Psychology," and "Myths and Modern Man." She read three paragraphs:

Text: "Both Jonah in the Old Testament story, and the hero Raven in an Eskimo tale, were swallowed by a whale (p. 172).

"On the other hand, myths may give a picture of the world as having fallen from a perfect state. The evil of the world, according to these traditions, resulted from man's failure to obey the will of God, and it is only by following the will of God that the world can be restored to its proper state. This is essentially the mythological standpoint of Christianity, Judaism, Islam, and many other religions (p. 188).

"A great many myths deal with the idea of rebirth. Jesus, Dionysus, Odin, and many other traditional figures are represented as having died, after which they were reborn, or arose from the dead" (p. 191).

Comment: "This book conveys to the student the story of Jesus [and other biblical stories] as myths . . . completely destroys . . . faith in the eyes of the student."

The salesman contended in reply that ". . . the word 'myth' has many, many different meanings. . . . I don't think . . . he [the author] implies that calling a story a myth says that it is untrue.

"Using the term 'myth' . . . is not intended to belittle . . . any religion, but to point up on the contrary, the importance of religious concept, in this case, myths, in the psychology of the individual."

Norma retorted in rebuttal, "I still have to stand on our statement about this book's attack on Christianity. . . . It seems strange that textbooks cannot contain favorable comments about Christianity, because this would be teaching religion. But attacks against

Christianity are condoned. The publisher states that 'there is no attack, direct or indirect, on Christianity, or any other religion.' This is a complete falsehood.

"Myth does not, and I repeat, 'not' convey to the students the idea of possibly being [not] true. Thus, to place Christianity with Greek myths, causes the student to equate the two. We checked a thesaurus and found synonyms such as imaginary, falsehood, fantasy, fiction, legend, and tradition for the word 'myth.' Under 'mythical' we found: unreal and fictitious. Under 'mythical deities,' we found many listings but in not one listing did we find God, or God the Father, God the Son, or God the Holy Spirit. Therefore . . . this book does equate the Bible as a myth. . . ."

X-Rated Texts Withdrawn

The Commissioner's hearing ended. Two weeks later the State Textbook Committee met to hear any further testimony which protesters and publishers' representatives wished to give. It was at this time that Norma presented the two Prentice-Hall books as "X-Rated" textbooks, with the Prentice-Hall man coming forward and requesting that one, *Sociology, an Introduction,* be withdrawn. So far as Norma knew, such action was unprecedented. She admired the salesman for having the courage to take such action.

The Textbook Committee met the next day to vote. They rejected the two Prentice-Hall books which Norma had termed "X-rated," Holt's *Introduction to Behavioral Science,* and Addison-Wesley's *Psychology: A Short Course* (1972). They accepted two Harcourt books: *Psychology: Its Principles and Applications* (1974) (not covered in this chapter) and *Sociology: The Study of Human Relationships.* Major changes were required of the latter book, including elimination of the student lab book and complete rewriting of the *Teacher's Manual.* They also accepted Allyn and Bacon's *Inquiries in Sociology* and Sadlier's *Psychology for You.*

The Commissioner removed the Allyn and Bacon book, leaving three of the original eight to be presented to the Board.

The Gablers filed their customary appeal on these books to the State Board of Education, and Norma returned to Austin in November. They felt they had a chance against *Psychology for You* when they noticed that the text recommended a "sex comic" written by the book's author. Norma brought the sex comic to the Board meeting.

Just before time for the coffee break, Joanne McAuley held up the comic book. The large-lettered title, *Ten Heavy Facts About Sex* aroused the Board members' curiosity, and during the break they rushed to see it.

They frowned at the provocative drawings of young women. They read the explicit captions that called pornography "harmless" and fears of homosexuality a "waste of time." They studied written advice for buying contraceptives. Then they asked to keep the "comic" overnight.

Curiously, *Psychology for You,* the book which included a reference to the "comic," was not brought up at the next day's board meeting. Nor did the controversial book appear on the Texas list, though it had been recommended by the State Textbook Committee. Norma and her friends surmised that privately the Board had allowed the book to be disqualified on the basis that it had not been entered properly into the Texas adoption procedures. This way the book would not carry the taint of rejection by Texas.

What mattered to them was that six of the eight books the Gablers had protested would not be used in Texas. Of the two, one was adopted with minor changes and the other would have to be extensively rewritten to meet Texas standards.

All in all, 1973 had been a very good year.

10

Battling the Bookmen

Ellie Hopkins, the Longview editor friend of the Gablers, had once advised them to study the background of the publishers and their representatives who came to Austin. They found that some publishing houses had been household names in education since the 19th century.

Some of the older houses still bore the name of their idealistic founders. D. C. Heath, for example, is reported to have once said, "Let me publish the textbooks of a nation and I care not who writes its songs or makes its laws."

This same concept was reiterated in the June 18, 1975 *Congressional Record* in a speech to the Association of American Publishers by Alexander J. Burke, Jr., president of McGraw-Hill Book Company. He stated ". . . textbooks both mirror and create our values." Burke then quoted Donald Taft, who 52 years ago noted: ". . . Public opinion is shaped by textbooks."

Some of the publishing firms had been bought by, or had merged with, "trade" publishers. For example, Row, Peterson, an elementary textbook firm, had in 1962 joined with Harper & Brothers, a general trade publisher. The result was the prestigious Harper & Row, which now publishes both school texts and general trade books. Others had been engulfed by corporate giants wanting to diversify. Random House was owned by RCA. Holt, Rinehart & Winston was a subsidiary of the Columbia Broadcasting System.

Ginn Incorporated was owned by Xerox. Along with these and others, a number of newcomers had also entered the profitable field.

The skyrocketing birthrate and knowledge explosion that followed World War II had made textbooks a strong growth industry. Yearly sales of elementary and high school texts had almost doubled between 1963 and 1970, from about $300 to $500 million annually.

While the school-age population had slowed, the demands for more up-to-date curriculum had kept increasing. Besides the standard student text and teacher's manual, many courses required work books, supplementary paperback readers, records, cassette tapes, filmstrips, and even movies. All this meant big profits for successful publishers and high royalties for their authors. A Harper & Row woman author in Illinois, the Gablers learned, had earned over $2,700,000 from sales of 67 million of her hardcover elementary readers.

The business of selling school texts was on two levels. In the Eastern states and throughout most of the Midwest and far West, books were sold to individual schools, districts, or counties. In the South and Southwest, books had to be approved at the state level in 22 states, then sold to counties, districts, and schools. But whether by state, or district, or both, salesmen had to deal with administrators, and/or professional committees, and/or school boards.

From time to time the Gablers heard believable stories of questionable practice in some states. The most jarring story came from a retired school administrator in a Midwestern state. He told them, "Publishers' representatives meet educators arriving at the airport for a convention. They hand over hotel and car keys with the implied promise of girls and booze."

The Gablers heard tales that, in the old days, books had been sold over dinner and drinks. Now publishers' representatives were even forbidden to speak to Textbook Committee members after a specific date. The competition was so keen and the stakes so large that it seemed certain the competitors kept an eye on one another.

Norma personally had high regard for most of the book salesmen who came to Austin. They were often her adversaries, but never enemies. She saw them as ordinary, decent, law-abiding businessmen who only wanted to make a living for their families.

As salesmen, they seemed willing to make whatever changes the Textbook Committee requested, though they couldn't always get their editors to go along. Norma felt some didn't like certain books any more than she did, but that they had to push the bad with the good. She knew how much the annual adoption meant to them. Most of a year's commission might be decided by a single vote. And it was said that if a sales representative didn't make the Texas list for three years he was replaced.

Most of these salesmen were going to Austin before Norma's first appearance in 1964. The State Textbook Committee had been created by the legislature in 1929 and charged with selecting a multiple list of books for state schools. The bookmen and competitors had all gotten to know one another and veteran TEA officials on a first name basis.

Norma got to know them too. They came grudgingly to respect her; a few perhaps, came to appreciate her. Macmillan's representative, for example, told her, "Mrs. Gabler, I often disagree with you, but I believe you're sincere and honest." One time he even sent a copy of Macmillan's annual report—"I hope you . . . note the pride that we take in our free enterprise economy," his note read.

The salesmen learned that Norma could not be cowed or intimidated. When one complained that she was building her case by taking quotes out of context, Norma shot back, "You'd better be glad I am. I'm doing you a favor." In another instance when a representative seemed to intimate that she was being devious, she reminded, "You'd better be glad I'm a Christian. I could play your game better than you can."

In the early days some wrote discourteous and condescending letters to the Gablers. Norma usually read their letters back in the public hearings with the demand that "respect be shown Texas parents and taxpayers." One representative, after being rebuked by a Board member for lack of manners, told Norma at the coffee break, "Mrs. Gabler, you surely have learned to read well." Norma replied, "You write and I'll read."

The salesmen learned to monitor home office responses to the Gablers' bills of particulars. One editor replied to Norma and Mel, "Your bill doesn't deserve an answer." Norma read this in the hearings. The publisher's book was rejected. The salesman warned the editor never to send another letter to the Gablers that didn't first go across his desk.

The representatives also came to realize that the Board was listening to her. For instance, one representative followed the familiar sales ploy of listing the states where his book had been "successfully" used. "I don't care how many places your books are used," Jack Binion snapped. "Just show this Board Mrs. Gabler's charges are not true."

The adversary atmosphere, with millions of dollars in sales hanging in the balance, fostered a brittle tenseness in the hearing room. Occasional moments of laughter helped ease the strain. Once as Norma came to speak she asked the man behind her if he would hold her books. He took them and said loud enough to be heard over the microphone, "You sure know how to hurt a fellow." The crowd broke up. He represented the publisher of the book to which she was objecting.

In another incident, when she was going full steam against a psychology book, a salesman in the crowd was waving the white handkerchief of surrender.

Some of the most interesting joustings came outside the hearing room. One morning Norma arrived early and found three men from an Eastern firm waiting for the doors to be opened. They remarked about the weather, then one said, "Mrs. Gabler, you really are not so bad are you?"

"Oh, I don't know about that," Norma grinned back. "I can be pretty mean sometimes."

He was not amused. "Mrs. Gabler, why don't you leave our company alone?"

"Why don't you put out a good book?"

"We do, but you keep it off the list."

Still teasing, Norma replied, "When did your company last put out a good book?"

Still serious, the representative said, "We put out a beautiful social studies program, and you kept it off the list."

"Oh, you mean the one with a beautiful little picture of a head cut off and the blood streaming down. It was in the second-grade book, I believe."

He flushed with the remembrance. "Well, uh, that was a poor choice of pictures. We're going to make some changes."

"It shouldn't have been there in the beginning. That's where you publishers make your mistake. Why don't you clean up your books before you submit them?"

The representative fell silent.

"Mr. ———, you know those pictures were sick. You are going to have to learn that Mel and I will give them a good going over. If we don't someone else will. Even the Committee has started checking very closely."

The representative tried a different tack. "Mrs. Gabler, do you realize how much influence you have in this state?"

"No, I don't. We don't even have an organization."

"Maybe you don't, but you have a lot of influence."

"How is that?"

"Well, there's that little rating sheet you and your husband put out on the books that make the list. A year or so ago you rated one of our books last in its division. In every district our salesmen went, people would remind them of the ranking."

He paused—perhaps hopeful for some expression of regret from Norma. When she said nothing, he turned acid. "Mrs. Gabler, you've ruined my sales for the past three years in Texas. I want you to get off my back."

Norma saw that his eyes had hardened. She could play tough too. "Mr. ———, remember that neat little dirty letter you wrote me a year or two ago?"

"I wrote you a lot of letters. Which one?"

"Oh, I think you know. It's this one." She pulled the letter from her attaché case.

He glanced at her and frowned. "Mrs. Gabler, you don't intend to read that today?"

"I will if I have to. You'd better be careful what you say about me."

The doors opened. "See you later," Norma said, still smiling. "I've got to cram for the exams."

When Allyn and Bacon representative Richard Carroll, an old acquaintance from the hearings, learned she would be going to Boston in July 1973, he invited her to "come by and meet some of my department heads."

"OK," Norma said, "while I'm there, I'll give you a call."

It was a return engagement to speak to the annual meeting of the New England Rally for God, Family, and Country. Norma called Carroll's office and was told he was on vacation. But his secretary insisted that she come to the publishing house anyway. "Everyone wants to meet you." Then a few minutes later a vice-president called back and insisted that Norma have lunch with him and a couple of other officials.

Norma took along a woman friend from Pennsylvania. In the taxi the friend was noticeably nervous. "Don't worry," Norma assured. "They won t bite you."

"But what do I say?" the friend asked fearfully.

"Just laugh and smile a lot. You'll find they're nice people just trying to do their job as they see it."

The vice-president who had invited Norma met them on the first floor and escorted them to the editorial offices. The offices were separated by shoulder high partitions. As they walked along an aisle, Norma felt on display. People kept looking up, wondering, she thought, "Which one is the woman who gives us so much trouble in Texas?" She smiled at each person whose eye she caught.

Their host took them to the executive dining room where two more vice-presidents joined them for a delicious meal. The conversation was friendly and spirited.

"Mrs. Gabler, I hope your next bill of particulars on us won't make us work so hard," the senior official joshed.

"We'll just do our homework," Norma replied, adding, "I bet you say, 'Here comes that old Gabler bill again.'"

"Oh, no, I don't," he assured. "When it comes in, I call my entire staff together and say, 'People, we have work to do.'"

The conversation continued pleasant. No barbs were exchanged. Norma and her friend left smiling.

"You see there was nothing to be afraid of," Norma remarked to her Pennsylvania companion on the way out. "Respect goes a long way in building good relationships. I don't see publishers as enemies, but just people whom we must persuade to put out good books."

The publishers knew by the '70s that the Gablers were becoming nationally known, particularly Norma because she was so frequently in the news. One salesman's face fell, in 1972, when he ran into Norma in Phoenix. "Mrs. Gabler, what are you doing here?" He was reassured to find she was not on his trail, but had merely come to speak to a parents' group. What he didn't know was that she had also been in consultation with certain members of the

Arizona Board of Education, including the Board president, Steve Jenkins, who was himself alarmed at the trend in textbooks. Jenkins had said publicly that because of the Gablers, he would prefer texts that had been accepted in Texas.

During this trip to Phoenix, she was interviewed by George Archibald, a young editorial writer and columnist for the *Arizona Republic* who was doing a series on education. Archibald had been reading the Gablers' materials and was "impressed" by their research. He said later, "I recognized them as responsible people, not the picky type who were always taking things out of context."

Except during vacations, Mel's job kept him from accompanying Norma on extended trips and hearings in Austin. He did go along on the two trips to Boston. After speaking there, they swung back through Washington, D.C., and spoke to a group at the Fourth Presbyterian Church where their oldest son, Jim, and his wife, Gloria, were attending.

"You started it all," Norma reminded her oldest son. "What do you think of us now?"

Jim replied with a twinkle, "You make a good team. I am convinced God gave you the mouth and Dad the brains."

It was a telling judgment. Since Mel had resigned his last heavy church responsibility in 1970 (they still attended regularly), he had been the researcher, organizer, and the chief writer of the annual bills of particulars from which Norma spoke at the hearings and which she also used as grist for speeches.

Still it was Norma who was receiving most of the accolades. In 1973 alone she was nominated for Texas Mother of the Year (and re-nominated in 1974), and recognized as "Outstanding Citizen Builder of Longview" by the Civitan Club. Mel and Norma together received the Award of Appreciation from East Texas Freedom Forum, and were awarded the Texas "Good Citizenship Medal" by the Sons of the American Revolution. During the next three years she received many other awards, including a prestigious "Award Appreciation" in 1975 from the Texas Senate and a special Education award from the Texas Mothers' Committee in the presence of Governor Dolph Briscoe, with both the immediate past and present Commissioners of Education attending in her honor.

Mel was that rare husband who could support his wife in the limelight and be proud of the honors she received. But the pressure of preparing reviews, answering mail, and keeping up with the world of education built to the point in 1973 where he had to cut back somewhere. He had to decide whether he should take early retirement from his job at Exxon Pipeline's district office in Longview.

In 1970, his close friend Fay Livers had helped him make the decision to concentrate on textbooks instead of church responsibilities. This time, all Fay said was, "I'll pray for God to show you what to do."

His retirement involved a high financial risk. For a number of years their textbook expenses had been $1,000 a year more than contributions received. This amount was a sizeable portion of Mel's salary as a clerk, not counting their time. To retire in 1973 when he was 58 would cut his annuity by well over half. They could get by, but could not continue to subsidize the purchase of research material, printing, postage, and other expenses, or pay for Norma's trips to Austin for several days each month. They had been getting by with only one secretary, but they now had enough work for several employees.

There was another consideration. Mel was concerned about his textbook workload and its effect on his job. His superiors seemed proud of what he and Norma were doing. In March the company magazine had run a long laudatory profile story of them. His fellow employees seemed not to resent the extra phone calls he received, but he usually worked a half hour late every afternoon to make up for any lost time. One fellow employee had remarked, "If I ever become a Christian it will be because of 'Gabe' (as Mel was known at work)."

When both Mel and Norma had the assurance that it was God's will for him to retire, they made another decision. They would set up a nonprofit public foundation that would allow gifts for the textbook work to be tax deductible. If financial support came in, they could pay office expenses, hire enough staff personnel, and perhaps receive a small allowance.

To receive a state charter as a nonprofit corporation, they needed a third trustee. One name stood out: Richard Gibson, a young Longview businessman, devoted to his family and active in his church.

Richard was the kind of Christian who, no matter how pressing his business, came to the midweek Bible study and went to Thursday night church visitation. His character was above reproach.

Richard agreed. He had long been interested in their work and on occasions had helped them financially. He had become deeply disturbed about textbooks when his daughter came home from school and told him that in class that day it was decided that, in certain situations, lying was better than telling the truth. Disturbed about whether it was his daughter's teacher or her textbook, he checked the teacher's edition of her fifth-grade social studies book. There it was in cold black and white. "I'll stand with you," he told the Gablers. "But the way the country is going, I'm not too optimistic."

So Mel retired, and he, Norma, and Richard Gibson incorporated as Educational Research Analysts. The newspapers took note across the state. In mentioning Mel's early retirement to devote full time to textbooks, the *Dallas Morning News* said editorially, "For the Gablers, civic responsibility goes far beyond voting and 'wishing someone would do something.' It's a refreshing and all-too-uncommon approach to citizenship these days."

Mel's giving up his work at the pipeline office came at a propitious time. This was the year of the grisly homosexual murders in Houston. He and Norma were able to spend more time than ever reviewing and preparing bills of particulars on the controversial psychology and sociology books.

After their 1973 victories, they asked the Board to adopt "a totally new and different approach" to the teaching of evolution and creation.

Let's begin giving students a choice by making "evolution" and "creation" optional subjects, rather than continuing to cram evolution down every student's throat in every subject as the only possible explanation for life; . . . Could it be the evolutionists are afraid that their case cannot stand comparison [with creation]? If they had confidence in their stand, they should gladly welcome all available evidence. If their case is this weak, why allow it to be forced on students? This isn't fair to the thousands of students who believe in creation.

. . . Those not familiar with the facts of science as they pertain to both evolution and creation will immediately claim that this is not possible, based on the very false assumption that evolution is science and creation is religion. Nothing could be further from the truth.

The Board didn't totally buy the request. But they went part way by voting unanimously in May, 1974 to insert the following amendment into adoption policy.

Textbooks that treat the theory of evolution should identify it as only one of several explanations of the origins of humankind and avoid limiting young people in their search for meanings of their human existence.

(a) Textbooks presented for adoption which treat the subject of evolution substantively in explaining the historical origins of man shall be edited, if necessary, to clarify that the treatment is theoretical rather than factually verifiable. Furthermore, each textbook must carry a statement on an introductory page that any material on evolution included in the book is clearly presented as theory rather than verified fact.

(b) Textbooks presented for adoption which do not treat evolution substantively as an instructional topic, but make reference to evolution indirectly or by implication, must be modified, if necessary, to ensure that the reference is clearly to a theory and not to a verified fact. These books will not need to carry a statement on the introductory page.

"Now a publisher is going to be made to stick to it even to rewriting parts of his books," Norma exulted to the Austin Associated Press reporter. "It [the amendment] is going to clarify things and say . . . that evolution is a theory and never convey to the student that evolution is a fact."

But when the Gablers saw the books proposed for adoption at the 1974 hearings, their jubilation cooled. This time evolution wasn't the big bugaboo. Instead, it seemed to them that the publishers were opening a Pandora's box filled with horror, violence, situation ethics, disrespect for authority, and "nonsensical" writing in elementary readers and language books.

This was the year that Jim and Gloria laughingly asked, "Can you find time in your agenda for the birth of a grandchild?" Norma and Mel vowed they would, requesting that they be kept informed. (A few months later Gloria delivered Kevin Scott Gabler.)

Around 500 books, in sets and series, were offered for adoption in 1974. In the years past, other petitioners had appeared at the hearings in Austin, but 1974 brought a host of citizens from all over the state. They came from Dallas, Fort Worth, Lubbock, San

Angelo, Houston, and Austin. Most of these had indirectly become concerned about textbook content due to the efforts, over the years, by Norma and Mel.

The Gablers filed on about 100 books and Norma brought a timer and alarm to Austin to dramatize the difficulty of covering all the material in so short a time.

She hit Macmillan's *Composing Language* series for grades one through eight, citing numerous instances of "invasion of privacy," "negativism," and "horror." For example, she objected to a suggestion in the teacher's manual for a sixth-grade book suggesting:

"Someone may want to create just the opposite of a pleasurable world, a world of horrors. This activity often appeals to reluctant creators. A world of horrors could be created in a song, in a story, or by cartoons and drawings" (p. 27).

She commented acidly, "Asking 12-year-olds to create a world of horror has reached the lowest depths. Encouraging the creation of a horror world, even if imaginative, would not help the student become a part of the real world in which he actually lives."

She objected to a seventh-grade play in Macmillan's *Composing Lauguage* "about an invalid woman who hears a murder being plotted through a wrong telephone connection. The last part of the play records her screams as she, turning out to be the victim, is knifed.

"This play is too violent and full of terror for seventh graders. [There is] no valid reason to include a play plotting a murder, unless this is the new aim of education."

She asked, "Why is it that the authors can write stories on stealing, kidnapping, horror, but never can write about morality? If the schools cannot teach morals, then let's stop teaching immorality."

Norma found the "same themes" in Follett's *The World of Language,* Books 1 through 8.

She pointed out "nonsense" poems in Harper & Row's *New Directions in English* language series.

"The grammar of . . . [this] series avoids rules and definitions. Rather, children learn inductively about the English language and its grammar; they then make their own generalizations about language (TE [Teacher's Edition], p. 33, grade 4).

". . . Little emphasis should be placed upon composition

skills. . . . It is important that the students know that their feelings . . . are . . . worth consideration in their own right (TE, p. 14, grade 4).

"Some students may not write what are considered complete sentences, some may not punctuate correctly, some may misspell words. What is important at this point is that they articulate their own ideas, that they are encouraged to value their own imaginations, not that they attend to every mechanical matter (TE, p. 212, grade 4).

"If the student uses 'ain't' instead of isn't, he should not be reprimanded or told that 'ain't' is bad. Instead, he should be told that there is another way of saying the same thing. . . . Drill on standard usage should be avoided (TE, p. 50, grade 5).

"Some children may want to try writing with their left hand if they are right-handed, writing from right to left, writing upside down, or writing in a circle. Encourage each child to make his own rules for writing and to stick to those rules (TE, p. 259, grade 3).

"Suppose school taught you only to obey. Would you like it? That's the kind of school many dog owners take their dogs to" (SE [Student Edition], p. 293, grade 3).

She strongly objected to the attack on fixed values:

"Always, we are concerned with estimation and with degrees of probability, not with absolutes. Children should know the difference between a wild guess and a careful hunch; they should be at home in the dynamic real world of probability rather than in the artificial world of certainty" (TE, p. 6, grade 2).

She strongly disapproved of Ginn's 360 Reading Program of 10 books for grades seven and eight, stating that much of the content was typified by a story called "The Snake" in the book *Awakenings* (p. 58). Her summation grabbed attention in the hearing room.

". . . It's about a beautiful little blond-headed boy about nine. He was to bring a jar of water to his uncle, who was plowing out in the field, and the uncle almost ran over the snake. Then he [the uncle] decided the snake was beautiful. But he went into great detail of making a big issue of it, how brutal the little boy was, because the little boy, naturally, as anybody would, killed the snake. . . . The uncle became very angry with him and . . . picked up the snake and tied it around the little boy's head. Now, if you don't think that's pretty gruesome, how would you like one to hook around your head—and the child could not get it off his neck."

She gave the D. C. Heath *Communicating* language grammar series for grades one through six the hardest drubbing, objecting to the teaching of violence and non-standard English, giving as examples instructions to teachers:

"Do not correct the grammar that you hear in the children's statements. Instead, listen for individual differences. When you have several write them on the chalkboard:

The bottom goat is more bigger than the middle goat.

The bottom goat is bigger than the middle goat.

"You should not suggest that either example is 'right' or 'wrong.'

". . . Do not insist on 'correct' answers to these questions. The questions are more valuable than the answers" (TE, p. 5, grade 1).

She objected to the frightening content for first-grade children including:

"Has anyone ever awakened and found a stranger looking at him?

"Has anyone ever seen a deserted house? Did you go in? (TE, p. 17, grade 1).

"Has a stranger ever talked to you and made you feel afraid? What happened? What could have happened?" (TE, p. 49, grade 1)

Norma objected to the third-grade students' *Dramatizing Creatively* (role playing or play acting):

"Two children are mad at a smaller child for tattling on them. They are threatening the small child. . . .

"Some children are playing with matches in an old garage. . . .

"Two children want to ring a fire alarm although there is no fire. . ." (TE, p. 189).

". . . After reading a story about cheating, third-grade students are told to:

"Talk about your own ideas.

"Most people think that cheating is wrong, even if it is only to get a penny, which is what Shan did. Do you think there is ever a time when it might be right? Tell when it is. Tell why you think it is right" (SE, p. 76).

Norma wanted to know why these books could condone immorality after having advised the teacher not to teach morals to students:

". . . The moral has been purposely omitted in order that the children, when talking about the story, may come up with their own conclusions" (TE, p. 90, grade 2).

In their bill of particulars the Gablers pointed out that a number of myths parallel Bible stories:

". . . One child might play a god and another child could be one of the god's creatures (Introduction, p. 8, grade 3).

"What else might the god in the myth have done in order to accomplish the same purpose?

"Suppose the god had taken the form of a wolf rather than a man. How might this change the actions in the story?" (Introduction, p. 7, grade 3)

She pointed out a passage in the grade 3 book where, at the close of a story about cheating, the students are to role play:

"Two third graders walk into a candy store. As they go in, one of them says to the other, 'I dare you to steal a pack of chewing gum' " (TE, p. 63).

She said that under "Telling Your Own Story" in the grade 4 book there are two pictures which show boys apparently stealing hubcaps and fruit. The student is instructed:

"Study these pictures. . . .

". . . you may want to tell it in the first person by using 'I' for your main character . . ." (SE, p. 113).

Norma summarized their bill on the Heath books: "These are from first to sixth grade. I cannot see the reasoning to want children to read horror stories, violence, disobeying the law, cruelty, under the guise of saying, 'This is education.' Now, if this is education, you would have to say we're uneducating our children."

Addison-Wesley's *Kaleidoscope Readers* for seventh and eighth grades were next on the list. She cited:

"Scott was sure that no one saw the gang 'borrow' that car. Anyway, they only took a short ride in it ("Two Blades of Grass", p. 30).

"This story makes stealing the car appear all right just because they only had a ride in it for a short time.

" 'You will have fresh blood to drink. The blood will make you strong' " (Three O'Clock Courage", p. 47).
"Someone would have to be sick to want that in a textbook.

"Don't do this. Don't do that,' Bob griped. 'Parents are antiques.'

" 'You said it, Bob,' said Jean. 'Times have changed. But parents don't know it. They're living in the Dark Ages.'

"Do these people sound like your family? Are you griped and grieved when your parents talk to you that way? Do you feel that you are already grown up?" (p. 63)
"These are derogatory remarks about parents and child discipline."

Among dozens of other citations from the books, she mentioned an activity centering on a story titled, "The Case of the Five-Saved and the Five-Doomed" (*Communicating,* Speech, Addison-Wesley [1972], p. 122).

"They [the students] have to decide which of the people are to live and who's to die, which is a very cruel thing." She read from the text:

"Pray to your Whitey God who died before He was born.
Pray to the Man whose dream of equality faded away as you,
Whitey, nailed Him to the cross. Take a good long look,
Whitey, and pray, because this time . . . you're going to burn,
baby, burn!"

Almost all of the publishers whose books the Gablers objected to "stood" on their written responses. Macmillan's representative did say that his company "as always, takes Mrs. Gabler's protest very seriously." In her rebuttal, Norma commended the publishers for replying to her and Mel's bills "with respect."

Primers of Violence

The other petitioners hit hard at the publishers in various areas, including the overabundance of disregard for authority, invasion of privacy, and violence that appeared in the books. They termed this the year for "bloodletting."

One woman singled out Scott Foresman & Company's basal readers, *Signposts* and *Milestones.* She held up copies of the books in which she had placed red tabs on the pages to represent each reference to death, violence, suicide, and killing. There were 147 tabs in *Signposts* and 195 in *Milestones.* One of the publisher's representatives told her, months later, that he and his colleagues had wanted to slide under their chairs when this happened. Three women petitioned against the Economy Company's basal readers.

These and other protesters ran the Commissioner's hearing to three days. When the verbal record was printed and added to the bills of particulars and publishers' responses, there were 24 volumes of reference for the Textbook Committee.

The Committee met, heard the pétitioners, and made its recommendations. Of the books and series previously mentioned, they accepted the Harper, Ginn, Houghton Mifflin, Macmillan, Economy, and Scott Foresman offerings. They rejected the Follet, Addison-Wesley, and Heath. A decision on Merrill's *Communications: Interacting through Speech,* protested by Joanne McAuley was held up until confirmation was received that the book was involved in the West Virginia controversy. Then the Merrill book was accepted for Texas on condition that substantial changes would be made.

The November Board meeting was a sizzler. One after another, Board members took publishers to task. A sampling from the record of statements and questions put to the bookmen:

"I personally don't follow the textbook people who say, 'We . . . only have this one little item in there that is questionable.' I don't want any idea in them that's questionable, . . . because that's where you get your foot in the door and keep pressing these issues, and I don't like it. . . .

"When we were children we knew about all these things going on (crime, violence, etc.), but our parents told us they were bad. When you let them read about them in this textbook, it adds an air of respectability that I don't like. . . .

"In several places [of the publishers' responses] they say they are going to replace a page, replace an article. Replace them with what? I'd like to see that, if I can."

After Norma made a presentation on nonsense words, a Board member reported:

"I saw recently that in California, in one of the colleges, out of 2700 freshmen, 50% of them had to take a refresher course in simple English composition. . . . We don't want to get in that shape. . . ."

After a salesman defended his book's use of nonsense words, the Board member replied:

"Well, they can't read, and we've been told they can't do math, and now it looks like they're not going to be able to speak English. . . . I can't see any relativity at all with the English language."

After Ginn and Company explained that the story "The Snake" was to teach allegory and propagandizing, a Board member said:

"I guess I'm obtuse—you're teaching allegory and . . . propagandizing, and the thing we hear is kids are not learning to read. Can't we teach reading without propagandizing and allegorizing and all these other things? . . . You go out and talk to these mothers and daddies, and they're not interested in allegory or propaganda or a lot of this other stuff. They want to know why kids can't read . . . and I really doubt that you're doing the job with this type of approach."

The Board demanded a long list of changes, and some members attempted to have 10 books removed from the list, but in the end they struck only one publisher's books from the Committee's recommendations.

The loser, the Economy Company of Oklahoma City, filed a $30 million libel, slander, and conspiracy suit against three women protesters (Mrs. Gabler was not involved) whom it claimed had "influenced" the State Board to reject the books. (One of the protesters had noted in the hearings that one of the Economy books included a "how-to-do-it guide for shoplifting," instructions on how to make metal knuckles, and a story that spelled out "how to cheat on tax forms.") Texas editorial comment ran strongly against the publisher. Said the *Fort Worth Star-Telegram* on November 26, 1974:

Whether the book contents were or were not acceptable as texts is not so important here as the overriding consideration of whether the Texas system of textbook selection will survive. We can't imagine a great amount of citizen participation in textbook selection if objections result in court judgments. . . .

A publisher is like any other businessman with a product to sell. If the product doesn't win acceptance, it doesn't sell.

In selling textbooks to Texas schools, acceptance means citizen review and public hearing. And anyone who offers his product under the procedure accepts the possibility of critical comment. . . .

In this age of consumerism, perhaps the State should

outline even more forcefully for publishers exactly what is involved in textbook selection in Texas, so there can be no misunderstanding about a "no sale."

At its March meeting the State Board passed a resolution:

A suit filed by the Economy Company . . . is of great importance to the State Board of Education and to all citizens of Texas interested in proper textbooks for the use of the school children of the state and the unfettered right to express opinions thereon. Therefore, the State Board of Education hereby requests that the Economy Company dismiss its suit against the three parties involved in the interest of maintaining an exemplary state adoption system. Should this not occur, the State Board of Education requests the Attorney General in his official capacity to immediately intervene in said suit (not in defense of the private litigants) or take appropriate action on behalf of all the citizens of Texas to ask for a judgment in said cause that will prevent intimidation and discouragement to citizens desiring to appear to protest textbook adoptions. . . .

The Economy Company did drop its charges against two of the petitioners, but the third, Mrs. Billy C. Hutcheson, had filed a counter suit, charging the publisher with libel, slander, and infringement on her constitutional rights, and she would not agree to their terms for dropping both suits. This action is still pending.

The Gablers followed these legal developments with interest. Their attorney assured them they had no worries so long as they stuck with the content of books being offered for adoption.

But it was not that way in West Virginia, where in 1974 conflicts over textbooks made the Texas altercations, by contrast, a tea party.

There, in embattled Kanawha County, the Gablers played an important role that was all but overlooked by national news media.

11

The Truth about West Virginia

By 1974 the Gablers were receiving almost daily long distance phone calls from parents asking help in protesting textbooks. The call from Alice Moore in Kanawha County (Charleston), West Virginia was critically important, though Mel and Norma did not realize it at the time. They were busy preparing bills of particulars for the '74 Austin hearings and treated it as a routine call.

Mrs. Moore said she was a first-term member of the Kanawha County Board of Education. Board policy had been to accept routinely the recommendations of the Textbook Selection Committee, but she had looked at some of the new books and had persuaded her fellow Board members to hold up purchase until they could see them also. She had been referred to the Gablers by the educational review organization America's Future, and wondered if they had any reviews on the Heath *Communicating Series* and other language arts books, speech books, and readers.

"We're working on the Heath books now for our Texas adoption hearings," Mel replied. "We'll send you what we have."

Daily as they reviewed these books, the Gablers airmailed the material but thought no more of the call until news stories began to appear about the battle brewing in West Virginia over textbooks. They started a file which grew larger as the busy summer passed into fall.

The national media carried stories that poorly educated fundamentalist, rural, coal-mining "creekers" were protesting school-books in opposition to better educated professional and business people in Charleston, who wanted the books to remain in the schools. It was ignorance against enlightenment, stubborn dogma-tism against progress, prejudice against tolerance, censorship against democracy. Some reports said protesters were racially motivated and did not want minority representation in texts. Others allowed that the protests might stem from a sense of frustrated powerlessness to stop the destruction of values of another era.

A more believable story came to the Gablers from a grapevine of friends and sympathizers across the country, some of whom had visited Kanawha County.

The people at the core of the protest were by no means poor and ignorant. Alice Moore, their leader, was a soft-spoken minis-ter's wife and mother of three. One was a middle-management executive in the State Department of Education and a former school principal. Another a suburban newspaper editor. Another a surgeon's wife. Another the wife of a well-known contractor. And so on. They contended that if the books couldn't teach morality, then they shouldn't flaunt immorality; if they couldn't promote absolute values, then they shouldn't push situation ethics; if they couldn't present the Bible and Christianity fairly, then they shouldn't indoctrinate in secular humanism.

The Gablers learned that Alice Moore was a latecomer to cur-riculum protests. She was first drawn into controversy when sex education came to Kanawha County.

She went into Charleston to look at the materials. She was ap-palled by the interference into family privacy and the value judg-ments demanded of second- and third-grade children. It was so much more than the mechanics of reproduction. The program was to teach children how to think, feel, and act about morals—a pre-rogative which she felt should be restricted to home and church.

She saw a newspaper announcement of a meeting of concerned parents. She attended and voiced her alarm. One thing led to another and within a short time about a dozen supporters were pushing her to run for the school board under the motto, "We need a mother on the school board."

The five-member board was responsible for a system of 44,000 children, but few people even knew the names of the members, and even fewer bothered to attend board meetings. Most members had served several six-year terms, and only one seat was being contested in 1970. Only sex education kept it from being another ho hum election.

Mrs. Moore's election seemed an impossible dream. The incumbent had strong organizational backing and five others were running—all men. Her supporters collected only about $2,500 in campaign funds and then spent most of this for billboards. They had only a few dollars left for newspaper and broadcast media.

The favored incumbent's mistake was to single out Alice for repeated attack. She was a censor, a bookburner, who wanted to impose her value system upon others. She wanted to run the schools. Rumors spread that her campaign expenses of at least $100,000 were being paid by H. L. Hunt. Every time Alice replied to a charge, she was in the news. A week before the election the *Charleston Gazette's* poll showed her running second to the incumbent, but he was still ahead by a two to one majority.

The clincher came when she appeared on television with several charred Bibles which a janitor had retrieved from a school incinerator. "And they [some supporters of the incumbent] have the nerve to call me a bookburner," she charged, holding up one of the Bibles.

After her surprise election, sex education was curtailed in Kanawha County Schools, The furor died down. But her concern that parents' and taxpayers' rights were being trodden upon increased as she came to believe that (1) the philosophy of education in general was to change values, (2) the board was little more than a mouthpiece for the school administration, and (3) federal aid to education was orchestrated from Washington along a network in the educational establishment that ran to local school systems and back to the federal capital. The Kanawha County school administration, she noted, would recommend an innocent-sounding resolution asking federal aid for the project, the board would pass it, and within days press releases would come out of Washington reporting public ground swell for appropriations to finance the program.

But her greatest worry soon became the textbooks which she felt were leading the way in values-changing. She found that the board was rubber-stamping recommendations of textbooks by the administration and the County Textbook Committee. In 1972 she got policy changed to require that the list of new books recommended for adoption each year be given to the board 30 days in advance, and that the books be put on public display.

The policy was followed in 1973, but in 1974 it was not. Instead of putting the recommended books on display, hundreds of different books were set out, making citizen review impossible. And the 1974 list of 325 language arts books was not given to the board until five days before the April 11 meeting when they were to adopt texts. The board majority agreed to adopt the books but to delay purchase with an option to accept or reject them at a later date.

Mrs. Moore took three books home. "The more I read, the more I was shocked," she was quoted as saying. "They were full of negative references to Christianity and God. There was lots of profanity and anti-American and racist anti-white stories. They presented a warped viewpoint of life, as if every black carried a knife, was locked into a slum, and was made to look inferior. In one book was the poem 'Growing Up to Be a Prostitute'; in another a story about a boy who thought only of running down men in a big Cadillac; in another a poem showing what a farce American freedom was. I was stunned. I had never thought they were this bad."

She then asked that all the books be sent to her house. After three big boxfuls arrived, she called the Gablers for reviews.

Next, she requested a private meeting of the board at which she passed around some of the books. One member agreed they were "rotten." Another said he didn't think they belonged in the classroom. But the board president consistently refused to give an opinion, saying, "Let's wait and see what the teachers have to say."

In the days immediately following, Mrs. Moore read more books and stayed in touch with the board members. When she sensed they were softening toward the school administration, she talked to the County Superintendent. He suggested a private meeting with teachers.

The minister's wife, so the Gablers subsequently heard, agreed to this, saying she was "not interested in a public protest." She felt the teachers would surely see the problems in the books, and also she did not want to be ridiculed by the news media as had happened in 1970. She explained, "I did not want it turned into a political fight during election time, knowing the press would accuse me of just trying to create a political issue for my side."

But the news was leaked—by a teacher, Mrs. Moore thought—to the *Charleston Gazette*. When a reporter called to ask if she was trying to keep some of the purchased books out of the library she answered as briefly as she could. Only a small story appeared on the back page of the newspaper.

However, on the basis of this story, the superintendent said the meeting should be a public meeting.

Those who came, in Mrs. Moore's judgment, were almost all teachers and their friends. Only the half dozen friends with whom she had discussed the books were there.

The meeting turned into a confrontation. Mrs. Moore held up a grammar book which she said instructed the teacher to tell students they could use their educated guesses at spelling and punctuation. A teacher spoke up. "Mrs. Moore, this book isn't for the college bound student, but for the student likely to be a dropout." Alice replied, "If there's any student that needs correct grammar, it's this student."

Then she turned to literature which she claimed encouraged stealing, disobedience of authority, and sexual immorality. She read from a literature supplement e. e. cummings' "Sonnet—Actuality 24" which begins "i like my body . . ."

"What is the purpose of having material like this in school?" she demanded.

When the meeting ended it was obvious to Mrs. Moore that the board members wouldn't cross the administration and were going to put the books in. She decided to take the books to the people.

WCHS-TV, Channel 8 in Charleston gave her that opportunity. The station first ran a week-long series of editorials in support of the books. One editorial even warned parents that they might wish to send small children from the room before certain excerpts from books were read. The commentator then said in effect, "If this upsets you, we want you to know these books have been in our schools for five years." The implication was that the material had been found acceptable, even though portions might be disturbing to small children. But the editorial blitz backfired and roused public sentiment against the books.

Mrs. Moore, naturally, demanded equal time. She read an editorial by Elmer Fike, editor of *Freedom's Ring* and an industrialist in the Charleston suburb of Nitro.

I have looked at examples of the new English books that are proposed for Kanawha County schools, and I am horrified. . . .

I object to this literature because I see very little in it that is inspiring or uplifting. On the contrary it appears to attack the social values that make up civilization.

Repeatedly it puts black against white, accentuating their differences and thereby stirring up racial animosity.

It dwells at length on the sexual aspects of human relationships in such an explicit way as to encourage promiscuity. . . .

It concentrates on the sordid aspects of life without ever suggesting that there is, or can be, a beautiful aspect. By so doing it promotes hopelessness and fails to motivate upward. . . .

Another book gives examples of answers to use when accused of shoplifting to avoid prosecution. These are not just isolated examples. It was the extent of this type of propaganda throughout the books that shocked me. Time-tested literary classics are crowded out by the type of writing I have described. You have to look through the books to believe it, and every parent and taxpayer should take the time to do it.

Aside from the fact that the philosophy is revolutionary and appears to attack the accepted values of our society, the series really doesn't do a very good job of teaching grammar. The course suggests that there are many dialects within our society and that the grammatical forms commonly accepted as right are not necessarily the correct ones, that expressions like "he don't understand" can be perfectly acceptable. . . .

. . . This brings up the real objection to this curriculum: Why spend money to teach the very things that uneducated people do naturally? Historically the goal of education has been to raise the level of society, but these books take the opposite view and aim to level society to the lowest common denominator. If that is the goal of education, then we don't need to spend a lot of money to do it. It would occur naturally.

She then read a descriptive poem from one of the Houghton Mifflin *Interaction* high school books about sex orgies on a bus that was probably more explicit than any lines ever spoken on the television station before.

"OK, my time is up," she concluded. "You've heard Mr. Fike's opinion and an excerpt from one of the books. You know what I think and you know what the management of Channel 8 thinks. Now it's up to you parents to decide what you want for your children."

Within two weeks, 12,000 county residents had signed petitions asking that textbooks be prohibited in the schools which:

Demean, encourage skepticism, or foster disbelief in the institutions of the United States of America and in the Western civilization. We submit that among these institutions are the following:

The family unit emerges from the marriage of man and woman;

Belief in a Supernatural Being, or a power beyond ourselves, or a power beyond our comprehension;

The political system set forth in the Constitution of the United States of America;

The economic system commonly referred to as free enterprise where the exchange of goods and services is governed by the forces of supply and demand rather than a central governmental authority;

Respect for the laws of the Nation, the State, and its subdivisions and for the judicial system which administers those laws;

The history and heritage of this nation as the record of one of the noblest civilizations that has existed;

Respect for the property of others.

The petition further asked that books be prohibited which:

Advocate, suggest, or imply that traditional rules governing the grammar and vocabulary of the English language are not a proper worthwhile subject for academic pursuit and do not, in fact, constitute the means by which well-educated people communicate most effectively.

Deal with religion in any manner—its beliefs, rituals, or literature. Inasmuch as it has been held unconstitutional for a tax-supported school to promote religious belief, we hold that it is equally unconstitutional to promote religious disbelief. Further, since the denial of supernatural forces is in itself a form of religion, the promotion of agnosticism or nihilism must also be unconstitutional.

Prior to this the executive board of the Kanawha County Council Parent-Teacher Association had declared its opposition to the books its members had read, and 27 ministers had condemned the objectionable books. The books had been endorsed by the West Virginia Human Relations Commission, the vice-president of the Charleston branch of the National Association for the Advancement of Colored People, and 10 clergy.

Over 1,000 parents showed up for the tense June 27 board meeting. Because the small auditorium would seat only 150, many crowded into the hallway, and most had to stand outside in the rain. In the hall the heat was turned up uncomfortably high. Speakers for and against the books were lined up to speak in alphabetical order. But at the last minute the list was juggled, permitting a minister proponent of the books to speak last. His speech, in the view of the book protesters, was a monologue of rage and ridicule against Alice Moore. At one point a couple of hippie-type youth began calling Alice and her people dirty names. Two big men promptly picked them up and took them outside.

The board voted three to two to adopt all the books, except eight which Mrs. Moore pointed out afterward were not the most objectionable. Yet the Charleston newspapers quoted the board president as saying 90% of the objectionable books had been removed.

She told reporters later, "Why didn't you ask me? I was the one objecting to the books."

She had been complaining about the D.C. Heath *Communicating* series and other elementary books. These, she decided, were far more objectionable than the high school books.

Other women secured a set of elementary books and took them around the valley to meetings.

The outlying coal-mining communities became aroused. This brought a new element into the controversy. The miners were tough. They knew the techniques of protest. Alice feared that if the board did not reverse its stand there would be violence.

Shortly before school was due to open on September 3, a mass protest rally drew 8,000 persons to the Campbell's Creek community in the upper valley, with 2,000 more being turned away by state police. The leader, Rev. Marvin Horan, a Free Will Baptist minister, called for a boycott of county schools. Alice and her friends did not know about the rally until just before it started, and they did not attend.

On September 3, the day school opened, more than 10,000 children were kept home, and there were picket lines around many schools. The next day an estimated 3,500 miners launched a wild-cat strike in sympathy with the protest movement.

The next few days were the worst in the county's history. There were exchanges of gunfire around schools. One man was shot through the heart by a "pro-textbook" leader. Schools, cars, and homes were firebombed. Several book protesters from the rural communities, including two ministers, were arrested for alleged violation of a court injunction forbidding the assembly of five or more persons. Calls for resignation were directed toward the super-intendent and the three board members who had voted for pur-chase of the books.

The board met and voted to remove the contested books, pend-ing a 30-day moratorium during which an 18-member Citizens Review Committee would examine the most controversial books. Three members and one non-voting alternate were to be appointed by each of the five board members, and three by the new board member-elect, who would chair the Committee. The argument was that only Mrs. Moore had really read the books, that the board couldn't make a fair decision until an examining committee had given their opinion. She didn't like the compromise, but she was put in a position of sounding totally unreasonable if she opposed it. Also, she believed that the board member who had voted with her against the books and the board member-elect would appoint to the Committee only persons who had expressed opposition to the books. This would make it at least a standoff.

The schools were then closed for a cooling-off period between September 12 and 16. Mrs. Moore asked the protesters to give the plan a chance. But she had hardly said the words when she re-gretted them, for the board member-elect appointed pro-textbook people. This left the protesters a minority of six.

The six minority Committee members and one alternate included a former principal, a former teacher, a housewife with a degree in business, a supervisor of computer programmers, a manufacturer's representative, and a businessman.

The date of the first meeting of the Review Committee had been set when Mrs. Moore called the Gablers. "Send us everything you have on the books the Committee is to review," she requested.

They were discussing various textbooks when Alice realized the Texas versions were different from West Virginia's. "You mean your books don't even have 'damn'?" she said incredulously.

"That's right," Mel assured her. "For four years we have had a state policy that books can't be adopted with profanity, obscenity, or blatantly offensive language. They can't even have a picture that would cause an embarrassing situation in the classroom."

"Well, I would never have believed it. We must be getting different editions up here."

"Tell the publishers you want Texas editions," Norma suggested. "Arizona does that."

"I'm amazed. Send me that policy. Maybe we can do something up here. Now before I hang up, do you have any advice for us?"

"Stay sweet and keep smiling," Norma recommended. "Don't let them get away with calling you a censor. Tell them the books have already been censored of morality and patriotism. Get the names of books and publishers in the paper. That unnerves them. And keep asking, 'Where are my rights as a parent and the rights of my children not to use the books?' "

Mrs. Moore passed the Gabler reviews to the minority Committee members. They and the 12 other Committee members, plus five teachers and principals as advisors, met two nights each week to compile and coordinate their recommendations on the five language arts books. In every instance, the minority's views were vetoed by the liberal majority.

Responding to an urgent West Virginia request, the Gablers flew to Charleston on October 5 for a whirlwind six-day speaking campaign. Both spoke at a city-wide rally to an estimated 8,000 persons the next afternoon (Sunday) in the Charleston ball park. The next day they separated, and were chauffeured up and down the valley, each speaking twice daily to groups of concerned parents.

One morning Norma substituted for Alice Moore in an appearance before a Charleston women's group. A half dozen women kept interrupting her. Finally Norma stopped and said, "I came here as an invited guest. In Texas we let the speaker speak without the rudeness of interruptions."

One woman kept talking.

"OK, let's put it this way," Norma said. "Either you or I will do the speaking."

The president then requested no more interruptions.

Still smiling, Norma continued speaking with her antagonist beating on her desk in frustration.

While in West Virginia, Mel and Norma learned firsthand about the arrogance of the Charleston press toward the protesters. One of the papers asked them to come in for an interview. They arrived to face a young man sitting behind a typewriter with his feet on the desk. He never stood up, but merely indicated that she and Mel take seats across the room. He asked a question and when Norma started across the room to show him a book, he held up his hands. "Hey, hey, I feel as if I'm being attacked," he said mockingly.

Norma glared at him. "Don't ever say that to me again. I don't attack anyone." Then she went back and sat down.

While the Gablers were in West Virginia they met with the minority members of the Review Committee for several hours. About a week later these members walked out of a Committee meeting in frustration, because their suggestions were not being considered by the majority. And they conducted their own independent review which consisted of approximately 500 contested pages of objections to the books.

The unrest resumed. There were more boycotts, more picketing. In some coal-mining communities women lay down in front of buses to keep them from moving. One group of women staged a "sleep-in" at board offices. The Charleston transit system was shut down. On October 26 there was an orderly protest march by over 8,000 persons, which a local TV station reported as the largest crowd ever to assemble in Charleston. Marching six abreast, they carried signs such as "teach English not revolution," and chanted:

> One, two, three, four,
> Tack it to the school door,
> Five, six, seven, eight,
> We don't want your books of hate!

The majority members of the Review Committee recommended that all the books be put back in the school system, with the provision that no student be required to use any book containing material offensive to any student's personal or parents' religious beliefs.

The minority members recommended that about two-thirds of the contested books be kept out of the schools.

The protesters waited to see what the board would do at their next meeting on November 8. They met in the Civic Center and the entire meeting was televised. Due to the fear of violence breaking out, Mrs. Moore and other protest leaders had already asked the protesters to stay home and watch the meeting on TV or listen to it on the radio. As a result, there were only about 30 people present and about 100 policemen prepared for a crowd. The board voted, with only Alice Moore dissenting, to return all the books to the schools, with only two exceptions. The Heath *Communicating* series for grades one through six and Level Four of the Houghton Mifflin *Interaction* series would be placed in the library for supplementary use by students whose parents gave written permission. (A *Gazette* poll, taken by an outside polling organization and published the same day, showed that 44% wanted all the books removed, 34% wanted some of the books removed, and 21% wanted all the books returned.)

By the same four to one vote the board adopted two other motions:

That no student be required to use a book that is objectionable to that student's parents on either moral or religious grounds. The parents of each student shall have the opportunity to present a written signed statement to the principal of the school, listing the books that are objectionable for that parent's child.

That no teacher is authorized to indoctrinate a student to follow either moral values or religious beliefs which are objectionable to either the student or the student's parents.

Mrs. Moore and other book protesters, however, had no confidence that the board or administration would police the procedures.

The boycotts and picketing began again. Thousands of children remained out of school. There were more demonstrations, more arrests, more rumors of threats of violence.

One of the school board members seemed tortured with indecision. He said he had wanted to hold off purchasing the books for a year, but now thought they should be used in the current school year. He mourned the permissiveness of the times and of the books, but he said academic freedom, school authority, and the very survival of the school system itself was in jeopardy. He was quoted as admitting, "The text material we are now getting is not the best, much because of pressure from the National Council of Teachers of English who have, we'll say, an extra-liberal view. This has been transmitted to the publishers, and in their rush to be in accord with the National Council of Teachers of English, they haven't got the best. There is much to be desired in the material they're producing in their hasty approach to be multi-ethnic." Yet he also spoke of fairness to the Kanawha teachers and giving consideration to their feelings.

Mrs. Moore was not sympathetic. "He says that in order to save the teachers' feelings, in order to be fair to the teachers, we'll feed this trash to our children for the next five years. I don't care how much the teachers who selected these books are offended. I don't care how much of a reflection it is on them, I'm concerned about the children who are going to be reading those books for the next five years."

Meanwhile, Elmer Fike, the suburban editor supporter of the book protesters, organized The Business and Professional People's Alliance for Better Textbooks. Fike and his friends felt the basic roadblock was that the protesters were not getting their objections into the media. Codes of decency prevented broadcast and print media from reporting certain passages from the books. The new group raised money for full-page ads and demanded that both Charleston newspapers print selected passages just as they appeared in the books. The newspapers reluctantly agreed. The result was probably the most profane family newspaper ads in the history of American journalism, with a full-page advertisement in the November 14, 1974 *Charleston Gazette* and the *Charleston Daily Mail*. They were filled with obscenities and curse words, documented by page references from four of the language arts series that had been returned to schools: The Webster Division, McGraw-Hill *Patterns in Literary Art* series; two Scott Foresman's series, *Galaxy* and *America Reads*; and McDougal, Littell & Company's *Man* series. This ad was taken entirely from the books placed back in the classroom for general use. The books placed in the libraries, to be used with parental permission only, were not quoted in the ad.

At the bottom of the full-page ad, they answered "half truths and innuendoes" spread by local and national media.

Context

We are criticized because we take excerpts out of context and present them unfairly, but it is only when they are in context that the total impact is recognized. Many of the selections do not sound so bad by themselves, but when they are taken in the context of complete anti-moral, antisocial, anti-American, anti-religious, anti-free enterprise, and anti-patriotic context our objections become more understandable. The complete lack of balance is one of the objectionable characteristics.

Multicultural

We are told that according to federal guidelines textbook content must be multicultural. We do not object. When, however, one cultural group objects to thousands of passages and another cultural group does not object to a single passage, it suggests that the books are monocultural in that they appeal to only one culture. As Superintendent Underwood is quoted as saying, "If public education is ever directed to a single group, it's the death of public education."

Censorship

We are accused of censorship, that we will not even accept such classics as *Jack and the Beanstalk,* or *Pinocchio*, or even the writings of Mark Twain. What is not said is that some of these classics have been changed to convey a different message than the original versions and that the liberals started the censorship when they insisted that classics ranging all the way from *Little Black Sambo* to *Huckleberry Finn* and *Little Women* be deleted.

Blind Prejudice

Some of the protesters have been criticized because they objected to the books before they had read them all. What has not been publicized is that past policy of the board had been that they would not read the books until they were adopted. Only because Alice Moore refused to honor this agreement and read some of the books was the public alerted to the content of the books.

Violence
It is implied that the book protesters are responsible for the violence, but, when violence has been directed against individuals, it has been the protesters who have suffered most. Furthermore, William Noel, who is alleged to have shot Phillip Cochran, was a member of the "Concerned Parents for Better Education," an organization whose name was changed immediately following the incident to "Kanawha Coalition for Quality Education," the most outspoken group of supporters.

Racism
The protesters are accused of racism, yet we supported the only black candidate running for the legislature. Mr. James Lewis [Episcopalian minister who led the book supporters] refused to do this. . . . Racism has been charged because some of the writings objected to were authored by blacks. When our president, Mr. Fike, obtained permission and appeared before the NAACP to state our position, he tried to read from a black author, George Schuyler, but was shouted down. When a white objects to a black author, it's called racism. When a black objects, it's acceptable.

Rights of Minorities
It is futile for us to try to convince people like James Lewis that our objections to the books are valid. We understand why certain groups object to *Little Black Sambo*, and we honor their objection. All we ask is that our group be given the same consideration. We do not insist that they agree with our position, but we do expect them to honor it. It is possible that if all minority objections were honored the schools might be reduced to teaching the basics, but would that be so bad?

The full-page ads turned the tide. Shortly afterward a Charleston newspaper poll found 81% of the people opposed to the books.

The board majority that had stood against "Sweet Alice," as the book protesters termed her, saw the handwriting on the wall.

The board met on November 21 under pressure and voted two stunning policies on future adoption procedures. With Mrs. Moore forcing a point-by-point vote, the first spelled out guidelines similar to the Texas requirements which the Gablers had sent.

Textbooks for use in the classrooms of Kanawha County shall recognize the sanctity of the home and emphasize its importance as the basic unit of American society.

Textbooks must not intrude into the privacy of students' homes by asking personal questions about the inner feelings or behavior of themselves or their parents by direct question, statement, or inference.

Textbooks must not contain profanity.

Textbooks must respect the right of ethnic, religious, or racial groups to their values and practices and not ridicule those values or practices.

Textbooks must not encourage or promote racial hatred.

Textbooks must encourage loyalty to the United States and the several states [all] and emphasize the responsibilities of citizenship and the obligation to redress grievances through legal processes. Textbooks must not encourage sedition or revolution against our government or teach or imply that an alien form of government is superior.

Textbooks shall teach the true history and heritage of the United States and of any other countries studied in the curriculum. Textbooks must not defame our nation's founders or misrepresent the ideals and causes for which they struggled and sacrificed.

Textbooks used in the study of the English language shall teach that traditional rules of grammar are a worthwhile subject for academic pursuit and are essential to communication among English-speaking people.

The second called for parent-teacher screening committees: Each board member would appoint three parents and one teacher to a screening committee for each subject area requiring new books in any given year. A 75% vote would be required to approve or retain any book submitted by a publisher. (Two months later, the board amended this to provide that a 75% vote would be required to *eliminate* any textbook.)

Mrs. Moore frankly told her supporters that as the present board was constituted, the victory was far from won. Board members would appoint to the Committee persons who agreed with their philosophy of education, and a committee favoring progressive education would stretch the guidelines as far as they could. She also noted that present board members were elected for six-year terms, and there was at present no legal redress for a recall vote.

An official investigation team sent by the National Education Association called the policy decisions "near capitulation to the anti-textbook forces." Enforcement of the guidelines, the NEA said,

> . . . would impose upon the public schools the task of indoctrinating students to one system of cultural and religious values, inflexible and unexamined.
>
> Retention of the guidelines could prohibit future history texts from telling the true story of Watergate because the story might cause some students to question the superiority of our government to all others; and it would surely, if told truly, contain profanity. Enforcement of these criteria could prevent history books from telling the true story of the black experience in this country, or of how the West was won, because those stories might offend the dominant race in this nation, might defame the nation's founders, and might induce students to question the opportunity that the nation has provided for the redress of grievances through legal processes. The guidelines would undoubtedly exclude from any future textbook the history of the present controversy in Kanawha County. Such a history, if truly told, would contain profanity and it would perhaps encourage racial hatred. If told from the viewpoint of the text opponents, it would clearly violate the guidelines concerning the obligation to redress grievances through legal processes.
>
> In short, the enforcement of these guidelines, as they are likely to be interpreted by their proponents, would destroy education in the Kanawha County public schools. Moreover, the textbook adoption procedures recently approved by the Board offer a method by which such a result could probably be accomplished. . . .
>
> Thus, if the anti-textbook forces in Kanawha County are able to obtain a majority on the Board of Education—or to further intimidate the present majority—their concept of "education" will surely prevail.

So stood the Kanawha County situation at the end of 1974. The controversy had received worldwide news coverage, almost all unfavorable to the protesters. Attention was centered on the boycotts, confrontations, and arrests while the issues were largely ignored. Three rural ministers, Marvin Horan, Avis Hill, and Ezra Graley, who was arrested three times, were generally credited with leading the protest, without it being stated that they came upon the scene long after Alice Moore and her supporters began questioning the books. The very limited involvement of the John Birch Society and the Ku Klux Klan was also widely mentioned.

The Gablers put out an end-of-the-year news release on the one-sidedness of the coverage.

West Virginia textbook protesters are generally portrayed as indulging in firebombings, shootings, and other violence. News reports have used statements such as, "shooting people," "Nazi tactics," "mob rule," and "ministers of anarchy."

The truth is practically all of the violence has been against, not by, protesters.

The shootings and bombing of automobiles, the Gablers reported, were all "against parents protesting textbooks." Nor had it been proved that the school dynamitings were by book protesters. Many of the jailed parents, they said, did not know they were guilty of violations until arrested for violating the court injunction. Besides the jailed ministers, those arrested included a mother with a six-week-old baby who had been sentenced to 30 days and held without bond.

The objectors, said the Gablers, were not simply "ignorant mountaineers who want their own brand of fundamental Protestantism taught. . . . We found them to be just like concerned parents elsewhere, except the West Virginians have had the courage of their convictions rather than submit to alien indoctrination of their children."

There was indeed much mis-reporting. As late as the spring of 1976, the following facts had not been printed:

The involvement of the John Birch Society was limited to sending a single reporter—as scores of other publications did—to research a story for the Society's *American Opinion* magazine. The one person in the protest movement labeled a "Bircher" had belonged to the Birch Society for only two weeks several years before. Ku Klux Klan participation amounted to five robed men driving onto school property, burning a cross, and then leaving, never to be heard of again.

It was also true that violence against the protesters went unreported.

Twice the master brake cylinder of Alice Moore's car was drained while she was on trips.

Twice in one night a man in a white Camaro drove by her house on a quiet street and fired a shot into the air in front of the red brick parsonage. The family was inside but no one was hurt. Thirty minutes before, she had received a death threat over the telephone.

For several weeks during the heat of the controversy, at least one male guard accompanied her everywhere she went outside the home. For two weeks after the shotgun blasts, armed defenders guarded the house. As many as 17 men were stationed on different streets surrounding their home.

And she was told that a private detective had traced her personal records back to Mississippi to see if her oldest daughter could have been conceived before marriage.

In defense of the press, it must be said that the protesters were reluctant to be interviewed. "Based on experience, we felt we wouldn't be treated fairly," Mrs. Moore says.

Coming from Texas, the Gablers, however, were not so wary. One of the writers with whom they talked gave perhaps the most objective analysis of the controversy.

Jeffrey St. John, a columnist for the Copley News Service, chided his media colleagues for one-sided reporting. They had given "complete and favorable coverage" to demands by women's liberationists and black militants that sexism and racism be excised from textbooks, but when white working-class fundamentalists made a similar demand in defense of their values, they were "branded bigots and book burners."

St. John saw the textbook conflict as "essentially a clash between two value systems." He wrote:

> On one side is the belief that once a parent turns a child over to a compulsory state-supported educational system, educators are free to mold and shape that child's mind to whatever value system serves the educational establishment's ends.
>
> On the other hand, parents in this community and many others . . . believe strongly in the fundamental teachings of the Bible, a love of country, and closeness of family.

The clash, he said, was in philosophical terms between humanism and fundamentalism, or "restated in personal terms, collectivism vs. individualism."

St. John further noted that the NEA had called the textbook revolt "the first serious challenge to its power and control to determine content without consent of parents," with the issue "one of book burners vs. enlightened education." To the contrary, he argued, the battle was between the "authoritarian educational establishment" and angry parents who are "fast realizing" they are losing control over their children in the legally compulsory public school.

West Virginia parents had been pressing for education to "cease being a privileged elitist sanctuary and open its doors" to "demands for democratization."

This, he said, was "particularly ironic" in view of NEA's asserted credo that education must serve democracy.

12

Charting the Future

The Gablers were scarcely noticed by the national news media in West Virginia. Yet, according to leaders of the protest there, their contribution was significant. "They showed us how to document our objection to a bad text by page, paragraph, and column," [1] says Larry Freeman, a minority member of the Textbook Review Committee. "They gave us encouragement when we needed it most," adds Alice Moore.

Mrs. Moore, however, doesn't think it fair to compare West Virginia to Texas in the battle for better schoolbooks. "The Gablers have been at it 15 years. We have just begun. Also they have powerful friends in Texas. The Churches of Christ and the Baptists, to mention two groups, are very strong there, not to mention the press and the business support they have received. Here most of the power structure either opposes us or ignores us. The State Department of Education is extremely antagonistic to our views, even though a recent college study determined that 95% of our population is fundamentalist."

An example of the effect board members can have when supplied with pertinent information came in 1975 after the Texas State Textbook Committee, TEA staff, and various publishers bowed to "women's liberationists" and accepted 1,651 generic

---

[1] Information about sources and uses of textbook reviews is given in Appendix III.

changes in elementary spellers and math books. They included changing "mother will bake a cake" to "father will bake a cake"; "when a woman marries a man, she becomes his wife" to "when a woman marries a man, she becomes a wife"; "Jill has a new dress" to "Jill has a new cap"; "the man climbed the telephone pole" to "the woman climbed the telephone pole"; and the removal of all bows from little girls' hair and changing "he" to "it." Some publishers had their presses rolling when the Texas State Board of Education met to ratify Committee recommendations.

Several protesters were against these changes, but could not legally appear before the Board on issues. They could, however, talk to individual Board members privately and let them know how they felt. Norma said, in effect, that the changes would be deleting "mother" from textbooks. " 'Mother' is very precious to me," she said. She asked that they "consider parents, not the feminist pressure groups who are trying to depict America in texts not as life has been or is, but as they want it to become—a completely egalitarian society. I don't object to a woman climbing a telephone pole," she declared. "But we don't want texts presenting this as a regular occupation for women when it isn't."

Norma said their most serious objections related to marriage and family. "They give the impression that a woman becomes a slave in marriage. A lot of them are keeping their maiden names. I like Mel's name. I like to be "Mrs. G.," and I think most other married women do too. Feminists feel that a husband ought to do housework. I say it's by choice. Mel will do anything around the house because he loves me. Whatever I do in the house, I do because I love him. They also act as if motherhood is second-class, a burden, when that's the highest privilege a woman can have. My point is that they're trying to force women into a role reversal that's against our culture and tradition and in some instances against the Bible."

When the Board met in official session, the vote was 18 to 1 to deny the generic changes requested.

The year 1975 was a small year as textbooks go in Texas. A budget shortage limited expenditures to $3.2 million and only spellers and a few other elementary books were up for adoption. Norma and Mel's objection to the spellers being offered, was to what they considered an almost complete absence of basics.

In Charles E. Merrill Publishing Company's *Spelling for Writing* (1976) grades one through six, they found teachers were instructed about the course, ". . . it leads children to truths about the language *as it is*, rather than to the half-truths of rules based on language as it *ought to be*" (TE, p. iii).

They referred to a story in the grade six book in which the student is to give another meaning for *white lies*. In the teacher's edition the answer is given as "harmless lies." Complaining to the Commissioner of Education about the teaching of "situation ethics," Norma said, " 'White lies: harmless lies' . . . all lies are harmful, even white ones. The publisher's response said, 'Lies can be harmful; nevertheless, some lies are less harmful than others.' I want to know since when?"

Concerning Harcourt Brace Jovanovich's *Harbrace Spelling* (1976), grades one through six, she told the Board what is expected of students having difficulty in spelling.

". . . Do not stress correct spelling if doing so would lessen pupil's eagerness to write (TE, Level 1, p. 37).

". . . Have him circle the words he thinks he can spell in the next unit. These will be the only words he will take on the Final Test. He can choose either new or review words" (TE, Level 3, p. 24).

"The publisher's reply stated,

". . . Once children have some success, they will want more. Chances are they will want to try to keep up with their peers once they see it's even remotely possible . . . to help them break out of a cycle of failure and frustration."

Not so, she said. "The publisher's reasoning is contrary to human nature. A child will not excel if not impelled to do so. Even adults will do no more than they have to do. How many persons will do a day's work if they can get their income by doing nothing?"

Speaking to the State Board of Education regarding Webster Division of McGraw-Hill's *Basic Goals in Spelling* (1976), grades one through six, she said, "Some of the teacher's instructions are unbelievable! Grades one through three have Dictionary Sound Signs. Beginning in the grade one book, the student is taught that whenever he sees an *e*, he is to think of the key picture *elephant*. (Every letter is given a key word, and instead of spelling cat *c-a-t*, the child is taught to spell *cat-apple-turtle*. Kangaroo would be *kite-apple-nail-girl-apple-rabbit-octopus-octopus*!) The instructions end with, 'Assign the page, and slump into your chair. If you did it right, you will be exhausted' " (TE, Grade 1, p. 108).

Press interest in '75 centered on protests by the well-organized women's liberationists, the concessions to them, and the veto of changes by the Board. The Gablers' bill and Norma's testimony against sight-reading and the lack of basics almost went unnoticed. But a wire services reporter did tell a fellow newsman, "Evolution was always a big news story, but that dispute never bothered me. I think she's really into something now with sight-reading. All over the country test results are showing schools are failing to teach the basics." [2]

The Gablers' call for a return to basics is a part of a broadening out from other issues which gained headlines in the past. For many years, Norma had attended almost every State Board meeting pertaining to textbooks but two years ago when friends from Dallas joined her, they began to attend State Board meetings each month. "We realized," she says, "that there is a lot more to education than just book content, and that the only way to become knowledgeable about other matters is to be there and offer input whenever practical." She and Mel have long been encouraging citizens in Texas and elsewhere to at least go to their local school board meetings and listen, as this is where the policies and decisions are made.

The Gablers intend to continue their energies in Texas where the state adoption process has forced extensive changes in many books that are now used in other states. They have no plans to start "branch offices" in other states. They feel that parents elsewhere should wage their own battles for better education. "In every state the situation is a little different," Mel says. "Besides, only residents of a particular state or district are entitled to protest there."

Progressive educators see the Gablers a little differently on this point. The word is out that Texas "troublemakers" and "censors" [the Gablers] are leading an all-out war against textbooks from coast to coast.

The Gablers refuse to take such credit and point to parents across the country who are rising up to fight for a return to tradi-

---

[2]For further information on reading problems and on phonics, see list of organizations in Appendix IV, and list of readings in Appendix V.

tional education. But the Gablers' pioneering role cannot be denied. The National Congress for Educational Excellence, an umbrella group for 350 parents' organizations, awarded Mel and Norma their Outstanding Parent Leadership Award in 1976.

While the Gablers are not living up to the "charges" of progressive educators, they have become a major source of information and inspiration for battlers in other states.

Their house is jammed with file cabinets bulging with reviews and clippings, and shelves of old and new textbooks. A half dozen young women workers keep typewriters and copy machines humming as material is prepared for mailing to meet requests that pour in daily from Oregon to Vermont.[3] Every room in the house, except the Gablers' bedroom, has textbook material, and there is a desk in there. When they have an overnight guest, a plywood work table is removed from the bed in the guest room, and boxes of books are removed from the adjoining bathroom. Their dream is to have an office building with an apartment adjoining.

Volunteer reviewers come in or work in their homes during the season for preparing bills of particulars for the state adoption hearings. Most are from the Longview area but some live as far away as Dallas. Once Norma was receiving a traffic citation (the first in her life) for skidding into another car on a rainslick street when her brakes locked. When the policeman realized who she was, he joked, "My wife will be angry when I tell her I gave you a ticket. She types reviews for you."

When H. L. Hunt was alive, rumors spread that the Dallas billionaire was their financial backer. (They never met or received any help from Hunt.) Once in a restaurant Norma overheard two women talking about "that rich Mrs. Gabler who flies all over the country in her own plane." The private plane referred to is owned by a Longview company. When the company has business in Austin or beyond, and Norma is going that way, the pilot gives her a lift.

Gossip aside, the Gabler foundation, Educational Research Analysts, runs on a thin shoestring. As recently as November, 1975 they were $2,000 behind when a gift brought them out.

They are reluctant to mount a fund-raising campaign, though contributions are tax-deductible. They fear their motives will be

---

[3]See Appendix VI for information on How to Take Action.

misconstrued. Also, they are by nature self-reliant and fiercely independent. And Mel further explains, "With so many requests to handle, we just don't have time to raise money. We just trust the Lord that it will come in."

Norma does most of the traveling while Mel stays home to manage the office. She takes along three or four cases of books, giving the appearance of a publisher's representative. Some groups give her an honorarium which she plows back into the work. A few have failed to even pay full travel expenses.

Her warmest audiences are parent and church groups and civic clubs. She may grab attention by holding up a book with a plain brown cover and say, "I'll bet you never saw an X-rated textbook. Well, I have some and you're welcome to look at them after the meeting. I won't read the words because I'm a lady." Or lift *Search For Freedom* and ask, "Did you know your children may be studying this 'sexy' history book?" The "Marilyn Monroe story" always gets laughs and captures interest.

Gaining attention, she will begin reading directly from the books. A frequently used excerpt is from a Houghton Mifflin literature series that tells about a mad killer thirsting for the blood of a little boy, followed by her comment: "Stories like this are not only in your children's textbooks but in films and on tapes prepared by publishers for use with textbooks. One sweet little high school girl told me in West Virginia she had nightmares for two weeks after listening to 'Diary of a Madman.' You'd think that with all the good literature available, publishers wouldn't print such trash. I don't know why they do. But I don't think children should be forced to read or hear it. However, that's my opinion. You be the judge about whether you want your children to have such material, paid for with your tax money."

She makes the same approach with morals. "Here's where a fourth-grade teacher is to tell the children that in some situations it may be all right to lie or steal. The children are to study the situations and then reach a group consensus on what action should be taken. The teacher is not to interfere or pass a judgment. That would be moralizing. Now you were young once and you know how children will rationalize any wrongdoing. Do you think fourth graders should be taught in school that it is sometimes right to break one or more of the Ten Commandments? Even if you believe that lying may sometimes be better than telling the truth, do you think fourth-grade children are old enough to know when? Might it not be infringing upon the rights of Christian parents to have their teaching contradicted by the school? Well, I don't think it's fair for the Bible and moral absolutes to be taken out of schools and situation ethics put in. Do you?"

To illustrate how textbooks have changed, she often compares the "old" and the "new" histories. "Mel and I read in the new histories that George Washington had a violent temper—period. We didn't know. We couldn't argue with the book until we found the same statement in an old history book by the same publisher, with an added qualification: 'George Washington had a violent temper, *but* he kept it under masterly control.' You see how the new history casts doubt on his leadership?

"We find examples like that all through the new histories. Our heroes are constantly put down and obscure characters put in to prove the author's point. I ask you: Has history changed or have the new books changed history?

"So many uplifting true stories about our nation's heritage have been left out. Stories that will inspire patriotism. Such as the one I'd like to tell you now from the War of 1812.

"The British had burned Washington and other cities and were laying siege to Baltimore. If they could take Baltimore, they would make a big step in their campaign to recapture the nation they had lost.

"While the guns were booming, a young lawyer was asked to accompany Colonel John S. Skinner on an official mission to secure the release of a prisoner on board the British flagship. But when they reached the ship, the British feared they had overheard plans to take the city, and detained them for the night.

"The young lawyer knew that only one little American fort was protecting the approach to Baltimore—Fort McHenry. He also knew that the beleaguered men in the little fort would soon be out of ammunition. He wondered if they would be able to stand their ground until the morning.

"All through the night the young lawyer walked the deck and watched the rockets whizzing through the air. You can imagine what he was thinking as he watched the fires along the river bank: 'The fort doesn't have a chance. How can anything be left?'

"At long last the first light of day broke through the foggy mist.

As he strained to look across the bay, suddenly the sun's rays pierced the gloom. There, there, hung Old Glory, our flag, all tattered and torn. Fort McHenry still stood proud and brave!

"Moved by the experience Francis Scott Key began to write:

'O say can you see, by the dawn's early light,
What so proudly we hailed at the twilight's last gleaming.
Whose broad stripes and bright stars through the perilous fight
O'er the ramparts we watched, were so gallantly streaming.'

"Doesn't this story of our national anthem make you proud of America? But,"—and her voice drops—"The new histories, at least the ones we have read, don't have that story and many, many others. Our children are being robbed of patriotic feeling. They're being denied much of the thrill of loving our country."

Men sit spellbound listening to Norma tell such stories, some with tears streaming down their faces. It is an emotional moment, a time when they are drawn into her concern for what she and Mel believe are the failures of the new histories.

At the end of the meeting there is always a line at the display table to read the textbooks. Often newspaper or broadcast reporters are first in line.

The Gablers continue to have warm rapport with East Texas newspaper and broadcast media. One area radio personality was even fired by his station's owner for alleged rude treatment of them. But sometimes in the large cities they are confronted by a skeptical or hostile interviewer.

Take the radio talk show host of WFAA-Dallas, whose mother sent him a clipping from Michigan about the Gablers. He invited them to appear and when they arrived with the cases, he asked what they had. "Textbooks," Norma said. "We read right from them. People believe us then."

"Not on my program," he growled and walked away. They followed him into the studio where they were to go on the air shortly.

"Don't say anything," Norma said to Mel. "This may be the first time we walk off and let the host have the mike to himself."

After they were on the air and had been introduced, Norma handed him an "X-rated" book, suggesting he start off with a little rhyme on page eight. He began reading and suddenly his eyes widened. "Bleep, bleep," he said. "I never thought I'd see a textbook I couldn't read over the air, but this is one, folks." The calls began coming rapidly till all eight lines were tied up.

When the off-the-air light flashed in the studio, the host ran over to the control room to show the book to the young newsman, repeating his amazement at not being able to read a text on the air.

The Gablers could see an engineer who would run out of the room during commercials. After his third trip out, he spoke to them. "You probably wondered what I was doing. I have a friend over on the television side, and I've been keeping him up to date on what's going on."

"Why don't you give it to him firsthand," Norma said, and handed him a book.

They were to be on two hours, but so many calls were waiting the host asked if they could stay an extra hour. They agreed and the excitement kept building.

One woman caller disagreed with the Gablers' criticism of an activity that called for each child to write his own epitaph. "It's good for children to be taught about death, because everyone dies sometime," she said.

"Well, you know there are spiritual issues involved here," Mel said. "Schools strictly enforce the Supreme Court ruling about religion. How do you teach about death without putting in the spiritual? How do you explain death otherwise? Myself, I know that I'm ready to die. I'm born again. I've accepted Jesus Christ as Lord and Saviour. But put yourself in the place of the student who is afraid of death. It could be very hard on him, especially if he has just lost someone close."

The caller then said she could see how death didn't belong in the classroom.

Later another WFAA personality, Dan Cutrer, had the Gablers on by phone for two hours. "By the way we have what we call an 'O'Hair listener rating' of from 1 to 10," he said during a commercial break. "Ten represents the audience we had when Madalyn Murray O'Hair was on."

"Where do we stand?" Norma asked.

"About ten and a half," he replied.

Another time in Dallas Norma debated with a local school board member on WFAA-TV's "Issues and Answers." Much of the time she agreed with Norma, even though the board member later admitted that the superintendent of Dallas schools had briefed her for two hours. The studio audience was even more with Norma and at the conclusion gave her resounding applause.

"Did you bring your audience with you?" the board member asked.

"No," Norma replied, smiling. "I thought they were your audience."

Out-of-state media people are more apt to be on guard. Just before Mel and Norma were to tape a broadcast at the University of Wisconsin for 10 stations, the woman interviewer predicted, "I'm sure I'll disagree with everything you say." Norma said that was her privilege and went ahead. When the half hour was up, the woman exclaimed, "You really have valid objections. I expected you to just moralize. You showed me right out of the books."

Sometimes press conferences are arranged; Norma's biggest was in Oklahoma City where three TV stations, a radio station, and the two newspapers sent reporters. Each of the broadcast crews had to take turns for their interviews, allowing those in the back of the line to hear previous interviews.

The last television reporter, a woman, wanted to know why Norma was opposed to pictures and stories of street demonstrations in textbooks.

"I'm against people being hurt and property destroyed," Norma said.

"I disagree," the reporter said. "I'm from Germany; shouldn't there have been an uprising against Hitler?"

"Didn't the people of Germany elect him to office?" Norma answered. "Couldn't they have taken care of him with the ballot?"

The reporter stopped the cameras and looked at Norma coldly. "You're not answering the way you should."

They began again. "You're trying to brand me a racist because I don't like violent protests in textbooks," Norma said. "Hitler is not the case here. We have a ballot box, a better way. We don't have to take to the streets."

Again the reporter stopped the camera and frowned at Norma. "You aren't answering the way you're supposed to."

"You're here to ask me questions," Norma replied. "You aren't going to put words in my mouth."

In Boise, Idaho, Norma was pressed hard by a television reporter who didn't really want to discuss the books. "Mrs. Gabler, there are many who say you and your husband are censors."

He put the mike before Norma. "We've complained about censorship for 14 years," she said. "The books were censored before we ever saw them."

He stopped and started again. "Mrs. Gabler, you talk a lot about offensive language in textbooks. How can you say this when the Supreme Court can't decide what is profane or obscene?"

Norma flashed a quick grin. "We don't worry over that. You may not know, but in Texas we know what's obscene and offensive. Our State Board voted not to accept any textbooks with offensive language or pictures that could cause embarrassment in classrooms."

Along with some reporters, the Gablers have often found teachers and other school personnel frosty.

When Norma senses this, she will go immediately to questions and answers. This enables her to get to what the teachers are thinking—usually that the Gablers are against new methods and are trying to restrict instruction to the views of a fundamentalist minority. Invariably, most teachers come up at the end and say, "We had no idea that you were asking for fairness and objectivity."

In Texas, numbers of teachers have thanked the Gablers. Repeatedly they hear, "Thank you for doing what we can't do. We've been appalled, too, but unless we serve on a selection committee, we have no say in choosing the books from which we must teach."

Occasionally, frustrated parents in another state will invite Norma to come for a publicity "blitz" to make the public aware of their problems. A Georgia group, Better Education for Georgia Today, had been trying for eight months to get a meeting with their State Board of Education about textbooks. Norma came for 11 days, speaking in the Atlanta area, appearing on a local radio station and answering calls for five hours. Before leaving, she advised the Better Education group to be patient. "The longer they go without hearing you," she said, "the more publicity you'll get."

Two weeks later they were invited to present their objections before the Board.

It was in Georgia that a woman administrator in the Atlanta school administration sent a long memorandum of misinformation about Norma to various people across the state. A friend in Atlanta obtained a copy for the Gablers. The administrator wrote about "Mrs. Gabler, who for years has represented herself as a professional textbook evaluator . . ." The description of Norma's travels and press "tirades" that followed included many more errors. The Gablers passed their copy of the memorandum on to their attorney. He immediately wrote the woman's supervisor, demanding a retraction and corrections.

Norma and Mel are continually asked if they believe the current trends in textbooks will be reversed. They are guardedly optimistic. "I think the pendulum is swinging our way," Norma says. "If the movement keeps gaining strength, we'll be going back to the basics —learning skills, traditional math, phonics, morality, patriotism, history that is really history, science that is science, and fair play for free enterprise economics. On my speaking tours I've found parents disgusted. No matter what kind of jargon the educators feed them, they see the results."

The Gablers do not believe publishers will stop producing "progressive" texts. "Realistically," says Mel, "what I think will happen is that the publishers will be forced to put out two sets of books if they want to stay competitive."

The spiral of alternative fundamental schools and private, church-related, and nondenominational Christian schools, the Gablers believe, will be a strong inducement for publishers to provide another set of books. They note that *Biology: A Search For Order In Complexity*, published by Zondervan Publishing House, which three major textbook publishers turned down, is in its fourth printing. Creation-Life Publishers are working overtime producing creation books for use in various science courses. Their most important contribution is *Scientific Creationism*, a handbook for teachers. The public school edition is strictly science with no biblical or religious content. Their new world history, *Streams of Civilization*, promises to be a major contribution to public and private schools interested in history presented objectively and in a scholarly manner. A Beka Book Publications has the largest assortment of texts with no humanistic bias, and has started producing texts for secular as well as Christian schools. Other publishers, such as Bob Jones University Press, are in the process of increasing the supply of acceptable texts. Textbooks from these and other publishers are included in the Gablers' "List of Recommended Books" [4].

---

[4] For names and addresses of publishers, see Appendix IV.

Because Texas textbook adoption law permits only publishers to press the advantages of their books, the Gablers and other protesters have wrongly been accused of being against all textbooks by secular publishers. "This is not so," Mel insists. "Whenever we can find a good book, we plug its merits in our mailings. We even condone books that are mildly objectionable when we feel they are the best in a particular field.

"We're not out to destroy any publisher," Mel declares. "We believe in free enterprise. We're simply trying to get publishers to see that they're missing a big market by not publishing books that millions of parents want."

Mel and Norma are hopeful that the big textbook publishers will take a cue from their general trade brothers. "Up until a few years ago their religious lines were mostly liberal," Mel notes. "They noticed that the sales of evangelical publishers were booming, and got on the bandwagon pretty fast. Today, publishers like Doubleday and Harper are signing up evangelical authors to write for the evangelical market. Of course, they still publish liberal books, too."

The Gablers don't see an alternate line of textbooks as any threat to public schools, no more than fundamental alternative schools are threats to the public system. "Perhaps the 'progressive' educators see the fundamental schools as a threat to their ideology," says Mel. "But the basic schools are in the best tradition of American democracy. They're tax-supported, integrated, and so popular that some have a long waiting list."

The Gablers list some of the features of these schools which capture parental confidence: Traditional curriculum; phonics beginning in kindergarten; basic math and grammar; spelling bees and math contests; classes grouped according to ability of students; assigned homework; grades that reflect actual achievement; promotion only on merit; high moral standards and patriotism; dress codes and strict discipline; respect and courtesy demanded.

The Gablers hold that education could change rapidly for the best if the progressive educational establishment would stop trying to enforce its own concept of what it thinks schools should accomplish. They do not believe this will happen. They believe that the establishment is pressing for complete control over curriculum and training and certification of teachers, with increased federal financing.

The Gablers would like to see the federal government get completely out of curriculum. They are encouraged by Arizona Rep. John Conlan's success in getting National Science Foundation funding for the *Man: A Course of Study* series (MACOS) cut off by Congress.

The National Education Association is the most visible promoter of the goals of progressive education. The NEA, the Gablers point out, has never denied its program for educator power. At the 1969 annual meeting, NEA president George D. Fischer urged teachers to form the country's most powerful political group to combat "a conspiracy" against education. The "conspiracy," he said, was composed of the Nixon administration, racist governors, private segregated schools, and private businesses offering to teach reading in public schools on contracts for pupil achievement. He predicted that in a decade NEA would grow to 4 million members, each earning $25,000 a year, with annual dues of 1% of salaries going to "elevate the status of educators and education." With that money and power, Fischer said, the NEA would win passage of a federal law legalizing teacher strikes and requiring school districts to negotiate with their teachers. The NEA, Fischer added, would also control who enters and leaves the profession and the training institutions.

Five years later, the NEA endorsed 310 congressional candidates and achieved a win record of 81%, the best among the nation's political lobbies. In 1974, the NEA also lobbied successfully for passage of the $25 billion bill extending the Federal Elementary and Secondary Education Act for school aid for four years.

By 1975, the NEA had grown more bold. At the 1975 convention, NEA president John Ryor called on the organization to get into presidential politics.

The Gablers worry that if the NEA reaches all its goals, an academic-political dictatorship could be established over public schools. Private schools, already hindered by bureaucracy, will be harassed till they fold or conform.

At the heart of this control will be a standardized, federally financed curriculum, administered and written by progressive educators. The Gablers concede that on the surface this sounds good to average parents. "But they need to consider," Mel warns, "that a powerful liberal group will gain even more control over what our children are taught, advance any ideology they wish, and do it in the name of representative democracy."

The Gablers obviously believe there is hope that this situation can be averted. They believe the failures of progressive education are now so apparent that a grass roots revolt is inevitable.

Even the most ardent progressives cannot deny there is much evidence for concern about American education in a society that seems to be retrogressing academically, morally, and socially.

Item: Average high school scores on the College Board Scholastic Aptitude Test have steadily dropped over the past 11 years. Other tests reveal similar trends in reading, writing, verbal comprehension, and math.

Item: Half of 440,000 11th and 12th graders tested in 1960 now say in a follow-up study by the U.S. Office of Education that their high school education has been no help in giving them special skills for jobs.

Item: A Senate Judiciary Subcommittee studying 75 school districts recently announced a "crisis" in school vandalism and violence. About 70,000 teachers are seriously injured in student attacks each year. Senator Birch Bayh, committee head, said "these hallways and playgrounds of fear and terror also account for an estimated $500 million of vandalism damage."

Item: In society at large, major crimes increased almost 50% during the past five years; 58% of all crimes were committed by persons under 25 years of age; up to $5 billion worth of goods are shoplifted each year, mostly by young people.

Item: Unwed teenage pregnancies keep increasing, as do abortions. The divorce rate keeps moving up. A Temple University sociologist found in a survey of 2,300 wives that 50% expected to eventually be involved in extramarital sex; one of every three aged 26 to 30 admitted they already had.

Item: A million American youth run away from home each year. Suicide is the second leading cause of death for youth ages 15-24. One of ten school-age children has moderate to severe mental and emotional troubles. Drug abuse and alcoholism have skyrocketed.

Item: The teaching of American history in our public schools "is in crisis," reports the Organization of American Historians after a detailed study in 50 states and the District of Columbia.

The OAH notes that because history teachers and texts have emphasized concepts rather than facts, college professors are "discovering that their students lack a sense of time and perspective about the past."

Item: Businessmen are concerned that 49% of the American people believe that big business is the source of much of what is wrong with the economy. A Gallup poll of 904 students in 57 colleges and universities showed an abysmal ignorance of economics. They agreed 88 to 10 that business is "too much concerned with profits and not with public responsibility"; they thought corporate profits average 45% (the correct figure is nearer 5%); they guessed a corporation with net earnings of $1 million would pay 25% federal income tax (the correct amount is 47%).

The Gablers do not blame progressive education for all of this, but they feel it must take a major share of the blame, particularly because of textbooks that "glorify" violence and lawbreaking, undermine basic institutions, and encourage students to believe that no system of morals is absolute. They note that social scientists almost unanimously agree that children become what they're taught.

When they began their crusade as "babes in the woods" in 1961, it was unpopular, almost traitorous, to criticize textbooks. Today there is a chorus of respectable voices calling for better books.

For example, the *Wall Street Journal* scolded the pro-textbook forces in West Virginia for proposing "that the way to broaden the sheltered, white, middle-class 1950's outlook is to confront it with the amoral, if not criminal, outlook fostered by . . . Eldridge Cleaver and the world of convicts." The *Journal* called on the "educated elite . . . to recognize that . . . the Kanawha County parents had a point."

U.S. Education Commissioner Terrell H. Bell frankly told the Association of American Publishers in a 1974 speech that some of their "current" juvenile literature in textbooks "appears to emphasize violence and obscenity and moral judgments that run counter to tradition, all in the name of keeping up with the real world." He called on the publishers to concentrate on "good literature that will appeal to children without relying too much on blood and guts and street language for their own sake."

In February 1976, Treasury Secretary William Simon urged the New York Chapter of the Public Relations Society of America to "counsel your bosses and your clients to take a close look at the [socialistic] teaching policies of schools and foundations being considered for corporate gifts. Otherwise the largess and the generosity of the free enterprise system will continue to finance its own destruction."

The Gablers are glad, as Mel puts it, "that people are waking up to see what the fuss is all about. But words are not enough. If experience is any teacher, we'll have to keep fighting till boards of education, administrators, and teachers demand that publishers give schools what parents want for their children."

Till that happens, Mel and Norma Gabler plan to keep on in the spirit of the logo on their letterhead: *A husband and wife team working for America's tomorrow—children.*

Epilogue

The Continuing Battle

Orginally published as *Textbooks on Trial* three years ago, the book ran through four hardcover printings and is now going into mass paperback. It has extended the fame of the Gablers as far away as Australia and New Zealand. It has provoked parental action, controversy among educators, and solemn warnings by many religious, political, and business leaders that the tide of destructive progressive education must be checked and alternatives in basics provided or the American public school system will surely go down the drain.

Most religious reviews have been A-positive. State Senator Gene Snowden of Indiana termed the documentary on the Gablers' work in Texas as "the most important book of the year. At last Christians can get an authoritative view of the reasons why so many of them have lost their young people in the last 20 years . . . . " Dr. Richard H. LeTourneau, President of LeTourneau College, wrote, "It expresses the right of concern and the right of indignation as to what was being foisted on our school systems through liberal and agnostic authors and publishers. And it demonstrates what *is* possible for individuals to do about it 'within the system.' " The National Educators Fellowship lauded the book for presenting the "full, personal story of the Gablers' long and lonely struggle with profit-motivated publishers who are reaping a harvest from the sale of unpatriotic, subversive, pornographic and anti-Christian textbooks that have been approved for public use." Such responses indicate the feelings of persons who do not subscribe to the secular, humanistic philosophy of progressive education.

Conservative organizations, not religiously oriented, have also lauded *Textbooks on Trial*. The Conservative Book Club made the Gabler story a monthly selection. *Human Events* magazine said the book proves that "objectionable textbooks can be removed if enough people make their removal a goal worth working towards." The Heritage Foundation in its 1977 "Education Update" said, "All citizens concerned about values clarification, humanistic education, evolution as fact, and distortion in social studies and history" should read the book. *America's Future*, the pioneer textbook reviewing agency for conservatives, declared the book will "shock any parent concerned with the education of his child, as well as any American concerned with the future of his country."

Perhaps the most provocative review was published by the *Dallas Morning News*. Reviewer Karol Virag said he had fled from Communist Czechoslovakia and become a naturalized American citizen "because of such teaching" as cited by the Gablers. He told the Gablers privately, "I saw in *Textbooks on Trial* the same kinds of socialistic quotes that appeared in Czech textbooks after the Communist takeover."

"I taught economics to boys and girls 14 and 15 years old," he recalled in his review. "The textbook was explicit in stating that Communism was incomparably superior to capitalism, that it was a sheer glory for a man to build himself a socialistic world, because capitalism was materialism at its worst: Wall Street gangsters, workers enslaved by greedy manufacturers, obsessed with obscene profits, greedy bankers cheating poor people out of their savings."

"When I read *Textbooks on Trial*," he concluded, "you could have knocked me over with a feather. Once a government decides on being an absolute supreme force, it has no use for an independent thinking citizen... [or] an independent, operating producer of goods; it needs only one thing—ignorant, unthinking masses."

Textbook publishers have taken note of the book. Some publishers immediately ordered extra copies for their editors and other staff members. And the Gabler documentary is required reading for salesmen going before boards of education and textbook committees.

One publishing executive, to whom the Gablers sent an autographed copy, admitted the Gablers' textbook critiques had in many instances resulted in improved school texts. *Textbooks on Trial,* he conceded, had given him a better understanding and appreciation of the Gablers' objectives.

Progressive educators have also taken note of the book. Let me cite just one example. Twelve such educators contributed to a special report on "organized censors" published by the Indiana Council of Teachers of English. Their 72-page book, in effect, is a manual of counteraction against textbook analysts and critics such as Mel and Norma Gabler. Said Edward B. Jenkinson, Professor of Education and Director of the Indiana University English Curriculum Study Center, in an editorial for the book:

> As I read about the work of the organized censors, I find myself applauding their hard work even though I disagree completely with their ideas. I must give the censors credit for their efforts; they are willing to spend countless hours preparing a campaign, organizing groups, reading reviews of books, and preparing the battle plans for their attacks.
> In short, they do their homework well.

It is significant that *Textbooks on Trial* has been cited many times by these professors of English in high schools and colleges. Gary Cox, a high school teacher in Kokomo, Indiana, alerts school personnel to the start of a "community-wide campaign" against school texts: " . . . A book called *Textbooks on Trial* will appear, first in religious bookstores, then in general bookstores and newstands . . . . "

Robert T. Rhode, an Associate Instructor in Education at Indiana University, quotes extensively from the book in his discussion "Are the Censors Confusing Humanism with Secular Humanism?" He concludes: "The Gablers and concerned parents like them rightfully have attacked the teaching of the religion of secular humanism in secondary and elementary schools. The laws of separation of Church and State in this country prohibit teaching anything that constitutes a religion." However, he believes that the Gablers and others may be confusing "the term 'secular humanism' with the educational philosophy called 'humanism.' " A secular humanist, in this writer's view, is one who belongs to the "secular humanist denomination"—a church of sorts. The humanism of progressive education, he contends, should not be identified with a humanist religious group. He has, of course, badly misread the Gablers. They object not to a humanist church, but to the ideology of secular humanism as they see it inculcated in the minds of children through textbooks.

Only one religious publication is known to have objected to the Gablers' views. A reviewer from *Church and State* magazine charged that, contrary to the Gablers' view, the old books were biased and distorted in favor of white middle class Americans, while ignoring minorities. The new books, he felt, were more realistic and presented minorities more fairly. Mel's response: "We hear that all the time from publishers and others who think the white middle class and their values are trash. We don't agree. Furthermore, we don't think the new books are fair to minorities because of the emphasis put on agitators and rioters, instead of highlighting minority persons who have made great positive contributions."

The liberal educational establishment is apparently now becoming alarmed over the crusades and protests by the Gablers and others. The protests keep gathering steam. And the media is increasingly becoming aware that the basic complaints raised by the Gablers and others about textbooks are no smokescreen.

An indication of this awareness was Norma's appearance on ABC-TV's "Good Morning America" in a face-off exchange with an old opponent from Texas hearings, Richard Carroll, a vice president of Allyn and Bacon. Program host David Hartman noted that textbooks are big business at sales of $600 million a year. He then asked Norma to present her charges. Specifically, what evidences of violence did she see?

"There's a fifth grade social studies text which teaches that a mother kills her own daughter and pulls the skin from the girl's face and hands," Norma said, "and which has a man eating his wife and little brother."

Carroll replied defensively, "No one can deny that out of the thousands of textbooks published that, through some human error in judgment, some violence gets in, but basically textbooks are not violent. The larger firms take all kinds of cautions to eliminate this." The Gablers' studies, however, have shown that major publishers are guilty of promoting violence.

In the continuing exchange, Norma cautioned, "We can't be too careful of what is put in the hands of children. Textbooks are changing the views and thinking of children. It's social education instead of academic knowledge. No wonder children can't read and write."

The publishing executive countered that most of the controversial texts were pegged for city schools. "These children have not achieved in school, and they must be motivated," he declared.

"Why then do we have to resort to violence to stimulate students?" Norma interjected. "Why teach them how to make brass knuckles out of garbage can lids? If this is stimulation, we don't need it."

The debate was frustratingly short for Norma. She couldn't possibly say one tenth of what she wanted to get across. She had brought books from which to present proof of her criticisms, but had been told by program consultants that she could not use them. After the program she showed some of the questionable passages to Hartman, and by her recollection, "he nearly came unglued" over some instances of violence.

More typically, the story of the Gablers' crusade has brought many invitations from parents groups for Norma to speak in their cities. For example, parents in Brainerd, Minnesota (pop. 12,000) invited her for a week. News of her coming provoked a division among teachers. Some said she was coming to attack them and they were definitely not using bad books. Others questioned the Christian commitment of the group sponsoring her visit. Pressure on a bookstore became so strong that the manager returned to the publisher copies of *Textbooks on Trial* that were to be sold in conjunction with her appearance.

Norma spoke first to a morning meeting of local ministers, where only two pastors had spoken favorably of the crusade for better textbooks. At noon she addressed community leaders at the Exchange Club, then appeared on broadcasts. By evening there was a decided lessening of tension. Before the week was up the local newspaper carried two articles commending parental concern over textbook content.

She made side trips during the week to St. Cloud and Park Rapids. In St. Cloud particularly there had been large parental turnout at school board meetings because of questions over school subject matter. At both cities response was overwhelmingly favorable to positions held by Norma. All copies of *Textbooks on Trial* brought by the sponsoring group were sold.

In July 1977 the Gabler crusade took on an international tone when Norma accepted invitations for six weeks of speaking engagements in New Zealand and Australia. She took along gilt-edged recommendations from Texas. Dr. J.W. Edgar, the recently retired Commissioner of Education in the Lone Star State, wrote New Zealand's Minister of Education, "She is held in the highest respect by Texas educators for her monumental efforts on behalf of Texas schools.... I commend her to you without reservation."

Norma arrived in New Zealand at a propitious time. *Man – A Course of Study* (MACOS) social studies series for fifth graders published in the United States was scheduled for the next school term. Angry parents who had heard that it taught wife-swapping, incest, and mercy killings were demanding that an investigation be held and that it be withdrawn. Additionally, a nationwide conference of the New Zealand National Party on education and repeal of laws related to abortion and homosexuality was coming up.

Two other related happenings helped highlight Norma's visit. A noted Danish anti-sex education crusader, Svend Aage Laursen, was then lecturing in the island country. Stories of educational decay in Britain were being given wide press coverage. One published quote came from E.R. Norman, Cambridge University lecturer in Modern British History: "What sort of society is it which allows educational theorists to put its inherited values up for auction in the classroom? The values of this country [Britain] are under threat."

Sponsored by the Concerned Parents Association of New Zealand, Norma spoke in every major city of the country. In most places she was introduced by the local mayor as an authority on education in America. She emphasized that United States education had shifted from basic academics to "values" education and that MACOS was only one example of the spread of the new approach to New Zealand. "This MACOS series," she declared, "is probably the most gruesome thing we have ever picked up. But I am not here to tell New Zealanders what to do. I think you know what to do."

An overflow crowd of parents jammed into the building where the National Party was holding its conference. First, the Party threw out a motion urging the elevation of de facto "living together" relationships to a level with marriage. Second, the delegates rejected a call for a referendum on repeal of laws related to abortion and homosexuality. Third, and most significant, the Party adopted by a large majority a historic resolution on parents' rights in selecting school curricula.

In view of the growing unrest regarding the contents of textbooks and related materials for use in classrooms, this conference urges that the National Government uphold the principle of parental participation in the school curricula:

(A) Parental and teacher selection in textbooks and related material for the classrooms.

(B) That less emphasis be placed on social education and that there be a return to skill and factual knowledge.

Norma was acclaimed as a major influence in attaining the victories of the National Party conference, and the parents' group began immediate plans to lobby for related legislation at the next meeting of the New Zealand Parliament. Shortly after Norma left for Australia, they wrote Mel for copies of Texas regulations on adopting schoolbooks for use as guides.

Norma was equally a celebrity in Australia where the mayors of large cities introduced her. At one lecture the Queensland premier's wife introduced her. But audience reaction was more mixed and in some places chaos almost prevailed.

One of her most memorable experiences occurred at Sutherland, a suburb of Sydney. She had spoken about violence and witchcraft in texts, citing one in which 12- and 13-year-olds were asked to role-play killers and victims. When she sat down, the chairman of the sponsoring parents' group invited audience response.

"What's the name of that book for murder?" a man yelled.

"It's ... " But the chairman was drowned out by the publishing representative who leaped to his feet, shouting, "I resent you calling my book a book for murder."

"Sit down and shut up," a voice bellowed, as the chairman gavelled for order.

"Why don't you tell her [Norma] the book is done in humor?" the salesman demanded. "And there are only eight stories about murder?"

The crowd was in an uproar. The chairman kept gavelling.

"Give him a chance," Norma shouted. "If he published the

book, the parents should have a right to ask him questions, and he should have a fair chance to defend his book."

The representative started talking about the book, mentioning that there were ten units with eight or ten stories in each unit. All the time he kept glancing at Norma, apparently in expectation that she would interrupt him. Once when he paused, she said, "Go right ahead." But the more he talked, the more he was booed and shouted at.

Finally, he was asked about the author of "these horror stories in your books."

"Oh, he's dead," he said quietly.

There was a brief hush, then, "How did he die?"

"He committed suicide." The salesman looked imploringly at the chairman. "I'd rather they ask Mrs. Gabler the questions."

At another meeting in Sydney, Norma had just finished reviewing MACOS and was taking up another text when an objector leaped to his feet. "Rubbish! Rubbish!" he stormed. "I've never heard such rubbish in my life."

Several persons began chanting, "Throw him out! Throw him out!"

At this point a dwarf of a man wormed his way to where the interrupter was still shouting, "Rubbish!" "C'mon old chap," he ordered. "Out with you. We came to hear the American lady speak. Out! Out!"

When the disturber balked, women began swarming towards him, swinging their purses. Norma looked on in open-mouthed amazement.

Meanwhile, the mayor had remained on the platform, observing it all. Norma noted that it was time for him to be leaving for the engagement which he had mentioned earlier. "Madam, I've forgotten about that," he grinned. "This is such fun. I wouldn't leave for anything."

But the interruptions and conflicts in the audiences were only sidelights of Norma's visit to Aussie land. In city after city, she left behind aroused and angry parents, demanding a role in the process of selecting school curriculum.

Since her trip to Australia the State Government of Queensland has banned from schools both the MACOS series and a similar program produced by The Australian Curriculum Development Center in Canberra. Of greater significance, the Queensland State Cabinet has ordered an inquiry into the state of education in Queensland with the widest possible terms of reference. A teacher supporter of the Gablers from the University of Queensland has written them: "It [the Cabinet] has called a halt to innovations, so that, for the first time in 100 years, there is to be a total review of education—what it all means and where we are heading."

Despite Norma's extensive travel, she and Mel have continued the battle in their home state. Says Mel: "The publishers think they can wear us and other parents down. They're wrong. As long as they keep presenting bad and inferior books for adoption in Austin, Norma and others will be there to call them to accountability."

Webster's New World Dictionary of the American Language, published by Prentice-Hall in 1976, for grades 7-11 came under fire in the fall of 1976 for indecent language and inappropriate definitions. Mel noted that a definition for *bed* was "a place to have intercourse." Texas State Commissioner of Education, Dr. Marlin Brockette, concluded that this and four other new dictionaries previously recommended by the State Textbook Committee have "blatantly offensive" language and Texas schools should continue using previously approved dictionaries.

Norma concentrated on ninth grade histories and a biology text.

She cited for the State Textbook Committee an example of indoctrination in the Hindu religion from the *Teacher Tactics* (guide) for the four volumes in Scott Foresman's ninth grade Spectra Program, *People of the World, 1977.*

p. 50: Suggestions for Procedures: 1. What is Hinduism like? Before the students begin to study the text, start them on the following exercise which is designed to teach an important point in this chapter. For the next several days, all those who are 5' 5" and over will be referred to as Satpuras and those 5' 4" or under will be Kistnas. All class members will observe the following rules (if applicable to your classroom situation).

a. All Satpuras may enter or leave the classroom through one door (to be designated by teacher); Kistnas may use either door.

b. Satpuras may not pass in front of Kistnas.

c. On any class day, any Kistna may trade seats with any Satpura before the tardy bell rings.

d. Satpuras may not sit on their chairs; they must sit on the floor next to their chairs.

e. Anytime a Kistna is called on to answer a question, he may designate any Satpura to answer it for him.

f. Satpuras may speak to Kistnas only if Kistnas address them first.

After the students have read pages 71-73, ask them for a working definition of reincarnation, caste, and universal soul.

Norma's comment:

The publisher tells me that "role-playing is a widely-used and effective device for teaching. This role-play involves caste, not religion." We will agree with the publisher that role-playing is very effective. This is why we are objecting. Following the lessons on the practice of Hinduism, there are pages in both the student's and teacher's editions on the flexibility of Hinduism and what it offers the individual. My greatest concern and objection is that it is illegal to teach religion in school classrooms.

From one of the student books (*India*, p. 75), Norma presented another example of teaching Hinduism:

One of the family: Hinduism is in one sense a religion of the home. Each household has its own god, like the Roman lares and penates [household gods], presiding over the day-long chores of the women-folk from his little niche [hollow in the wall] by the entrance to the kitchen. His is an honored position and he is the friend of all, from the children who love the tinsel and the saffron [yellow coloring] on his plaster forehead, to the women who make of him a real friend and confidant. And although the men may not pay their respects to their home god every day, they never fail to show their respect by devotions at festival times in the prescribed manner.... He is more than a god and a friend; he is a member of the household. A friend, yet a God. How soothing to the children sleeping in the dark! How precious to the girl who prays for a husband as handsome as [the god] Krishna, as powerful as [the god] Siva! How comforting to the wife sorrowing over the health of her young or the death of a bullock!

Norma's objection: "This description is laced with opinionated comments about this Hindu god."

Her bill of particulars had cited the book on Japan (pp. 65-69) as teaching that arranged marriages would be good for America. The publisher denied this: "The text does not say, nor does it imply, that arranged marriages would be good for America." Norma countered in the public hearing by reading from the text:

p. 65: This is a reminder, even on her wedding day that she is not to expect her husband to be faithful to her, nor is she to be jealous when [her husband takes an interest in other women] . . . .

p. 66: Unromantic? Perhaps. But I think the Japanese way has certain advantages over our own. In Japan one still gives great weight to the wisdom of one's elders when taking the most important step in life.

p. 67: . . . Even American friends of mine, men, have told me that they no longer think romantic reasons are the best reasons for marrying. The Asian way, they say, is much more sensible . . . .

Norma's comment: "This text not only implies but promotes cultural change. It asks students to consider Japanese customs of marriage—the parental arrangement system."

Norma further quoted from the discussion on Japanese customs:

p. 69: Love or physical beauty were not the only qualifications considered by either parents or son. They assumed that if Mitsunori were interested in these qualities, he could find them outside of his home.

Her objections: "The statement encourages unfaithfulness among marriage partners. This story is a very poor choice for teaching World History. Interesting, isn't it? If you don't enjoy or love your wife, then run around with other women."

Moving to the section on "Soviet Union Workers," Norma compared the "rosy" description of life under Communism with "the sheer hatred this text conveys for the American economic system."

p. 36 (Student Edition): Under communist rule the Soviet Union has become an industrial giant, greatly changing the lives of its workers. The masses are no longer peasants, nor are they poor. Today people in the Soviet Union work as mechanics and doctors, as miners and farmers. There are jobs for almost every worker. Although there are not many luxuries available to most citizens, few have to worry about the necessities of life—a vast change from the time of the czars.

p. 124 (from an interview with a woman taxi driver): "What baffles me," she continued, "is how you people over there put up with capitalism. You're so progressive in other ways. You could overthrow it if you really tried. You just have to follow our example—no! You can do it a lot better than our example. And with all your wealth and learning—just think what a magnificent life you'll have."

"What's so wrong with capitalism?"

"What's wrong with capitalism? It's contrary to human nature, that's what's wrong with it. We know the West is rich, really rich. That you live far better than we, that everyone has a car. But I wouldn't swap for anything. Not so much because of the exploitation and lack of freedom and all that, but the feeling it gives you. You know the country doesn't belong to you. You exist to do the work of the capitalists. And besides, capitalism eats a person and cripples him psychologically. It's an evil thing."

"What is it that cripples people?" I asked.

"Private property. You know what private property means. It means jealousy and greed and hate. Your neighbor gets rich for no reason on dividends; you feel insulted and bitter. Is he better than you? Not a bit! Then why should he have more? Because he's crafty and cruel, or dishonest or lucky. You might work twice as hard and give society twice as much—and get a tenth in reward. Why? Because he or his father owns shares of stock. It's not decent or fair—not human. No thank you, that's not for me."

Norma's response: "This is blatant Marxist propaganda."
We realize that this is quoted as the opinion of a woman taxi driver, but it was selected for use in this text, and the question is, "Why?" We read some counteracting statements [elsewhere in the book], but the overall impact is to change student values toward the concept of those who are blind to the advantages, benefits, and superiority of our in-

comparably better system. At the very least it would plant seeds of doubt.

Norma further noted that 56 pages were devoted to the religion of Islam, while very little was told about Christianity. The publisher's representative replied that American students could learn about Christianity elsewhere. "Yes," Norma said, "but what is the excuse for the material included about Christianity? The three and one half pages on little-known Servetus emphasize the most undesirable features about both Protestants and Catholics. Example: "Catholics burned Protestants. Protestants burned Catholics." (p. 453)

Overall, Mel and Norma assessed 1976 as a good year for the parents. The contested histories and several other objectionable books were rejected by the State Textbook Committee. The State Commissioner of Education removed ten more books, and, after the final protest, the State Board of Education eliminated four others.

The year 1977 also brought great results. Nine out of eleven books objected to by the Gablers were not adopted and one had to have major changes.

On other fronts the battle goes on with results indicating that the crusaders for more objectivity and balance in textbooks are gaining ground.

A number of school boards have adopted the Creation Research Society's *Biology: A Search for Order in Complexity* as a supplementary text to evolutionary oriented books. In Indiana the creationist text was adopted by several local school boards, then thrown out by court order because "the creation view is religious," completely disregarding the fact that evolution is just as religious. In Texas, the Dallas School Board's adoption of the book as a supplementary text was permitted, despite a storm of opposition by evolutionists. The Dallas controversy resulted in a debate between creationists and evolutionists, sponsored by Americans United for Separation of Church and State. As at similar debates, the evolutionists relied more on diatribe, personal invective and emotion, while the creationists stuck strictly to presenting scientific models and evidence. For example, the opening remarks of evolutionist Ken Gjemere in Dallas were: "We chopped their [the creationists] heads off in California; we chopped their heads off in Arkansas; we will chop their heads off in Indiana, and—look out—here comes the axe in Dallas!"

The evolutionists' thesis in Dallas and elsewhere was that creationism should be banned from the classroom on the basis that it would be teaching religion. The creationists continued to argue that both evolutionist and creationist models of origin and development should be taught without reference to the Bible or any other religious view.

In many places school administrators have felt the heat and dispatched clear-cut orders to employees of their systems. In South St. Paul, Minnesota, Superintendent of Schools, Ray I. Powell, decreed that teacher counseling in areas of abortion and birth control must stop immediately. "This is an inherent right of parents and must not be denied," he declared. Superintendent Powell further ordered the expansion of teaching that will enhance parental values, specifically:

—Preservation of the family unit.
—Feminine role of wife, mother and homemaker.
—Masculine role of guide, protector, and provider.
—Advocacy of home and family values.
—Respect for family structure and authority.
—Enhancement of womanhood and femininity.
—Restoration of morality.

One of the greatest defeats suffered by progressive educators occurred in Frederick County, Maryland, the home of many bureaucrats who commute to their positions in Washington, D.C. Upset parents first prodded the Frederick County Civic Federation into authorizing a study of curricula and teaching methods in the county school system. This resulted in two reports by Mary Williams, titled "Big Brother in Education" and "What Is Replacing the Three R's in Education." She stated in her introduction to the first:

Psychiatric techniques such as value clarification, sensitivity training, game simulations and socio-drama in the classroom began as a device for handling disruptive youth. The public did not consider that once the door was opened to handling disruptive youth in the classroom, educationists would then proceed to try to mold every child. Monies are now being funded to go right to the cribside in the home, under the guise of helping the disadvantaged.

Frederick County, aided by federal funds, has not escaped. Here and across the nation, innocent people, seduced by behavioral scientists, probing busy-bodies, experimenters and do-gooders have been duped into implementing "innovative programs." Have you heard about some ninth grades grappling with decisions concerning death? It's called death education. Has your 10th grade daughter ever had to role-play being an unmarried pregnant girl living in a ghetto? Has your son, under the guise of deciding on a vocation, been asked to quickly list 20 things he likes to do and then to check what Mother and Dad might like to do from that same list? Has your sixth grader ever been asked to fill out such open questions as "if I were the color brown, I would be... " and "if I were the color green, I would be... " Have you seen any little "All About Me Diaries" or any papers where your child wrote about his or her faults? Did you know that if your child's friend is on drugs, he or she is instructed that it's unacceptable to tell his parents or the police? If your teenager was going with a boy or girl you didn't like would you want the school authority to suggest to your teenager that his objective should be to keep the friend, get his parents to change their minds about the friend and to get those parents to have more respect for his or her judgment? These are some of the symptoms of big brother in education and they occurred in Frederick County.

In essence educationists have assumed that they are to decide what changes are needed in society and teachers are to accomplish these changes. Textbooks and audio visual materials are being developed by such big publishing companies as Harcourt, Brace, and World; Scott Foresman; Macmillan; and Houghton-Mifflin to implement those ideas.

Despite the ever-mounting sums spent on education, SAT scores have steadily dropped over the past 12 years. Now we want to spend more funds to do something about our growing ranks of "functional illiterates." Could it be that all this emphasis on what educationists term the "affective [feelings and emotions] domain" has interfered with the development of intellectual capabilities? Also in reference to the affective domain, why should teachers decide what students should feel about subject matter, themselves or society? Teachers can be as wrong as anyone else.

Venereal disease, teenage pregnancies and crime are steadily rising. Does this have any connection to value clarification which stresses that each person should select those values which are comfortable to him? Value clarification, in essence, teaches that there are no absolute standards. Would this help cause an adversary relationship between the parent and child in those homes where the parents teach that there are absolute standards?

The reports were documented by statements from educators and quotations from curricula. Parents read them and descended on the Board of Education. The Board questioned school administrators and the staff curriculum committee. When satisfied that the charges had merit, the Board mandated sweeping policy statements to its employees. The directives are expected to serve as guidelines to other school boards struggling with similar problems.

The Frederick County Board decreed:

—Any persuasion of humanism that promotes a religious or irreligious belief is in violation of the constitutional separation of church and state . . . . Such persuasive techniques are not legitimate areas of curriculum in the Frederick County School System.

—Values, value clarification, and moral education will not be taught in the Frederick County School System as courses in and of themselves or through a series of contrived situations without specific approval by the Board of Education.

—Situation ethics, according to the secular humanist, affirms that "ethics is autonomous and situational, needing no theological or idealogical sanction. Ethics stem from human need and interest." This concept must not be promoted . . . . Situation ethics . . . is strictly prohibited.

—Group therapy, involving staged encounters which are used to break down behaviors and defenses so that more effective reactions can be constructed by a carefully designed management program, will be excluded from all curricular areas.

—Survival games . . . (which) puts people in hypothetical

situations and causes them to make life-death decisions based on their values... could cause undue emotional stress and as such are invalid techniques to use in the instructional program.

—Sensitivity training which involves encounter groups and in-depth analysis of personal feelings shall not be practiced in the public schools in Frederick County.

So the battle goes on, and the Gablers are cheered by the successes of others who share their belief that textbooks mold nations, and therefore schools are to impart knowledge and skills and not to change the values held by most Americans.

Appendix I

How Textbooks Are Adopted in Various States
The following states have state textbook adoptions:

ALABAMA
St. Supt. of Ed.
Dept. of Ed.
St. Office Bldg.
Montgomery, 36130

ARKANSAS
St. Supt. of Ed.
Dept. of Ed.
Little Rock, 72201

CALIFORNIA
Supt. of Pub. Instr.
Dept. of Ed.
721 Capitol Mall
Sacramento, 95814

FLORIDA
Commissioner of Ed.
Dept. of Ed.
Tallahassee, 32304

GEORGIA
St. Supt. of Schools
Dept. of Ed.
Atlanta, 30334

HAWAII
Office of the Supt.
Dept. of Ed.
P. O. Box 2360
Honolulu, 96804

IDAHO
St. Supt. of Pub. Instr.
Dept. of Ed.
Len B. Jordan Bldg.
Boise, 83720

INDIANA
Supt. of Pub. Instr.
Dept. of Ed.
Room 229 St. House
Indianapolis, 46204

KENTUCKY
Supt. of Pub. Instr.
Dept. of Ed.
St. Office Bldg.
Frankfort, 40601

LOUISIANA
St. Supt. of Ed.
Dept. of Ed.
Baton Rouge, 70804

MISSISSIPPI
St. Supt. of Ed.
Miss. Txbk. Purchasing Board
P. O. Box 1075
Jackson, 39205

NEVADA
Supt. of Pub. Instr.
Dept. of Ed.
Carson City, 89701

NEW MEXICO
Supt. of Pub. Instr.
Dept. of Ed.
Santa Fe, 87501

NORTH CAROLINA
Supt. of Pub. Instr.
State of North Carolina
Raleigh, 27602

OKLAHOMA
Supt. of Pub. Instr.
Dept. of Ed.
Oklahoma City, 73105

OREGON
St. Supt. of Ed.
Dept. of Ed.
942 Lancaster Dr. NE
Salem, 97310

SOUTH CAROLINA
St. Supt. of Ed.
Dept. of Ed.
Columbia, 29201

TENNESSEE
Office of Comm.
Dept. of Ed.
130 Cordell Hull Bldg.
Nashville, 37219

TEXAS
Commissioner of Ed.
TEA, 201 E. 11th St.
Austin, 78701

ARIZONA*
St. Supt. of Pub. Instr.
Dept. of Education
1535 West Jefferson
Phoenix, 85007

UTAH
St. Supt. of Pub. Instr.
Dept. of Ed.
Salt Lake City, 84111

VIRGINIA
Supt. of Ed.
Dept. of Ed.
Richmond, 23200

WEST VIRGINIA
St. Supt. of Schools
State Dept. of Education
Charleston, 25305

If you live in the above states, write to the address shown for textbook procedures and/or other information.

In the states *not listed,* you will have to obtain textbook adoption procedures locally. For other information, write the Department of Education in your state capital.

*This state has a textbook *selection* procedure and furnishes a list of 3 to 5 *suggested* rather than adopted books per subject.

Appendix II

Values Clarification
To Build or Destroy Basic Values?
by Mel Gabler

For years, schools took a neutral stance on morals. Gradually, neutrality changed to attacks on moral standards, until student beliefs or values were under attack in both textbooks and school programs.

Then a seemingly wonderful solution appeared—a "values education" program which is sweeping through schools like wildfire. The descriptions of these programs delight the many parents who consider the teaching of morality a school responsibility. Students are to clarify, that is, evaluate their values or beliefs by coming to their *own* conclusions based on the following seven criteria:

Choosing:
1. Must be freely chosen. (Anything *taught* is authoritarian imposition so cannot be a "true" value.)
2. Must be chosen from alternatives. (Variables must be considered with no indication from the teacher that any values are fixed or are of more importance than other values.)
3. Must be chosen after careful consideration of the consequences of each alternative. (How many children will know the consequences?)

Prizing:
4. Must be prized or cherished.
5. Must be publicly affirmed. (Makes it difficult to back down.)

Acting:
6. Must be acted upon. (Example: If the choice were that premarital sex is acceptable, find someone and practice it.)
7. Must be acted upon regularly. (To establish it firmly as the chosen behavior.)

To qualify as a "true" value, *all* seven criteria must be met.

Traditional values do *not* qualify if they have been taught, because students received those beliefs through "authoritarian indoctrination." They were not chosen of the students' own free will. Thus, values previously taught by the home, church, or school are eliminated. Religious faith held by students is not valid since it cannot meet the criteria listed.

In their instructions to teachers, prominent proponents of Values Clarification say guided discussion is disastrous for the consideration of values such as honesty. With no absolute values considered, a seed of doubt about the firmness and validity of traditional values is planted each time a choice of alternatives is made.

Even proponents of Values Clarification concede that it is based entirely upon relativism or "situation ethics" (the philosophy that circumstances determine whether an action is right or wrong). Granted, some students may select absolute, moral positions; but since teachers are prohibited from favoring any moral stand, decisions will be heavily influenced by peer group knowledge and peer pressure. How many students will be able to stand firm in their religious faith while being constantly confronted by relativism in a public school classroom? In most instances there will be secular teachers and an intense atmosphere of "group consensus" against any individual student deviating from the norm of the class. At the very best they gradually and usually unknowingly, receive an indoctrination in situation ethics. Thus, in practice, Values Clarification *destroys home taught values.*

Values Clarification programs are presented so favorably that few Christians realize they are based upon humanistic relativism, in direct opposition to the Judeo-Christian ethic. Values Clarification is supposed to allow each student to form his *own* values, but in practice the student merely *trades* his personal convictions for the norm of the group. Thus, it produces students with no fixed values, and they are set adrift in the sea of life as a raft without oars, sails or rudder.

Some suggested sources of information:
1. *Values Changing—Whose Values?* booklet by Jo Ann K. Abrigg, 3915 Windsor Road, Youngstown, OH 44512
2. *Why Are You Losing Your Children?* and *The Religion of Humanism in Public Schools,* as well as additional valuable books are available from *The Barbara Morris Report,* P.O. Box 412, Ellicott City, MD 21043
3. *Secular Humanism and the Schools: The Issue Whose Time Has Come,* booklet by Dr. Onalee McGraw, available from the Heritage Foundation, 513 C St., N.E., Washington, D.C. 20002
4. *Values Clarification . . . And Values, A Review,* by Mrs. William Stiefel, Rt. 4, Hwy. Y, Box 292, Watertown, WI 53094
5. "The Assault on the Family," available from PRO Publishers, P.O. Box 1569, Melbourne, Fl 32901.
6. "Secular Humanism," booklet by Daniel McGarry in two parts, Educational Freedom Foundation, 20 Parkland, Glendale, St. Louis, MO 63122.

Appendix III

Much textbook content appears so natural, reasonable, and convincing *in context* that the reader tends to accept it at face value. Since the subtle "questionable" content must be located through tedious line-by-line examination, detailed reviews can save countless hours of painstaking work.

1. Uses:
   a. To facilitate determining your view of the book(s) in question. Always consider the questioned portions *in context*.
   b. Concerned teachers can use them to correct and/or skip "questionable" content. While this is certainly applicable to public schools, it is particularly pertinent for private Christian schools. Here, unless the dedicated teacher guards against it, students will be indoctrinated with the very philosophies their school was formed to counteract.
   c. Use the reviews at home with your children to give them objective coverage if the school is not correcting the books' indoctrination.

2. Sources:
   a. As the major textbook clearing house, the Gablers have thousands of textbook reviews—their own, plus reviews from many other states. Most are by page, paragraph, and line, prepared by parents for parents, and consider the age level and knowledge of the student. They concentrate on pointing out "questionable" content, not from the viewpoint of teaching aids, etc. Order from Educational Research Analysts, Box 7518, Longview, TX 75602, giving title, publisher, and copyright date. Many are quite lengthy, and are photocopied as ordered, entailing considerable time and expense compared to printed matter. Detailed instructions on *How to Review* may also be requested.
   b. *America's Future* has been providing textbook reviews for many years. Their reviews are summary type, prepared by college professors of stature. The Gablers encourage the use of these reviews, though a number of them tend to be lenient. *America's Future* recommends about one-third of the approximately 600 texts on which America's Future has reviews. Write to America's Future, 542 Main St., New Rochelle, NY 10801.

215

Appendix IV

Recommended Sources and Publishers

The Gablers can furnish a listing of textbooks they consider acceptable. The list is kept up-to-date in order to add more books whenever possible. Suggestions for additions are welcomed. Write to them at: Educational Research Analysts, P.O. Box 7518, Longview, TX 75602.

1. *A Beka Book Publications,* 125 St. John Street, Pensacola, FL 32503. Publisher of texts without a humanist basis developed by Pensacola Christian Schools. They have a complete phonics program, a wide variety of readers, the God's World science series, traditional math texts and workbooks, primary history books, grammar books for elementary and high school, and a high school literature series.

2. *A.C.E.* (Accelerated Christian Education), P.O. Box 2205, Garland, TX 75040. Complete curriculum, K-12.

3. *Bible-Science Association,* Box 1016, Caldwell, ID 83605. Publishes a monthly Bible-Science Newsletter. Also publishes five magazines at different age levels, called Science Readers, in two series—one for Christian schools, and one for public schools. Conducts seminars, distributes and sells creation materials, and distributes two radio programs.

4. *Bob Jones University Press,* Greenville, SC 29614. Produces texts with separate teacher's editions for Christian schools. Now available: Bible K-12; Science 1-11; Biblically sound scientific audio visual materials. Coming: Christian texts in all other disciplines.

5. *Christian Light Publications, Inc.,* P.O. Box 1126, Harrisonburg, VA 22801. Publishes textbooks for Christian schools. These are being used in schools of various church affiliations. Catalogs available upon request.

6. *Citizens for Constructive Education,* P.O. Box 25704, Seattle, WA. A fundamentalist citizen-parent group publishing periodic newsletter concerning education issues.

7. *Creation-Life Publishers,* P.O. Box 15666, San Diego, CA 92115. Publishes textbooks developed by the Institute for Creation Research, 2716 Madison Avenue, San Diego, CA 92110, an affiliate of Christian Heritage College. A handbook by Dr. Henry Morris, entitled *Scientific Creationism,* is designed for use with any subject touching on origins. The text is available in both public school and Christian school editions. A world history textbook, *Streams of Civilization,* suitable for both Christian and public schools is in second printing. Co-published with Mott Media.

8. *The Creation Research Society,* 2717 Cranbrook Road, Ann Arbor, MI 48104. Voting members must be scientists holding at least a master's degree. Publishes a quarterly devoted to reports on scientific activity and acts supporting creation.

9. *Creation-Science Research Center,* P.O. Box 23195, San Diego, CA 92123. Publishes Science and Creation Series, student and teacher supplementary textbooks. Sixteen years' experience monitoring science and social science textbooks for California, creating drastic improvements.

10. *L.I.T.E.,* 9340 W. Peoria Ave., Peoria, AR 85345. Citizen-parent group publishes well researched and documented newsletter on current trends in education.

11. *Mott Media,* Box 236, Milford, MI 48042. Publishes textbooks for Christian schools and colleges as well as public schools. Texts available include *Economics,* World History, Creative Writing, teaching fiction, tutoring, Christian education. To come: a revision in conjunction with the Creation Research Society of *Biology: A Search for Order in Complexity.*

12. *National Council for Better Education,* P.O. Box 81, Andover, MA 01810. Publisher of books for parents and educators addressing contemporary problems in U.S. public education.

13. *National Educators Fellowship,* P.O. Box 243, South Pasadena, CA 91031. An organization of Christian professional educators, mostly in public schools, dedicated to restoring Christian principles in education. NEF has local chapters, holds an annual national conference, and publishes a monthly magazine called *Vision.*

14. *Reading Reform Foundation,* 7054 East Indian School Road, Scottsdale, AZ 85251. An international organization devoted to restoring the alphabet to its proper place. Anyone concerned about reading problems—parent or teacher—should contact this organization which is reporting amazing solutions to reading difficulties. Concentrates on phonics only—not content.

15. *Rod and Staff Publishers, Inc.,* Crockett, KY 41413. Publishing Bible-based textbooks for Christian schools since 1964. Free Curriculum Guide and School Catalog available upon request.

16. *Victor Books,* P.O. Box 1825, Wheaton, IL 60187. Has a good creationist resource book, *Creation: A Scientist's Choice* by Zola Levitt.

17. *Zondervan Publishing House,* 1415 Lake Drive, S.E., Grand Rapids, MI 49506. A biology textbook based on scientific creationism was completed in the early 1970's sponsored by the Creation Research Society. *Biology: A Search for Order in Complexity,* and the accompanying teaching aids and laboratory manual are in their second editions and are used in hundreds of private Christian schools and some public schools.

Appendix V

Recommended Readings

1. *Family Choice in Education: The New Imperative,* by Dr. Onalee McGraw. The Heritage Foundation, 513 C Street, N.E., Washington, D.C. 20002. Explores the First Amendment in relation to education.

2. *Fundamentally Speaking,* by Dr. Henry S. Myers, Jr., the originator of the fundamental schools movement. Strawberry Hill Press, 616-44th Ave., San Francisco, CA 94121.

3. *Johnny Still Can't Read — But You Can Teach Him At Home,* by G.K. Hodenfield and Kathy Diehl. Appeared as articles in nearly 300 newspapers during 1976. The valuable series is now available as a booklet from Mrs. Dean Diehl, 554 N. McDonel St., Lima OH 45801.

4. *Poison Drops In The Federal Senate* (1886) by Zach Montgomery, reprinted by St. Thomas Press, P.O. Box 35096, Houston, TX 77035. Documents with United States Census figures the huge increase in crime, poverty, suicides, etc. in almost an exact parallel with the transfer of education from the private to the public sector.

5. *Professor of Phonics Gives Sound Advice,* and other excellent materials, by Sister Monica Foltzer. A very effective program for teaching reading. Available from St. Ursula Academy, 1339 E. McMillan St., Cincinnati, OH 45206.

6. *Public Education — River of Pollution,* by Joseph P. Bean, M.D., and its sequel, *The Source of the River of Pollution.* Available at $1.00 each from Educator Publications, P.O. Box 333, Fullerton, CA 92632.

7. *Storming the Citadel: The Fundamental Revolution Against Progressive Education,* by Richard Vetterli. Educational Media Press, Box 1852, Costa Mesa, CA 92626.

8. *Why Johnny Can't Add,* by Dr. Morris Kline of NYU. Vintage Books, New York. Identifies the failure of "modern math."

9. *Why Johnny Can't Learn,* by Opal Moore. A veritable encyclopedia of valuable background information concerning the plans, methods, etc. used to promote the present educational philosophy. Published by Mott Media, P.O. Box 236, Milford, MI 48042.

Appendix VI

How to Take Action

The Gablers share here some of the information and wisdom their seventeen years of experience has provided them.

In the area of textbook content definite gains can be made by those wanting more objective subject matter in schools—probably more than in any other area for an equivalent amount of time and funds expended. However, please do not expect sudden victories. The requirements are simple: work, persistency and prayer. The effect is vital, because *children become what they are taught*. For this reason, until textbooks are changed, one must expect a continuing decrease in honesty, decency and morality, and a continuing increase in illiteracy, crime, violence.

It is important to realize that textbooks were about 97% Christian/moral when our nation was founded. Our forefathers intended the United States to become and to remain a Christian nation. An 1852-1853 study by the U.S. House of Representatives determined this, and it was verified in 1893 by a U.S. Supreme Court ruling.

However, the Christian/moral influence was gradually eliminated on the pretext that the State has no right or authority to teach religion. This vacuum has been filled with the philosophy/religion of humanism, faith in man rather than in God. Today textbooks are nearly 100% amoral or humanistic, even though two U.S. Supreme Court rulings (1961 Torcaso case; 1964 Seegar case) stated that Humanism is a *religion*. It is evident that the educational system is leading our nation directly down the path of amoralism and humanism contrary to our forefathers' intent.

Interestingly, Supreme Court rulings give stronger support to traditional values and parental rights than is generally known. For example, with regard to the case which supposedly removed Bible reading and prayer from public schools, all Justices concurred in stating, "There is nothing in this decision ... inconsistent with the fact that school children ... are officially encouraged to express love of our country ... and belief in God." (Engle v. Vitale, 1962). Further documentation concerning Court rulings is available from CITIZENS FOR GOD & COUNTRY, P.O. Box 137, McLean, Virginia 22101.

Thus, it is vital that concerned citizens work to correct distorted textbook content. Individuals do not need to be specially trained, skilled or educated, but they do need to be thoroughly prepared.

The essential time to protest objectionable books and to propose positive alternatives is *before* the texts are adopted and purchased. It is at the adoption stage that victories are more likely to be obtained. Begin by determining your state's adoption procedure. Then obtain copies of texts to be offered and examine them for questionable material. A line by line examination is necessary to detect subtly damaging content.

219

We advise participants to do their "homework" thoroughly and to contact Board members, Committee members and community leaders in advance, so that their cases are won before these individuals are publicly confronted. It is very important that a book be protested *only after* careful and personal examination by the protester.

Observation of established procedures is a must. Discourteous treatment can be expected from some, but remember that when truth is being upheld one will always encounter some opposition. Do not give up; persistency will pay off!

Follow these suggestions for remaining on the offensive:

Teachers' rights   Administrators will most likely say that they defend the rights of teachers to teach questioned material. Ask if they also defend the rights of teachers to *not* teach this material. Many teachers are sympathetic to parents' viewpoints, but feel obligated to support the educational establishment's stand.

Television   A favorite reply to complaints about books loaded with violence is that children see much violence on television. Reply, the TV can be turned off, but in a classroom a child receives forced indoctrination as a member of a captive audience. Ask how many teachers allow students the option of *not* reading questionable materials.

Academic freedom   You may be accused of trying to destroy the teacher's academic freedom. Ask about the freedom of students who do not want to be taught subject matter that violates their standards and values. Ask about the rights of parents who do not want certain material forced on their children. Does not academic freedom include the right *not* to read questionable subject matter?

Censorship   If you are called a censor or book burner, you should advise that you are merely pointing out the censorship that took place when negative content was selectively chosen by the authors. Point out that most books which teach morals, encourage the work ethic, teach basic academic skills, stress individualism, favor our country, etc., have long been removed from schools and destroyed or burned in the interest of "progressive education."

Relativism   When you object to Values Education, frequently educators will accuse you of wanting to indoctrinate students with your "biased" views. They maintain that students should be given the opportunity to develop their "own" values. See Appendix II for further explanation.

Realism   If you point out negative, depressing, morbid, and profane content, you may be told that children must be given realism lest they be like hothouse plants, unable to cope with "real" life. First, point out that the so-called realism found in many textbooks applies to a very limited sector. Ask those who favor such books if they or their friends live in the "real" world portrayed by such negative content. Tell them *your* friends and associates don't live or talk in such a way. Second, point out that realism isn't all negative. Ask why students aren't given constructive realism as well, through the use of positive, character-building materials.

Emotionalism   When school officials try to place you on the defensive as an "emotionally overwrought" parent, ask them if *they* have read the books thoroughly. Question *them* on content. If they have not read the books, or have done so cursorily, they have clearly placed themselves in the absurd position of defending a text with which they are not personally familiar.

Detailed advice concerning further "do's and don't's" can be obtained by requesting it from the Gablers at their mailing address. The above are only a few examples.

You need not be intimidated. You have a strong case. Stand up for your principles and exercise your own thinking, but be reasonable. While remaining on the offensive, be careful to maintain tact, courtesy and cheerfulness. A smile and pleasant manner will gain credibility and respect. Do not attack authors, teachers or other individuals. Keep the focus of debate upon the material involved.

The improvement of textbooks depends upon concerned citizens. Much time and effort are required, but it is definitely worthwhile. Where people have become concerned and spoken up, students have received better textbooks.

Closely related to textbook content are various programs and practices such as PPBS (Planned Program Budgeting System), sensitivity training, behavior modification, as well as films and outside readings. Each of these is a field in itself, amplifying the problems inherent in humanistic curriculum.

Numerous parents' groups have concentrated in these areas even more than in textbook content. Much helpful information can be obtained from these groups which are scattered throughout the country. Names and addresses for parents' organizations can be furnished by the Gablers upon your request.

Norma travels from coast to coast, sharing her burden with concerned citizens, speaking to civic, church, school and parents' groups, and giving interviews to newspapers, TV and radio stations. She goes wherever requested if her schedule permits. Sponsoring groups are expected to provide travel and lodging expenses in addition to an honorarium.

The Gablers can provide much additional printed material, including textbook reviews (see Appendix III), over 300 forms pertaining to textbook content and related problems, as well as research material on educational innovations. All their helps are available on a contribution basis by writing to them at the following address:

The MEL GABLERs
P.O. Box 7518
Longview, Texas 75602

Appendix VII

A eulogy written by Don Gabler's brothers appeared in the *Borger News-Herald* on September 12, 1971:

Eulogy to Don Allen Gabler
(Feb. 27, 1952—Aug. 23, 1971)

In a day when men seem to pursue earthly possessions such as money, status, power, and security, one wonders where it will all lead. Often, men attempt to correct the problems caused by these pursuits by trying to change the "outer" man. But they are "missing the boat" and accomplish little.

Occasionally, someone starts with himself. He knows he can't really change anyone else unless he himself changes. People like this seldom "move mountains" in an earthly sense, but they leave the world a little better than they found it. They change the face of mankind just like the constant assault by the oceans on the seashores and the winds on the land gradually change the face of the earth.

Such a person was Don. . . . Everyone who ever knew Don benefitted from him in some small way. Perhaps it was his desire to see a job well done; some act of kindness; an understanding ear; or just a friendly smile. Regardless, you were just a little better because of him.

Now, it seems strange that the Lord would take such a life, but we know that "all things work together for good to them that love God." Just as the gardener picks the best roses in the garden first, God takes those whose purpose in life has been fulfilled. Man may not understand God's purpose for giving life, and then taking it, but it's there, *if* we are willing to look for it.

Maybe one purpose God had for taking Don home was to remind those of us who remain that earthly things are soon gone, but the love and concern one shows to others will last; that those things the world can't buy are the only permanent treasures; that God wants the "inner" man. He wants the man that "lives *in* God"—not the man who just "talks about God." And in return, He gives us a joyful life now and throughout eternity.

It's wonderful to know that we can see Don again, and that the next time we see Don we can join him forever, without worries or problems. But the least we· can do for him now is to look to God in prayer and thought, asking the Holy Spirit to help us seek lasting treasures so that we too may leave the world just a little bit better.

—by his brothers